Compact and Flexible Microwave Devices

Scrivener Publishing
100 Cummings Center, Suite 541J
Beverly, MA 01915-6106

Publishers at Scrivener
Martin Scrivener (martin@scrivenerpublishing.com)
Phillip Carmical (pcarmical@scrivenerpublishing.com)

Compact and Flexible Microwave Devices

Edited by

Dilip Kumar Choudhary

Indrasen Singh

Manoj Kumar Singh

and

Amit Kumar Jain

Scrivener Publishing

WILEY

This edition first published 2025 by John Wiley & Sons, Inc., 111 River Street, Hoboken, NJ 07030, USA and Scrivener Publishing LLC, 100 Cummings Center, Suite 541J, Beverly, MA 01915, USA

For more information about Scrivener publications please visit www.scrivenerpublishing.com.

Wiley Global Headquarters
111 River Street, Hoboken, NJ 07030, USA

For details of our global editorial offices, customer services, and more information about Wiley products visit us at www.wiley.com.

Library of Congress Cataloging-in-Publication Data

ISBN 9781394275557

Cover image: Generated with AI using Adobe Firefly
Cover design by Russell Richardson

Set in size of 11pt and Minion Pro by Manila Typesetting Company, Makati, Philippines

Printed in the USA

10 9 8 7 6 5 4 3 2 1

Contents

Preface

In recent years, the rapid evolution of wireless communication systems, wearable technologies, and miniaturized electronic platforms has spurred an increasing demand for microwave devices that are not only compact and efficient but also mechanically flexible and adaptable. The convergence of these design requirements presents exciting challenges and opportunities in the field of microwave engineering. This edited volume, *Compact and Flexible Microwave Devices*, brings together recent advances and cutting-edge research that address these pressing needs.

The book aims to serve as a comprehensive reference for researchers, engineers, and graduate students working at the intersection of microwave technology, materials science, and applied electromagnetics. Contributions from leading experts across academia and industry cover a broad spectrum of topics, including novel materials and fabrication techniques, reconfigurable and metasurface-based devices, wearable and conformal antennas, flexible RF components, and system-level applications.

Each chapter has been carefully selected to offer both theoretical insights and practical design strategies, enabling readers to understand the underlying principles while also gaining hands-on knowledge of modern fabrication and characterization techniques. Special emphasis has been placed on the integration of compact and flexible devices into real-world applications, such as Internet of Things (IoT), biomedical diagnostics, remote sensing, and next-generation communication systems.

We extend our deepest gratitude to the contributors for their valuable chapters and to the reviewers for their insightful feedback. This volume is the result of their collective expertise, effort, and dedication. We also thank the editorial and production teams for their support throughout the publishing process.

It is our hope that this book will inspire further innovation and interdisciplinary collaboration, ultimately contributing to the advancement of flexible and miniaturized microwave technologies that shape the future of communication and sensing systems.

Dilip Kumar Choudhary
Vellore Institute of Technology,
Vellore, India

1

A Systematic Survey on Wearable Biomedical Sensors Using Flexible Microwaves Devices

Warisha Fatima[1], Shailendra Kumar[2], Mohd Javed Khan[2*] and Indrasen Singh[3]

[1]*Department of Physics, Integral University, Lucknow, India*
[2]*Department of ECE, Integral University, Lucknow, India*
[3]*School of Electronics Engineering VIT, Vellore, TN, India*

Abstract

Microwave devices play a vital role in medical sensors and imaging technology, offering non-invasive monitoring and diagnosis. The Internet of Things (IoT) framework is pivotal in healthcare, with radio frequency and microwave technologies enabling wireless sensory data transmission. Wireless power transmission is crucial for wearable, portable, and flexible sensors without bulky batteries. Electronic health (e-health) leverages digital and communication technologies to enhance healthcare delivery and outcomes. Wearable biomedical sensors revolutionize health maintenance, collecting physiological data for personalized insights, early detection, and continuous monitoring. These sensors encompass accelerometers, gyroscopes, heart rate monitors, skin temperature, electrocardiograms (ECG), and blood oxygen levels. They empower users with real-time health information, including blood glucose levels and heart rate patterns, benefiting those with cardiovascular diseases and the elderly through remote monitoring systems. Flexible materials like fabrics and polymers enhance sensor adaptability to body contours. Microwave devices enable non-invasive tissue characterization and tumor monitoring, offering insights into tumor features and dielectric properties. Ongoing research explores novel applications and technological advancements to enhance the functionality and adaptability of microwave-based wearable gadgets in healthcare and beyond.

**Corresponding author*: mjkhan.ec@gmail.com

Dilip Kumar Choudhary, Indrasen Singh, Manoj Kumar Singh and Amit Kumar Jain (eds.) Compact and Flexible Microwave Devices, (1–24) © 2025 Scrivener Publishing LLC

Keywords: Wearable sensors, real-time monitoring, microwave devices

1.1 Introduction

Interest in wearable health monitoring devices has grown as a result of the quick development in wireless communications and physiological sensing technologies [1, 2]. Wearable sensors can be used for monitoring and diagnostic purposes. They are currently capable of motion detection in addition to physical and metabolic sensing. The extent of the issues that these advances could potentially aid with is difficult to overemphasize. Many people with neurological, cardiovascular, and pulmonary conditions, including seizures, hypertension, dysrhythmias, and asthma, may benefit from physiological monitoring for both diagnosis and continued care. Motion detection technology installed in a home may help reduce the risk of falls and maximize a person's freedom and involvement in the community [3–7]. A potential new method of gathering physiological data without causing patients any inconvenience is through wearable wellness and physical activity monitoring devices [8–10]. Various operating techniques can be used by microwave sensor devices, depending on the needs of the particular application [11, 14]. Wearable microwave sensing devices work by probing biological tissues with electromagnetic waves to record complex physiological data with amazing accuracy and precision. This innovative method gets around several of the drawbacks of conventional monitoring approaches, including discomfort, obtrusiveness, and limited mobility. These sensors allow people to monitor their health continuously by blending in perfectly with regular clothing. This allows for early detection of abnormalities and proactive management of chronic illnesses [16–21]. These technologies include time-of-flight (ToF) approaches for accurate ranging, frequency-modulated continuous wave (FMCW) radar for distance measuring, and Doppler radar for motion detection [22–26]. Furthermore, developments in microwave technology have produced extremely selective and sensitive sensors that can pick up on minute alterations in the target's characteristics [38, 39]. The Wireless Body Area Network (WBAN) [41], which typically consists of several tiny, portable, ultralow powers, effective biosensors, is an example of a recently developed health monitoring gadget. Through dedicated networks, wearable gadgets with sensors positioned throughout the body may communicate [29]. Figure 1.1 shows that the size of the worldwide market for wearable medical devices was estimated at USD 30 billion in 2022 and is projected

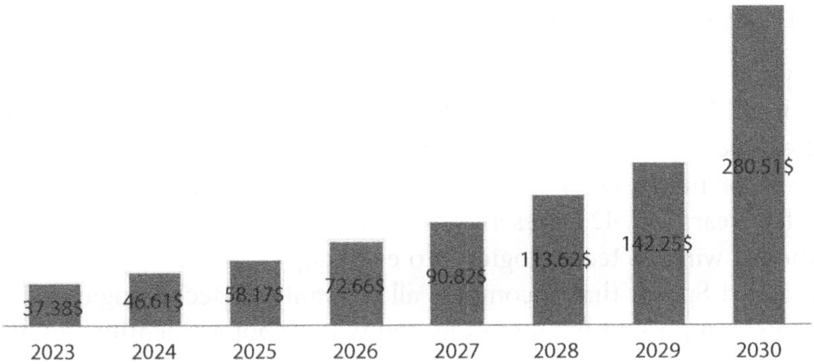

Figure 1.1 Wearable devices market in 2023-2030 in US dollars. Source: Precedence Research.

to reach approximately USD 300 billion by 2032, with a compound annual growth rate (CAGR) of 25.1% anticipated over the forecast period of 2023 to 2032 [48].

This research attempts to shed light on the revolutionary potential of microwave wearable sensors in transforming healthcare monitoring and spurring the transition to proactive, individualized healthcare paradigms by combining views from a variety of diverse viewpoints.

1.2 Literature Survey

A literature survey on wearable biomedical sensors reveals a growing market in developing safer and more efficient methods for essential tasks. The development and uptake of these sensors have been driven by the rising incidence of chronic illnesses and the increased focus on preventative healthcare [34, 35, 37]. This study explores wearable biological sensors' prospective uses, difficulties, and technological developments. Below, we provide a summary of key findings and insights from existing literature. In order to present an overview of cutting-edge technology and wearable devices intended for use in the electronic healthcare framework, the paper is divided into three sections, each of which covers one of these three subjects in detail. Systems for the indoor positioning are dealt with in subsection 1.2.1. Subsection 1.2.2 is concerned with the wearable sensors dealing in fall detection. Subsection 1.2.3 gives an overview of the microwave wearable sensing devices.

1.2.1 System for Indoor Positioning

Every application must have the ability to automatically identify items and people. RFID is remote object identification and localization technology that can be applied to patient monitoring. The domain of RFID and wireless sensor networks (WSNs) has experienced substantial growth in the past few years [40, 42]. Presently, there is a tendency to incorporate state-of-the-art wireless technologies into everyday locations, converting them into Smart Spaces that encompass all relevant IoT technologies. RFID is extremely important because of its ability to remotely identify and distinguish objects and people, even in congested areas and electromagnetically challenging conditions, such as private residences or retirement communities. The idea behind this is that it's getting more and more crucial to keep an eye on how senior citizens move and behave in order to spot any age-related conditions or issues early on (such as senile dementia and Alzheimer's disease) [43]. The following section shows how such devices, by witnessing individuals as well as non-intrusively evaluating their patterns of behavior, can be used effectively to localize people in their daily lives. Many data points can be stored on an RFID chip and then sent to the cloud for additional processing [45, 47]. An antenna-like electronic circuit board and a microchip are integrated into tags, also known as RFID "transponders," which are able to transmit radio signals that contain information, primarily the tag's distinctive identification number [63]. According to how they obtain energy to react to an RFID reader, tags can be categorized as "passive" or "active," depending on whether they're equipped with their own source of electricity and frequently transmit their ID signal or if they only use the tiny energy that the reader emits and collects via a small antenna [49]. A few RFID tags are "semi-passive," meaning they use tiny batteries and only send out signals when they detect a reader signal. A device called an indoor positioning system (IPS) makes it possible to track and locate people or items in limited spaces, usually buildings where GPS signals might not be available or dependable [50]. IPS uses a variety of techniques and tools to precisely pinpoint the location of an object or person. This final technology, as shown in Figure 1.2, foreshadows the use of multiple UWB receivers (also known as anchors), dispersed extensively throughout the testing room, and a substantial length of time for the analysis of the incoming data. The primary benefit is that it makes it possible to prevent the possible effects of fading and shadowing, which might happen at specific frequencies indoors. In order to analyze people's movements and the relative heights of the tags, a suitable data processing unit was developed and used to estimate the distance of the tags from the reader in addition

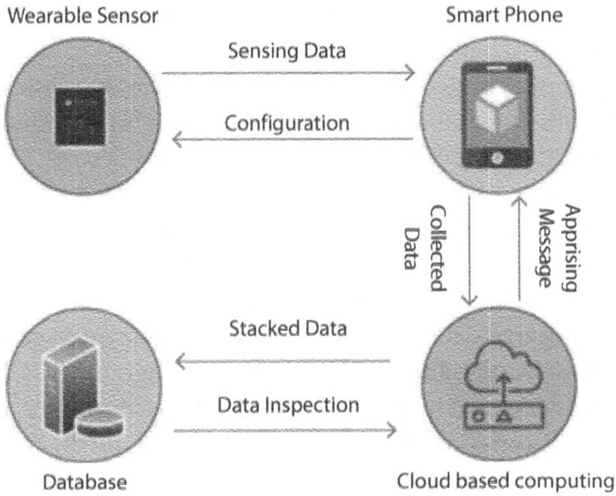

Figure 1.2 Localization and tracking system using wearable sensors [51].

to the computation of the two angular positions that were previously displayed. The reader's evaluation of the strength of the received signal indicators (RSSI) allowed this process to be completed. In this regard, Figure 1.2 describes a system where a wearable sensor gathers data, which is then sent to a smartphone. The smartphone forwards an alert to cloud computing for analysis, while also storing the data in a database for review, showcasing a streamlined process for real-time localization and tracking.

1.2.2 Fall Detection System

A fall detection system is a piece of technology intended to identify when someone falls, especially in circumstances when they might not be able to ask for assistance on their own. The system may sound an alert to notify emergency services, caregivers, or other designated contacts when a fall is detected. While some fall detection systems are put in homes or care facilities, others are integrated into wearables like smart watches or pendants. The diagram shown in Figure 1.3 provides a visual representation of a fall detection system utilizing deep learning and wearable sensor data. It captures the process from the initial fall detection by the sensor, through data transmission over the GSM network, to the delivery of an alarm message to a designated receiving terminal. The system's reliance on satellite communication indicates its potential for wide-area coverage, ensuring that alerts are promptly communicated, and assistance can be mobilized quickly, enhancing safety for individuals prone to falls, particularly the elderly or those with mobility challenges [62, 64].

This study demonstrated that the existing microwave system may reliably identify falls in senior adults who live alone in communities or in cohousing, obviating the requirement for continuous care. Usually, these systems use sensors like gyroscopes or accelerometers to identify abrupt motion changes that point to a fall. These sensors for detecting falls in wearable device-based fall detection systems are integrated into the wearable device via a wrist band, for example, that the subject wears. These systems track several data, including pulse oximetry, oxygen saturation (SPO2), heart rate variability (HRV), electrocardiogram (ECG), and kinematic properties detected by magnetometers, gyroscopes, and accelerometers. These sensors provide the tilt angle orientation, pitch, and oscillation information. For data processing and event classification, the retrieved information is routed to the computation unit. To find the linear and angular acceleration, utilize the accelerometer and gyroscope values. There were two accelerometer sensors: a chest sensor and a thigh sensor. The system underwent two stages of classification: first, it created an inconsistent signal lasting five seconds and paused if the accelerometer unexpectedly crossed a threshold. Five seconds later, the body position was evaluated by the system based on the orientation of the sensor. Under the assumption that the individual is standing, it can be assumed that the sensor's x axis aligned with the thigh was zero. Comparably, the system detects lying and validates the fall event if the x axis of the sensor positioned at the chest was high. The sensor's output was transferred via the ZigBee network to a PC, where all processing was done remotely in order to save battery power. Using a single accelerometer to track extremely complicated human movement is challenging. A fresh layout was suggested with six accelerometers that were positioned on the thighs, wrists, and neck [28]. Although the system had a high degree of accuracy, its numerous sensors made it difficult to utilize in everyday situations. Regarding a waist-borne fall detection device, multiple fall detection algorithms provided varying levels of performance. To determine which of the twenty-one distinct algorithms was most appropriate, an analysis was conducted [32]. The use of Wi-Fi or radar as fall detection sensors represents the final significant advancement in sensor technology after 2014. It looks into fall detection from a whole new perspective without using a new sensor. This type of fall detection method's primary concept is utilizing wireless technology to monitor changes in the environment and establishing a connection between human activity and wireless signals [12]. In addition to protecting users' privacy, it enables users to carry out daily tasks organically and constantly without

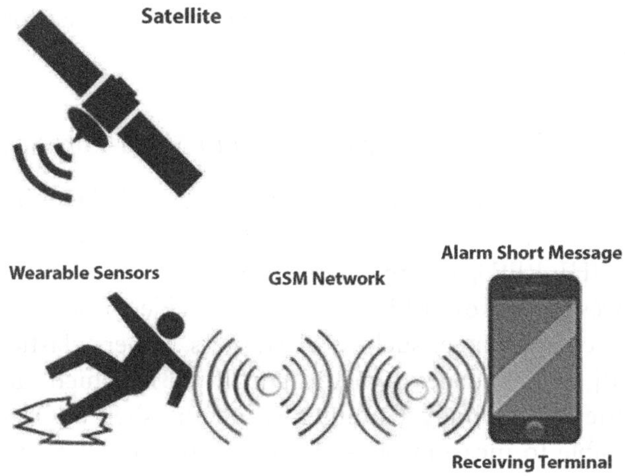

Figure 1.3 Diagrammatic illustration of the fundamental workings of a deep learning-based fall detection system that uses data from wearable's sensor.

wearing any equipment on their bodies [27]. This offers a fresh path into the future. A relatively non-invasive technology called WiFall is offered, which is an interesting example of a totally remote fall detection system. The physical layer channel state information (CSI) is used to detect human movement indoors before learning the specific patterns linked to falls and other behaviors that are of interest. The sensing, learning, and alerting components are the three core parts of the WiFall system. According to the trial data, WiFall had an average false alarm rate of 15% and 90% detection accuracy [65–67].

1.2.3 Wearable Sensor Device

The incorporation of radiofrequency (RF) and microwave technology to create wearable and passive sensors has drawn a lot of attention in recent years. Reliability, light weight, dainty size, and miniaturization are important considerations in the construction of cutting-edge microwave peripheral sensing systems. Even though radar is a highly well-known microwave technology, researchers are nevertheless interested in RF sensing since it has the ability to monitor novel biological characteristics and drastically simplify sensing systems. This segment examines various developments in RF-based wearable sensing covering the design of antennas and tags, their uses, read-out circuits, and constituent incorporation in the demanding electromagnetic environment that wearables are used in. The first publicly accessible platform discussed is UHF RFID, which is used for single and multi-parameter sensing.

1.2.3.1 UHF RFID: From Identification to Multi-Port Sensing

In the 860–960 MHz range, Ultra High Frequency (UHF) Radio Frequency Identification (RFID) is a well-established technology. Compact transponders enable UHF RFID, an expandable technology, to operate at intermediate distances [13]. Now RFID antennas are able to be mass-produced in any form or substance, such as elastomers, paper, plastics, washable e-textiles [30], and bandages of medical quality [31], which can be applied straight to the human body. Commercial-off-the-shelf (COTS) tags have made it possible to measure physiological values like temperature, pressure, and moisture. Chemical properties (such as pH and chlorides) and bio-electric signals (such as skin resistance, ECG, and EMG) are also sensed by additional experimental equipment [32, 33]. Compressing several functionalities onto a single device is an additional benefit. Multi-port RFID devices can be produced by boosting the total quantity of implanted ICs, which in turn increases the number of sensors that can be operated simultaneously. It can serve as a single antenna with numerous embedded ICs, or alternatively they can be designed as an array of single-IC antennas placed closely to one another. The Identification Division Multiplexing (ID-DM) technology multiplexes the gathered sensor data on-the-air. It enables the management of multiple data at once using the accepted EPC protocol, based on the ID associated with every IC. Sensor-oriented multi-chip RFID systems can function in one of two ways: either in a multi-parametric sensing mode, where each port operates independently and provides useful data, or in a single-parameter sensing mode, where each port constructively contributes to only one piece of outcome.

Multi-chip RFID systems that are focused on sensing have two possible modes of operation: (i) multi-parametric sensing, where each port functions independently and provides relevant data, or (ii) single-parameter sensing, where each port coherently contributes to a single output data. Here, a number of wearable RFID sensors that employ both strategies are evaluated to show how bio-friendly materials and RFID sensing can be used to give wearables new capabilities in a non-pervasive way. Figure 1.4 presents a systemic illustration of wearable sensor devices used in e-health. It shows a network where individuals (User 1, User 2, User N) are equipped with wearable biosensors. These devices collect health data and transmit it to a server via a data transmission system. The server processes and stores this information in a cloud database, which is accessible to health

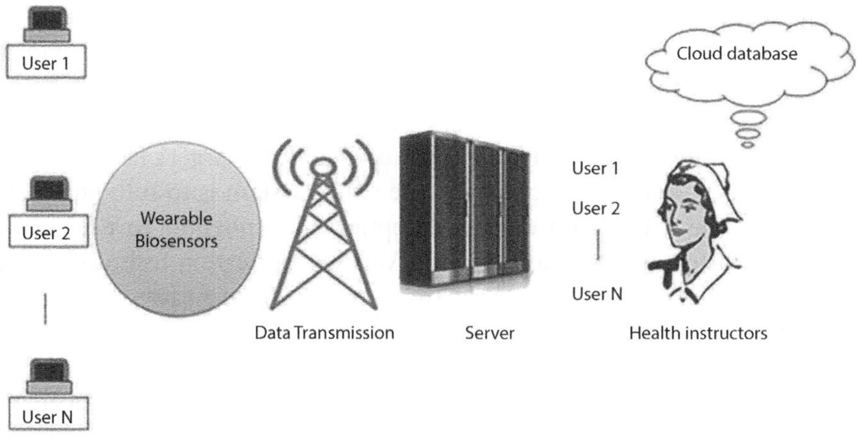

Figure 1.4 Systemic illustration of wearable sensor devices used in e-health.

instructors. This setup enables continuous health monitoring and allows instructors to provide personalized feedback or interventions, illustrating the potential of wearable technology in enhancing healthcare delivery and patient outcomes [72].

1.2.3.2 Bio-Radar in Microwave Wearable Application

Even though radar is a highly well-known microwave technology, researchers are nevertheless interested in RF sensing since it can monitor novel biological characteristics and drastically simplify sensing systems. Vital indicators, like cardiac and respiratory signals, can be recorded by radar systems, eliminating the need for touch sensors or electrodes. These devices typically send electromagnetic pulses (EM waves) in the direction of the subject's abdominal wall based on the Doppler effect, which are then reflected and picked up by the radar. The physiological intelligence is contained in the phase modulation of the received signal, which is interpreted as a result of the chest-wall displacement altering the EM waves' travelled route [41]. The system in question, hereinafter referred to as the "Bio-Radar system," offers a variety of features that allow for uninterrupted surveillance that can detect variations in vital sign patterns and, in turn, assist in identifying unexpected events, such as a car driver's fatigue or a baby's airway obstruction during sleep [41]. Patients who are bedridden and in a serious condition can also be observed, and this may aid in the diagnosing process. It is also possible to use it for psychological purposes, such as measuring stress response. Bio-radar applications that leverage wearables and semi-wearable integration may necessitate complete set-up integration in customized objects. This improves the primary system's low-key nature and expedites the manufacturing process, and it gives the person being watched greater comfort. Antennas are an important component in the bio-radar context that determine the radar's and the target's field of sight. Consequently, one way to empower the entire system is to fully integrate them into the application objects deception. It is possible to use textile antennas to achieve this purpose [44]. Various fabrication techniques can be employed to create wearable electronic textiles from a variety of materials. The ultimate use is always linked to the materials and fabrication techniques chosen. Because of this, the study of e-textiles requires knowledge of multiple disciplines, including textiles, materials, electronics, mechanics, and computer engineering [15]. The diagram in Figure 1.5 illustrates a biosensor system designed to monitor sweat concentration. It features a sensor applied to the skin, likely on the arm, which absorbs sweat to analyze its composition. The sensor transmits data as a microwave signal to a chip that interprets the parameters. This chip is responsible for recognizing the specific sweat parameters and displaying the results on a screen. This technology could be pivotal for health monitoring, allowing for non-

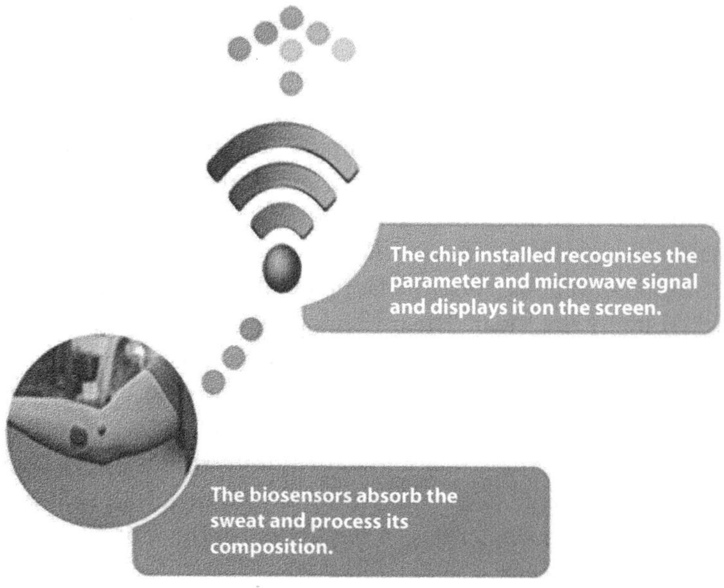

Figure 1.5 Biosensors detecting sweat concentration.

invasive tracking of physiological changes through sweat analysis, potentially providing insights into hydration levels, stress, and other health-related metrics [77].

1.3 Procedure and Working

1.3.1 Sensor Architecture

- **Frequency Selection:** Take into account the intended use when selecting an appropriate frequency range. Microwave sensors typically function in the GHz band.
- **Antenna Design:** Create antennas that are appropriate for wearable technology. Antennas that are conformal, flexible, and compact are frequently favored.
- **Sensor Configuration:** Choose the sensor arrangement that best suits the particular parameter that needs to be measured. For example, a radar-type sensor would work well for breathing monitoring.

1.3.2 Principle of Measurement

- Recognize the relationship that exists between the target physiological parameter and microwave signals. For example, differences in heart rate or respiration can alter a tissue's dielectric characteristics, which microwave sensors can pick up on.
- Based on the needs of the application, select a suitable sensing method, such as impulse radar, frequency-modulated continuous wave (FMCW) radar, or Doppler radar.

1.3.3 Signal Encoding

- Utilize the microwave sensor to gather raw data.
- To obtain pertinent data on the metabolic parameter, use signal processing techniques including feature extraction, filtering, and noise reduction.
- When analyzing and interpreting signals, make use of sophisticated algorithms like machine learning techniques for anomaly or pattern identification.

1.3.4 Calibration and Verification

- To guarantee measurement accuracy and dependability, calibrate the sensor system.
- Verify the sensor's performance with controlled trials and by contrasting it with other systems or techniques.
- As needed, iterate the calibration and design processes to increase precision and dependability.

1.3.5 Connectivity with Wearable Technology

- Include the microwave sensor in a wearable form factor, like a clothing item, wristband, or patch.
- Make sure the wearable gadget is cozy, unobtrusive, and appropriate for extended usage.
- Include the electronics required for power management, wireless transmission, and data processing.

1.3.6 Examining and Implementing

- To evaluate the wearable sensor system's usability, dependability, and performance, put it through a rigorous testing process under real-world circumstances.
- Resolve any problems or restrictions found throughout the testing process.
- Install the sensor system for planned uses, such as wellness management, sports performance tracking, or remote health monitoring.

1.3.7 Perks of Microwave Wearable Sensors

- **Portability:** Because compact wearables are small, light, and convenient to carry, users can wear them all day without feeling burdened. Without limiting mobility, this portability allows for constant tracking and monitoring of multiple parameters.
- **Comfort:** Designed to be worn directly on the body, compact wearables frequently have soft materials and ergonomic layouts that provide comfort even after extended use. There is a decreased chance of discomfort or annoyance for users,

which improves their entire experience and encourages them to wear the device consistently.

- **24/7 Monitoring:** Wearable devices may be worn constantly because of their lightweight design and tiny size, which makes it possible to monitor health indicators, activity levels, sleep cycles, and other metrics around-the-clock. This ongoing observation offers a thorough picture of the health and behavior of users throughout time.
- **Real-Time Feedback:** Vibrating alerts, LED indicators, or notifications on linked devices are examples of real-time feedback methods that are frequently included in compact wearables. Users' motivation and engagement are increased because they may make decisions regarding their productivity, fitness, or health right away thanks to this instant feedback.
- **Wireless Communication:** To synchronize data with computers, tablets, or smartphones, a lot of small wearables use wireless communication technologies like Bluetooth or Wi-Fi. The frictionless data transfer, online storage, and remote monitoring made possible by this wireless link improve accessibility and data-sharing possibilities.

1.3.8 Imperfections in Wearable Sensors

- **Accuracy and Reliability:** The accuracy and reliability of wearable sensors might fluctuate depending on the innovation and application. The precision of measurements can be impacted by variables such sensor drift, motion artifacts, ambient interference, and user variability, which could result in inaccurate data interpretation.
- **Maintenance and Calibration:** To maintain correct readings over time, some sensor devices need to undergo routine maintenance and calibrating. Users may find this process laborious, and there may be a period of time when the device cannot be used.
- **Data Security and Privacy:** Health indicators, activity patterns, and location data are just a few examples of the private information that wearable sensors may gather. It is crucial to protect the privacy and security of this data, but if the right security measures aren't taken, wearable technology could be subject to hacking, data breaches, or unwanted access.

- **Cost:** Some consumers may find it burdensome to pay a substantial upfront cost for high-quality wearable sensors with sophisticated features and capabilities. Furthermore, recurring expenses like software upgrades or cloud service subscription fees could raise the overall cost of ownership.

1.4 Next-Generation Wearables: A Strategic Plan for the Future

The combination of state-of-the-art technology, user-friendly design, and easy integration into daily life is embodied by future-oriented wearables. These wearables provide sophisticated surveillance of health, personalized instances, and improved connection, going beyond a basic activity tracker. Numerous new avenues for wearables research have been made possible by developments in RFICs, materials, packaging, and machine learning (ML) approaches for the recognition and classification of vital signs. In order to facilitate the emergence of a new generation of wearable devices, we have highlighted in this section the primary application regions and study disciplines that will witness additional growth. ML algorithms more accurately correlate several physical and biochemical characteristics to overall health or particular disorders than a single modality can. The second part provides a snapshot of the current uses of microwave systems in healthcare and highlights areas where further advancements could hasten the widespread implementation of wearables in novel biomedical uses.

1.4.1 Troubleshooting for Microwaves and Extended Inspection

Applications utilizing impedance, capacitive, and permittivity sensing on physiological variables including skin impedance, its rhythms, pulses, and arterial pressure, and biochemical indicators like fluids and blood sugar levels have been successfully documented for unobtrusive microwave probing via wearables. It is evident that their therapeutic applications will depend on how accurate and robust they are in real-world situations. Enhanced integration of these RF sensors with specialized read-out circuitry for a better read range and more thorough comparisons with current clinical-grade sensors may be possible in future research. Additionally, techniques to protect privacy will have to be created to stop third parties from listening in on private information. Other bio parameters like blood pressure and blood glucose levels have been handled utilizing a variety of techniques, ranging from SILO [36] to reflectometry employing a lab-based Vector Network Analyzer (VNA) [46]. Such measuring sets must be repeatable and portable in order to support clinical studies and long-term assessment. Before the circuits are widely used, the issues of dependability and usability must be resolved in order for them to pass the rigorous testing in a clinical context. Multidisciplinary microwave-accredited medical also includes wearable microfluidic biosensing. In recent years, the use of microfluidics for on-body diagnostics in applications related to biology has been investigated [52]. Scholars studying wearable technology are nowadays quite interested in biological sensors. These kinds of sensors can track atmospheric chemical constituent levels and biochemistry (e.g., to assist monitoring persons working in dangerous conditions). Biochemical sensing is possibly the most complicated from a design perspective since it frequently needs the collection, processing, and disposal of bodily fluids. Though studies regarding wearable biochemical gauges have proved sluggish to advance, they have recently accelerated thanks to advancements in micro and nano manufacturing technologies. Subsequent portable microfluidic technology might make use of microwave sensor technology with additional study on microwave microfluidic sensors, especially adaptive and customizable devices [53, 54]. But this would depend on getting hold of small-form-factor, sensitive collecting circuitry; current developments like single-chip VNAs [55] may make substantially miniaturized wearable electromagnetic to so-THz sensing [56] possible.

1.4.2 Implantable Microwave Technology

Implantable equipment can be added to or used in conjunction with "wearables" in some situations where the quality of the obtained signals is crucial. High data rates coupled with great spatial resolution, non-intrusive biological signal capture are necessary for future-oriented implantable medical devices including brain-machine interfacing. Brain-computer interfaces, or BCIs, are very interesting because they can capture in real time neural impulses from the brain for the purpose of diagnosing neural illnesses like epilepsy [68, 69], and controlling artificial limbs with signals from the cortex motor [70, 71]. In order to control symptoms, such as Parkinson's illness [73, 74], epilepsy [75], spasms [76, 78], convulsions [79], vertigo [80, 81], Tourette syndrome (TS) [82, 83], and pains, BCI can be used to influence the brain or nerve systems [52]. Cognitive decline, depressive disorders, schizophrenia, drug addiction, anxiousness, obsessive compulsive disorder, and other conditions are at present being studied using brain monitoring and stimulation techniques. Because smaller wearables and implantable devices result in more sensor volume, a simpler sealing and implantation procedure, better spatio-temporal resolution, and less harm to tissue, research to reduce their size has therefore been ongoing [58, 59]. The use of body-centric microwave technology in next-generation healthcare includes implanted gadgets like brain-machine interfaces. These necessitate high data rates and high spatial resolution biological signal capture that is non-invasive. As a result, attempts to reduce the size of wearable and implantable devices have been ongoing since doing so increases sensor density, facilitates wrapping and implantation, improves spatio-temporal resolution, and causes the least amount of tissue damage [57]. A dispersed network of mm-size nodes realises the conceptual notion of a closed-loop systems neural interface as shown in the diagram. To improve the results of brain stimulation, closed-loop systems have been suggested. In order to control brain processes and consequently signs and symptoms, instantaneous feedback can be obtained by selecting neuro-stimulation characteristics according to the electrical impulses collected on linked neurons. Figure 1.6 describes a closed-loop neuronal recording and stimulation apparatus. It features neural chips integrated into the brain, which are connected wirelessly to an external data processor like a laptop. This setup enables two-way communication, allowing for both the recording of neuronal activity and the delivery of stimulation signals. The wearable power and data component suggests a portable aspect to the system, facilitating real-time interaction with the neural interface. Such technology could be pivotal in advancing neuroscientific research and developing treatments for neurological disorders by providing precise monitoring and control of brain activity.

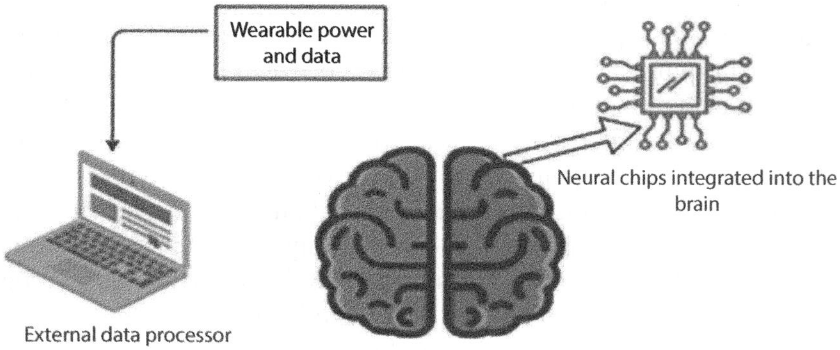

Figure 1.6 Diagrammatic representation of a closed-loop neuronal recording and stimulation apparatus.

1.4.3 Medications Using Microwaves

Another important research path is the transition from microwave-enabled wearable healthcare diagnostics to wearable medicines. For example, microwave hyperthermia is a tried-and-true method of treating cancer [60]. However, the possibility of employing wearable textile antennas for hyperthermia on a basic breast-shaped spectre has only been somewhat investigated [61]. Diagnostics and therapeutic wearables both have their share of difficulties. Assessments of efficacy of treatments and feedback systems for wearables for neuro-stimulation and hyperthermia presently rely on assessments made by qualified experts. Because of the field and power distributions throughout a wide range of body and tissue types, the results can be unpredictable. Research procedures for these kinds of research are usually complex since it is hard to design human body-controlled trials or realistic phantoms that replicate a wide range of physical and biological factors. The ability of simulation technologies to depict intricate bodily circumstances is likewise restricted. Sophisticated multi-physics modeling of tissues, organs, and bodies with dynamic parameters that align well with both anatomical and molecular features are required to overcome this impediment. In uses, boosting signal frequency improves spectrum and spatial clarity spontaneously and may allow field engagement with biomolecules for sense. Power consideration, interference, sounds, and body artifacts in radio frequency technology remain significant obstacles. Treatment for hyperhidrosis can also involve microwave hyperthermia. Regardless of the outside temperature. Hyperhidrosis is a disorder in which a person generates excessive amounts of sweat over and above their usual bodily requirements. Focusing the glands that produce sweat under the arms, miraDry® has created a minimally invasive treatment that uses microwave hyperthermia to decrease sweating and treat basic underarm hyperhidrosis. The flesh beneath the arms is shielded by a cooling device while microwave energy is being administered [84]. To optimise the absorption of energy close to the dermal/hypodermal interface an applicator with a cooling mechanism and a collection of four waveguide antennas was developed [85].

1.5 Conclusion

It's important to explore a variety of topics while talking about the outcomes and discoveries of wearable microwave sensors, including performance measures, usability, possible applications, and constraints.

A wearable health monitoring technique's main goal is to enable people to live autonomous, active lifestyles in their comfortable homes while providing seamless, ongoing, non-intrusive wellness and bodily health monitoring. A person's health condition can now be continuously and non-intrusively monitored at a very low cost thanks to the significant technological advancements of the past few years. These advancements have made it possible to manufacture and use tiny, inexpensive sensors, actuators, circuits for electronics, and robust computers. Numerous advantages stemming from wearable technologies' small form factor include wireless communication, wireless mobility, comfort, ease, continuous monitoring, and integration with daily life, real-time feedback, and customisation. Because of these benefits, small wearables can be used for a variety of tasks, such as measuring fitness and health and enhancing productivity. Sensitive personal data, including activity patterns, location data, and health measures, are gathered by wearable sensors. It is crucial to protect the privacy and security of this data; if the right security measures aren't taken, wearable technology could be subject to hacking, data breaches, or unwanted access. In order to address usability issues, user-centric design techniques, clinical validation studies to determine the effectiveness of microwave sensors for medical usage, and ethical considerations to guarantee user data confidentiality and privacy should be the main areas of future research and development. In conclusion, microwave wearable sensors are a remarkable technical development with enormous promise across many industries, but especially in sports, healthcare, and wellness management. Compared to conventional monitoring techniques, these sensors provide a number of benefits, such as non-intrusiveness, continuous monitoring capabilities, and ease of integration into daily life. The performance test has shown the microwave wearable sensors' accuracy, sensitivity, and real-time monitoring capabilities, underscoring their potential for use in lifestyle management, sports performance tracking, and remote patient monitoring. To guarantee dependable and strong performance in real-world scenarios, however, issues including signal interference, motion artifacts, and environmental influences must be resolved.

References

1. Boric-Lubecke, O., Lubecke, V.M., Jokanovic, B., Singh, A., Shahhaidar, E., Padasdao, B., Microwave and wearable technologies for 5G, in: *2015 12th International Conference on Telecommunication in Modern Satellite, Cable and Broadcasting Services (TELSIKS)*, IEEE, pp. 183–188, 2015, October.

2. Vijayan, V., Connolly, J.P., Condell, J., McKelvey, N., Gardiner, P., Review of wearable devices and data collection considerations for connected health. *Sensors, 21*, 16, 5589, 2021.
3. Aroganam, G., Manivannan, N., Harrison, D., Review on wearable technology sensors used in consumer sport applications. *Sensors, 19*, 9, 1983, 2019.
4. Castillejo, P., Martinez, J.F., Rodriguez-Molina, J., Cuerva, A., Integration of wearable devices in a wireless sensor network for an E-health application. *IEEE Wireless Commun., 20*, 4, 38–49, 2013.
5. Kim, J., Chou, E.F., Le, J., Wong, S., Chu, M., Khine, M., Soft wearable pressure sensors for beat-to-beat blood pressure monitoring. *Adv. Healthcare Mater., 8*, 13, 1900109, 2019.
6. Brady, S., Carson, B., O'Gorman, D., Moyna, N., Diamond, D., Combining wireless with wearable technology for the development of on-body networks, in: *International Workshop on Wearable and Implantable Body Sensor Networks (BSN'06)*, IEEE, pp. 4–pp, 2006, April.
7. Padash, M., Enz, C., Carrara, S., Microfluidics by additive manufacturing for wearable biosensors: A review. *Sensors, 20*, 15, 4236, 2020.
8. Huang, J., Yu, X., Wang, Y., Xiao, X., An integrated wireless wearable sensor system for posture recognition and indoor localization. *Sensors, 16*, 11, 1825, 2016.
9. El Gharbi, M., Fernández-García, R., Ahyoud, S., Gil, I., A review of flexible wearable antenna sensors: design, fabrication methods, and applications. *Materials, 13*, 17, 3781, 2020.
10. Chen, C.Y., Hsieh, C.W., Liao, Y.H., Yin, T.J., Implementation of wearable devices and indoor positioning system for a smart hospital environment, in: *2018 International Symposium in Sensing and Instrumentation in IoT Era (ISSI)*, IEEE, pp. 1–5, 2018, September.
11. Paolini, G., Masotti, D., Costanzo, A., RFID Reader and Wearable Tags for Smart Health Applications, in: *2021 XXXIVth General Assembly and Scientific Symposium of the International Union of Radio Science (URSI GASS)*, IEEE, pp. 01–03, 2021, August.
12. Paolini, G., Masotti, D., Antoniazzi, F., Cinotti, T.S., Costanzo, A., Fall detection and 3-D indoor localization by a custom RFID reader embedded in a smart e-health platform. *IEEE Trans. Microwave Theory Tech., 67*, 12, 5329–5339, 2019.
13. Wang, Y., Wu, K., Ni, L.M., Wifall: Device-free fall detection by wireless networks. *IEEE Trans. Mob. Comput., 16*, 2, 581–594, 2016.
14. Waheed, M., Afzal, H., Mehmood, K., NT-FDS—A noise tolerant fall detection system using deep learning on wearable devices. *Sensors, 21*, 6, 2006, 2021.
15. Escobedo, P., Bhattacharjee, M., Nikbakhtnasrabadi, F., Dahiya, R., Smart bandage with wireless strain and temperature sensors and batteryless NFC tag. *IEEE Internet Things J., 8*, 6, 5093–5100, 2020.

16. Costanzo, A., Augello, E., Battistini, G., Benassi, F., Masotti, D., Paolini, G., Microwave devices for wearable sensors and IoT. *Sensors*, *23*, 9, 4356, 2023.
17. Hiremath, S., Yang, G., Mankodiya, K., Wearable Internet of Things: Concept, architectural components and promises for person-centered healthcare, in: *2014 4th International Conference on Wireless Mobile Communication and Healthcare-Transforming Healthcare through Innovations in Mobile and Wireless Technologies (MOBIHEALTH)*, IEEE, pp. 304–307, 2014, November.
18. Miorandi, D., Sicari, S., De Pellegrini, F., Chlamtac, I., Internet of things: Vision, applications and research challenges. *Ad Hoc Netw.*, *10*, 7, 1497–1516, 2012.
19. Costanzo, A. and Masotti, D., Wirelessly powering: An enabling technology for zero-power sensors, IoT and D2D communication, in: *2015 IEEE MTT-S International Microwave Symposium*, IEEE, pp. 1–4, 2015, May.
20. Movassaghi, S., Abolhasan, M., Lipman, J., Smith, D., Jamalipour, A., Wireless body area networks: A survey. *IEEE Commun. Surv. Tutor.*, *16*, 3, 1658–1686, 2014.
21. Grosinger, J. and Michalowska-Forsyth, A., Space tags: Ultra-low-power operation and radiation hardness for passive wireless sensor tags. *IEEE Microwave Mag.*, *23*, 3, 55–71, 2022.
22. Wagih, M., Weddell, A.S., Beeby, S., Rectennas for radio-frequency energy harvesting and wireless power transfer: A review of antenna design [antenna applications corner]. *IEEE Antennas Propag. Mag.*, *62*, 5, 95–107, 2020.
23. Lu, X., Wang, P., Niyato, D., Kim, D., II, Han, Z., Wireless networks with RF energy harvesting: A contemporary survey. *IEEE Commun. Surv. Tutor.*, *17*, 2, 757–789, 2014.
24. Bito, J., Hester, J.G., Tentzeris, M.M., Ambient RF energy harvesting from a two-way talk radio for flexible wearable wireless sensor devices utilizing inkjet printing technologies. *IEEE Trans. Microw. Theory Tech.*, *63*, 12, 4533–4543, 2015.
25. Lyu, H., Wang, Z., Babakhani, A., A UHF/UWB hybrid RFID tag with a 51-m energy-harvesting sensitivity for remote vital-sign monitoring. *IEEE Trans. Microw. Theory Tech.*, *68*, 11, 4886–4895, 2020.
26. Reeder, B. and David, A., Health at hand: A systematic review of smart watch uses for health and wellness. *J. Biomed. Inf.*, *63*, 269–276, 2016.
27. Hinde, K., White, G., Armstrong, N., Wearable devices suitable for monitoring twenty four hour heart rate variability in military populations. *Sensors*, *21*, 4, 1061, 2021.
28. Bianco, G.M., Occhiuzzi, C., Panunzio, N., Marrocco, G., A survey on radio frequency identification as a scalable technology to face pandemics. *IEEE J. Radio Freq. Identif.*, *6*, 77–96, 2021.
29. Wagih, M., Wei, Y., Komolafe, A., Torah, R., Beeby, S., Reliable UHF long-range textile-integrated RFID tag based on a compact flexible antenna filament. *Sensors*, *20*, 12, 3435, 2020.

30. Simorangkir, R.B., Le, D., Björninen, T., Sayem, A.S.M., Zhadobov, M., Sauleau, R., Washing durability of PDMS-conductive fabric composite: Realizing washable UHF RFID tags. *IEEE Antennas Wirel. Propag. Lett.*, *18*, 12, 2572–2576, 2019.
31. Panunzio, N. and Marrocco, G., Second skin project: Biointegrated wireless sensors for the epidermal monitoring and restoring of sensorial injuries, in: *2021 IEEE International Conference on RFID Technology and Applications (RFID-TA)*, 2021, October, IEEE, pp. 173–176.
32. Mazzaracchio, V., Fiore, L., Nappi, S., Marrocco, G., Arduini, F., Medium-distance affordable, flexible and wireless epidermal sensor for pH monitoring in sweat. *Talanta*, *222*, 121502, 2021.
33. Besnoff, J.S., Deyle, T., Harrison, R.R., Reynolds, M.S., Battery-free multichannel digital ECG biotelemetry using UHF RFID techniques, in: *2013 IEEE International Conference on RFID (RFID)*, IEEE, pp. 16–22, 2013, April.
34. Marrocco, G., RFID grids: Part I—Electromagnetic theory. *IEEE Trans. Antennas Propag.*, *59*, 3, 1019–1026, 2011.
35. El Arif, R., Su, W.C., Horng, T.S., Chest-worn heart rate variability monitor with a self-injection-locked oscillator tag. *IEEE Trans. Microw. Theory Tech.*, *70*, 5, 2851–2860, 2022.
36. Tseng, C.H., Tseng, T.J., Wu, C.Z., Cuffless blood pressure measurement using a microwave near-field self-injection-locked wrist pulse sensor. *IEEE Trans. Microw. Theory Tech.*, *68*, 11, 4865–4874, 2020.
37. Lee, C.S., Wu, C.Y., Kuo, Y.L., Wearable bracelet belt resonators for noncontact wrist location and pulse detection. *IEEE Trans. Microw. Theory Tech.*, *65*, 11, 4475–4482, 2017.
38. Benassi, F., Paolini, G., Masotti, D., Costanzo, A., A wearable flexible energy-autonomous filtenna for ethanol detection at 2.45 GHz. *IEEE Trans. Microw. Theory Tech.*, *69*, 9, 4093–4106, 2021.
39. Rizzoli, V., Costanzo, A., Masotti, D., Lipparini, A., Mastri, F., Computer-aided optimization of nonlinear microwave circuits with the aid of electromagnetic simulation. *IEEE Trans. Microw. Theory Tech.*, *52*, 1, 362–377, 2004.
40. Loss, C., Gouveia, C., Salvado, R., Pinho, P., Vieira, J., Textile antenna for bio-radar embedded in a car seat. *Materials*, *14*, 1, 213, 2021.
41. Yavari, E., Rahman, A., Xu, J., Mandic, D.P., Boric-Lubecke, O., Synchrosqueezing an effective method for analyzing Doppler radar physiological signals, in: *2016 38th Annual International Conference of the IEEE Engineering in Medicine and Biology Society (EMBC)*, 2016, August, IEEE, pp. 263–266.
42. Anishchenko, L., Challenges and potential solutions of psychophysiological state monitoring with bioradar technology. *Diagnostics*, *8*, 4, 73, 2018.
43. Fernández, J.R.M. and Anishchenko, L., Mental stress detection using bioradar respiratory signals. *Biomed. Signal Process. Control*, *43*, 244–249, 2018.

44. Paracha, K.N., Rahim, S.K.A., Soh, P.J., Khalily, M., Wearable antennas: A review of materials, structures, and innovative features for autonomous communication and sensing. *IEEE Access*, *7*, 56694–56712, 2019.
45. Patron, D., Mongan, W., Kurzweg, T.P., Fontecchio, A., Dion, G., Anday, E.K., Dandekar, K.R., On the use of knitted antennas and inductively coupled RFID tags for wearable applications. *IEEE Trans. Biomed. Circuits Syst.*, *10*, 6, 1047–1057, 2016.
46. Kandwal, A., Nie, Z., Igbe, T., Li, J., Liu, Y., Liu, L.W., Hao, Y., Surface plasmonic feature microwave sensor with highly confined fields for aqueous-glucose and blood-glucose measurements. *IEEE Trans. Instrum. Meas.*, *70*, 1–9, 2020.
47. Cataldo, A., De Benedetto, E., Schiavoni, R., Monti, G., Tedesco, A., Masciullo, A., Tarricone, L., Portable microwave reflectometry system for skin sensing. *IEEE Trans. Instrum. Meas.*, *71*, 1–8, 2022.
48. Wagih, M., Malik, O., Weddell, A.S., Beeby, S., E-textile breathing sensor using fully textile wearable antennas. *Eng. Proc.*, *15*, 1, 9, 2022.
49. Liu, Y., Yu, M., Xia, B., Wang, S., Wang, M., Chen, M., Ye, T.T., E-textile battery-less displacement and strain sensor for human activities tracking. *IEEE Internet Things J.*, *8*, 22, 16486–16497, 2021.
50. Tajin, M.A.S., Amanatides, C.E., Dion, G., Dandekar, K.R., Passive UHF RFID-based knitted wearable compression sensor. *IEEE Internet Things J.*, *8*, 17, 13763–13773, 2021.
51. Wang, M., Yang, Y., Min, J., Song, Y., Tu, J., Mukasa, D., Gao, W., A wearable electrochemical biosensor for the monitoring of metabolites and nutrients. *Nat. Biomed. Eng.*, *6*, 11, 1225–1235, 2022.
52. Su, W., Cook, B.S., Tentzeris, M.M., Additively manufactured microfluidics-based "peel-and-replace" RF sensors for wearable applications. *IEEE Trans. Microw. Theory Tech.*, *64*, 6, 1928–1936, 2016.
53. Cook, B.S., Cooper, J.R., Tentzeris, M.M., An inkjet-printed microfluidic RFID-enabled platform for wireless lab-on-chip applications. *IEEE Trans. Microw. Theory Tech.*, *61*, 12, 4714–4723, 2013.
54. Chung, H., Ma, Q., Sayginer, M., Rebeiz, G.M., A Packaged 0.01–26-GHz single-chip SiGe reflectometer for two-port vector network analyzers. *IEEE Trans. Microw. Theory Tech.*, *68*, 5, 1794–1808, 2020.
55. Liu, S., Orloff, N.D., Little, C.A., Zhao, W., Booth, J.C., Williams, D.F., Nauwelaers, B., Hybrid characterization of nanolitre dielectric fluids in a single microfluidic channel up to 110 GHz. *IEEE Trans. Microw. Theory Tech.*, *65*, 12, 5063–5073, 2017.
56. Nikolova, N.K., Microwave imaging for breast cancer. *IEEE Microw. Mag.*, 12, 7, 78–94, 3077–3079.
57. Rahmani, H. and Babakhani, A., A wirelessly powered reconfigurable FDD radio with on-chip antennas for multi-site neural interfaces. *IEEE J. Solid-State Circuits*, *56*, 10, 3177–3190, 2021.

58. Muller, R., Le, H.P., Li, W., Ledochowitsch, P., Gambini, S., Bjorninen, T., Rabaey, J.M., A minimally invasive 64-channel wireless μECoG implant. *IEEE J. Solid-State Circuits*, *50*, 1, 344–359, 2014.
59. Ha, S., Akinin, A., Park, J., Kim, C., Wang, H., Maier, C., Cauwenberghs, G., Silicon-integrated high-density electrocortical interfaces. *Proc. IEEE*, *105*, 1, 11–33, 2016.
60. Tammam, E., Said, A.M., Ibrahim, A.A., Galal, A., II, About the interstitial microwave cancer ablation: Principles, advantages and challenges. *IEEE Access*, *8*, 49685–49694, 2020.
61. Mukai, Y. and Suh, M., Development of a conformal woven fabric antenna for wearable breast hyperthermia. *Fashion Text.*, *8*, 1, 7, 2021.
62. Zhi, W.J., Wang, L.F., Hu, X.J., Recent advances in the effects of microwave radiation on brains. *Mil. Med. Res.*, *4*, 1–14, 2017.
63. Preece, A.W., Iwi, G., Davies-Smith, A., Wesnes, K., Butler, S., Varey, A., Effect of a 915-MHz simulated mobile phone signal on cognitive function in man. *Int. J. Radiat. Biol.*, *75*, 4, 1999.
64. Tak, J. and Choi, J., A wearable metamaterial microwave absorber. *IEEE Antennas Wirel. Propag. Lett.*, *16*, 784–787, 2016.
65. International Commission on Non-Ionizing Radiation Protection, Guidelines for limiting exposure to electromagnetic fields (100 kHz to 300 GHz). *Health Phys.*, *118*, 5, 483–524, 2020.
66. Kim, J., Khan, S., Wu, P., Park, S., Park, H., Yu, C., Kim, W., Self-charging wearables for continuous health monitoring. *Nano Energy*, *79*, 105419, 2021.
67. Tian, Y., Guan, W., Li, G., Mehran, K., Tian, J., Xiang, L., A review on foreign object detection for magnetic coupling-based electric vehicle wireless charging. *Green Energy Intell Transp.*, *1*, 2, 100007, 2022.
68. Schulze-Bonhage, A., Long-term outcome in neurostimulation of epilepsy. *Epilepsy Behav.*, *91*, 25–29, 2019.
69. Kusyk, D.M., Meinert, J., Stabingas, K.C., Yin, Y., Whiting, A.C., Systematic review and meta-analysis of responsive neurostimulation in epilepsy. *World Neurosurg.*, *167*, e70–e78, 2022.
70. Gosselin, B., Recent advances in neural recording microsystems. *Sensors*, *11*, 4572–4597, 2011.
71. Benabid, A.L., Deep brain stimulation for Parkinson's disease. *Curr. Opin. Neurobiol.*, *13*, 6, 696–706, 2003.
72. Limousin, P. and Martinez-Torres, I., Deep brain stimulation for Parkinson's disease. *Neurotherapeutics*, *5*, 2, 309–319, 2008.
73. Wu, C. and Sharan, A.D., Neurostimulation for the treatment of epilepsy: a review of current surgical interventions. *Neuromodulation: Technol. Neural Interface*, *16*, 1, 10–24, 2013.
74. Marks, W.J., Deep brain stimulation for dystonia. *Curr. Treat. Options Neurol.*, *7*, 3, 237–243, 2005.
75. Ostrem, J.L. and Starr, P.A., Treatment of dystonia with deep brain stimulation. *Neurotherapeutics*, *5*, 320–330, 2008.

76. Kringelbach, M.L., Jenkinson, N., Owen, S.L., Aziz, T.Z., Translational principles of deep brain stimulation. *Nat. Rev. Neurosci.*, *8*, 8, 623–635, 2007.
77. Vanneste, S. and De Ridder, D., Noninvasive and invasive neuromodulation for the treatment of tinnitus: an overview. *Neuromodulation: Technol. Neural Interface*, *15*, 4, 350–360, 2012.
78. Hoare, D.J., Adjamian, P., Sereda, M., Electrical stimulation of the ear, head, cranial nerve, or cortex for the treatment of tinnitus: a scoping review. *Neural Plast.*, *2016*, 2016.
79. Pedroarena-Leal, N. and Ruge, D., Toward a Symptom-Guided neurostimulation for Gilles de la Tourette syndrome. *Front. Psychiatry*, *8*, 219987, 2017.
80. Moisset, X., Lantéri-Minet, M., Fontaine, D., Neurostimulation methods in the treatment of chronic pain. *J. Neural Transm.*, *127*, 4, 673–686, 2020.
81. Hofmeister, M., Memedovich, A., Brown, S., Saini, M., Dowsett, L.E., Lorenzetti, D.L., Clement, F., Effectiveness of neurostimulation technologies for the management of chronic pain: a systematic review. *Neuromodulation: Technol. Neural Interface*, *23*, 2, 150–157, 2020.
82. Deer, T.R. (Ed.), *Interventional and Neuromodulatory Techniques for Pain Management*, Elsevier/Saunders, 2012.
83. da Silva Freitas, T., de Monaco, B.A., Golovac, S. (Eds.), *Neuromodulation Techniques for Pain Treatment: A Step-by-Step Guide to Interventional Procedures and Managing Complications*, Springer International Publishing, 2022.
84. Sammons, J.E. and Khachemoune, A., Axillary hyperhidrosis: a focused review. *J. Dermatological Treat.*, *28*, 7, 582–590, 2017.
85. Johnson, J.E., O'Shaughnessy, K.F., Kim, S., Microwave thermolysis of sweat glands. *Lasers Surg. Med.*, *44*, 1, 20–25, 2012.

2

Metamaterials in 5G and the Path towards 6G: Enabling Advanced Wireless Communication

Mohd Javed Khan[1], Saif Ahmad[1], Indrasen Singh[2*] and Zeenat Fatima[3]

[1]*Dept. of ECE, Integral University Lucknow, UP, India*
[2]*School of Electronics Engineering VIT, Vellore, TN, India*
[3]*Dept. of ME, University of Polytechnic, Integral University Lucknow, UP, India*

Abstract

The transition from 4G to 5G wireless communication technology has seen tremendous advances in data speeds, connectivity, and network capabilities. As the telecom industry prepares for the next frontier, 6G, metamaterials have emerged as a transformational force. This chapter discusses the applications and prospective contributions of metamaterials in the context of 5G networks, as well as their anticipated role in shaping the foundation of 6G networks. Metamaterial-based antennas and beamforming technologies have played a critical role in satisfying the growing need for data-intensive applications, delivering unprecedented speeds and reliability to users. Metamaterials are poised to revolutionize the manipulation and control of electromagnetic waves in this higher frequency spectrum as terahertz frequencies become a focal point for communication. Smart surfaces, particularly reconfigurable intelligent surfaces represent yet another frontier in which metamaterials will play a significant role. When strategically installed in communication contexts, these surfaces promise to optimize signal propagation, reduce interference, and greatly improve overall network performance. The chapter dives into the possibilities of metamaterial-enabled smart surfaces in altering the 6G network communication landscape.

***Keywords*:** 4G, 5G, metamaterials, beamforming

**Corresponding author*: indrasen.singh@vit.ac.in

Dilip Kumar Choudhary, Indrasen Singh, Manoj Kumar Singh and Amit Kumar Jain (eds.) Compact and Flexible Microwave Devices, (25–48) © 2025 Scrivener Publishing LLC

2.1 Introduction

2.1.1 Background

The background of metamaterials in the context of 5G and potential applications in 6G lies in the quest to meet key challenges and enhance the capabilities of wireless communication systems. Metamaterials are engineered materials designed to exhibit properties not found in nature, particularly in the manipulation of electromagnetic waves. In the transition from 4G to 5G and the ongoing exploration of 6G, the application of metamaterials has become increasingly significant. Here is the background of metamaterials in the evolution of wireless communication. The unique capabilities of metamaterials make them a promising avenue for innovation and optimization in the evolving landscape of 5G and the anticipated era of 6G [14–16].

2.1.2 Role of Metamaterials

Metamaterials play a pivotal role in modern technology, particularly in the field of telecommunications, including 5G and potentially future 6G communication networks. Metamaterials play a transformative role in various fields, including telecommunications, optics, and medical imaging. These artificially engineered materials possess unique properties not found in naturally occurring substances, often bending light or electromagnetic waves in unconventional ways. In telecommunications, metamaterials enable the development of compact antennas capable of receiving and transmitting signals with improved efficiency and range. In optics, they open doors to unprecedented control over light propagation, leading to the creation of ultra-high-resolution lenses and cloaking devices. In medical imaging, metamaterials enhance the capabilities of diagnostic tools by manipulating electromagnetic waves to produce clearer and more detailed images of the human body. Overall, metamaterials hold immense promise for revolutionizing technology across numerous disciplines, offering unprecedented control over the behavior of light and electromagnetic radiation.

Here are some key roles of metamaterials [32]. Metamaterials are engineered materials designed to have properties not found in nature, such as negative refractive index or specific frequency response. This enables precise control over electromagnetic waves, allowing for the manipulation of signals in novel ways. In communication systems, metamaterials can be used to design antennas with unique properties. Metasurface antennas, for example, enable beamforming, allowing for the precise direction of signals. This is crucial for enhancing signal strength and overcoming obstacles in the path of the signal. Metamaterials offer the ability to create structures with subwavelength features. This enables the miniaturization of devices and components, leading to more compact and efficient communication devices. By manipulating the propagation of electromagnetic waves, metamaterials can be employed to enhance the resolution and quality of signals. This is essential for applications such as high-definition video streaming, augmented reality, and virtual reality.

Metamaterials can be designed to exhibit specific frequency-dependent responses. This allows for the creation of advanced filters and selective components, which are valuable for managing signal interference and optimizing spectrum utilization in communication networks. Metamaterials can contribute to the development of energy-efficient communication systems. By controlling and directing the flow of electromagnetic waves, they enable the design of more efficient antennas and devices, reducing energy consumption in wireless networks. Smart metasurfaces, which can dynamically control the properties of electromagnetic waves, play a crucial role in 6G communication. These surfaces enable adaptive signal propagation, allowing networks to respond to changing conditions and optimize communication paths in real time. In the context of 6G, metamaterials with quantum properties can contribute to the development of secure communication systems. Quantum metamaterials can be designed for quantum key distribution and other quantum communication protocols, enhancing the security of data transmission. Metamaterials can be integrated with artificial intelligence (AI) algorithms to create adaptive and self-optimizing communication networks. AI-driven systems can leverage the unique properties of metamaterials to dynamically adjust network parameters, improving overall performance and efficiency. As technology advances, metamaterials hold the potential for even more innovative applications. These might include advanced cloaking devices, metamaterial-based lenses for advanced imaging, and other applications that push the boundaries of what is currently possible. In summary, the role of metamaterials in communication technologies, especially in the context of 5G and 6G, is multifaceted, ranging from signal enhancement and beamforming to energy efficiency and security. Their unique electromagnetic properties make them valuable tools for overcoming the challenges and pushing the capabilities of modern and future communication networks.

2.2 Basics of Metamaterials

2.2.1 Definition and Characteristics

In the context of 5G and potentially 6G communication networks, metamaterials refer to engineered materials with unique electromagnetic properties that are strategically designed to enhance the performance and capabilities of wireless communication systems. These materials play a crucial role in addressing the challenges associated with high-frequency and high-data-rate communication by providing innovative solutions for signal control, beamforming, and interference management [33]. Metamaterials in 5G and 6G are designed to manipulate and control the propagation of electromagnetic waves, enabling improved signal quality and reliability. This includes the ability to focus signals, steer beams, and shape the electromagnetic field for optimal communication. Metasurface antennas based on metamaterials are utilized for beamforming, allowing for the precise control of signal directionality. This is essential for achieving high data rates, low latency, and efficient use of available spectrum in 5G and future 6G networks [13]. Figure 2.1 show pictorial represntation of beamforming null stearing process.

Metamaterials can be engineered to exhibit specific frequency responses, allowing for selective transmission or blocking of certain frequency bands. This characteristic aids in frequency division, reducing interference and optimizing spectral efficiency in advanced communication systems. Metamaterials enable the miniaturization of components and devices

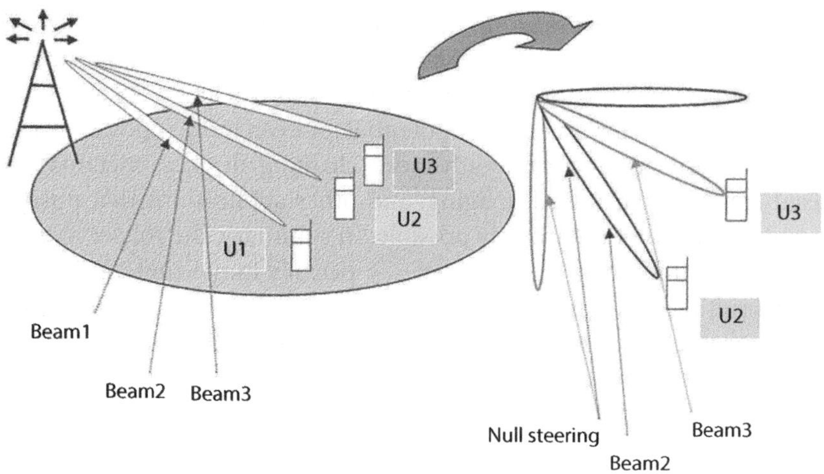

Figure 2.1 Beamforming null steering.

operating at millimeter-wave frequencies, a key aspect of 5G and potentially 6G communications. This supports the development of compact and efficient communication systems with improved integration capabilities [18]. Smart metal surfaces that can dynamically adjust their properties in response to changing conditions are integral to 5G and 6G networks. These surfaces allow for adaptive signal control and optimization, addressing challenges associated with dynamic environments and diverse user requirements. Metamaterials designed for low-loss characteristics contribute to reducing signal attenuation and improving the overall efficiency of communication systems. High-gain structures using metamaterials enhance the reach and coverage of wireless networks. Metamaterials play a role in managing interference in crowded frequency bands. By selectively controlling the transmission and reception of signals, they contribute to minimizing interference and enhancing the reliability of communication in dense urban environments. In the realm of 6G, quantum metamaterials may be explored for applications related to quantum communication. These materials could contribute to the development of secure communication protocols based on quantum key distribution and other quantum technologies.

The integration of metamaterials with AI algorithms allows for intelligent and adaptive communication systems. AI-driven metamaterials can optimize network parameters in real time, improving the overall performance and efficiency of 5G and 6G networks. Metamaterials in 5G and 6G communication open the door to innovative applications, including advanced wireless connectivity, augmented reality, holographic communication, and other futuristic technologies that demand high data rates, low latency, and reliable connectivity. Understanding and leveraging these characteristics enable the development of metamaterials specifically tailored for the unique challenges and requirements of 5G and future 6G communication networks, contributing to the advancement of wireless communication technologies.

2.2.2 Types of Metamaterials

Metamaterials are engineered materials with properties not found in nature, often designed to manipulate electromagnetic waves. In the context of 5G and potential future generations like 6G, metamaterials play a crucial role in improving the performance of communication systems. Some types of metamaterials used or considered for application in 5G and 6G are presented below [34, 35].

2.2.2.1 *Electromagnetic Bandgap (EBG) Structures*

EBG structures are periodic arrangements of conducting elements that exhibit bandgap properties. These structures can be used to control and manipulate the propagation of electromagnetic waves, reducing interference and enhancing the performance of antennas in 5G and 6G systems. Electromagnetic bandgap (EBG) structures are engineered materials designed to control the propagation of electromagnetic waves within a certain frequency range. These structures consist of periodic arrays of conducting elements or dielectric materials, creating a bandgap where certain frequencies of electromagnetic radiation are forbidden from propagating. EBG structures find applications in various domains such as antenna design, microwave engineering, and electromagnetic interference mitigation. In antenna design, EBG structures are utilized to suppress surface waves, improve antenna efficiency, and reduce mutual coupling between antenna elements. In microwave engineering, they find applications in the design of low-loss transmission lines, filters, and resonators. Additionally, EBG structures are employed to mitigate electromagnetic interference (EMI) by suppressing unwanted radiation and reflections. Their ability to manipulate electromagnetic waves with precision makes EBG structures indispensable in modern communication systems, radar technology, and electromagnetic compatibility design.

2.2.2.2 *Frequency Selective Surfaces (FSS)*

Frequency Selective Surfaces (FSS) are thin and periodic structures that allow specific frequencies to pass through while reflecting or blocking others. They are used to design efficient and selective filters for wireless communication systems. FSS are specialized structures engineered to control the transmission or reflection of electromagnetic waves at specific frequencies or within certain frequency bands. These surfaces typically consist of periodic arrays of conductive elements or apertures etched onto a dielectric substrate. By carefully designing the geometrical parameters of the elements and their spacing, FSS can exhibit unique electromagnetic properties such as selective filtering, polarization manipulation, and wave impedance matching.

In practical applications, FSS find extensive use in various fields such as antenna design, random construction, and electromagnetic shielding. In antenna design, FSS are employed as frequency selective radomes to protect antennas from environmental effects while allowing desired frequencies to pass through. They also find application in creating compact and multifunctional antennas by integrating FSS directly onto antenna surfaces. Moreover, FSS are essential components in microwave devices and systems, where they serve as filters, polarizers, and reflectors. Their ability to selectively control electromagnetic waves based on frequency makes them invaluable in radar systems, wireless communication networks, and satellite communications. Additionally, FSS are utilized in electromagnetic shielding to prevent unwanted interference and radiation leakage in sensitive electronic devices and equipment. Overall, Frequency Selective Surfaces play a crucial role in modern electromagnetic engineering, enabling precise control over electromagnetic waves for a wide range of applications across telecommunications, aerospace, and consumer electronics industries.

2.2.2.3 Reconfigurable Metamaterials

These metamaterials can dynamically change their properties in response to external stimuli, such as an applied voltage or magnetic field. Reconfigurable metamaterials offer flexibility in adapting to different communication scenarios and optimizing performance. Reconfigurable metamaterials represent a cutting-edge class of materials that can dynamically alter their electromagnetic properties in response to external stimuli such as voltage, temperature, or magnetic fields. Unlike traditional static metamaterials, which have fixed properties determined by their structure, reconfigurable metamaterials offer unprecedented versatility and adaptability. These materials typically incorporate active elements such as varactors, liquid crystals, or MEMS (Micro-Electromechanical Systems) to achieve tunability. By changing the state of these active components, reconfigurable metamaterials can modify their electromagnetic response, including their effective permittivity, permeability, and scattering properties.

The applications of reconfigurable metamaterials span a wide range of fields. In communications and radar systems, they enable adaptive antennas and beam-steering devices capable of dynamically adjusting their radiation patterns in real time to optimize performance. In imaging and sensing applications, reconfigurable metamaterials facilitate the development of tunable lenses, filters, and cloaking devices, allowing for enhanced resolution and versatility. Furthermore, reconfigurable metamaterials hold promise in areas such as energy harvesting, where they can optimize the absorption of ambient electromagnetic radiation across different frequencies. Additionally, they find applications in biomedical devices, where tunable metamaterials can be utilized for controlled drug delivery, biosensing, and non-invasive medical imaging. Overall, reconfigurable metamaterials represent a paradigm shift in material science and electromagnetic engineering, offering unparalleled flexibility and functionality for a wide range of technological applications. As research in this field progresses, the potential for innovative uses and breakthroughs continues to expand, promising exciting developments in the near future.

2.2.2.4 Plasmonic Metamaterials

Plasmonic metamaterials utilize the unique properties of surface plasmons to enhance light-matter interactions. In the context of 5G and 6G, plasmonic metamaterials can be employed to develop compact and high-performance components like antennas and waveguides [1, 17]. Plasmonic metamaterials hold significant promise for advancing the capabilities of 5G communication systems. By harnessing the unique properties of surface plasmons, these metamaterials can potentially overcome some of the key challenges facing 5G networks, such as limited bandwidth and signal interference. Plasmonic metamaterials offer the ability to manipulate and control electromagnetic waves at the nanoscale, enabling the development of compact and efficient components for 5G devices and infrastructure. In 5G antennas, plasmonic metamaterials can enhance performance by enabling antenna miniaturization and improving radiation efficiency. These metamaterial-based antennas can operate at higher frequencies while maintaining strong signal strength and coverage, essential for the high data rates and low latency requirements of 5G networks. Additionally, plasmonic metamaterials can be integrated into 5G base stations and repeaters to enhance signal propagation, mitigate interference, and optimize spectrum utilization.

Furthermore, plasmonic metamaterials offer opportunities for advanced signal processing and beamforming in 5G systems. By exploiting the subwavelength confinement of electromagnetic fields enabled by plasmonic structures, researchers can develop novel beam-steering techniques for directing signals with unprecedented precision. This capability is particularly valuable for millimeter-wave communication in 5G, where beamforming is essential for achieving reliable and high-capacity links. Moreover, plasmonic metamaterials hold potential for enhancing the security and privacy of 5G networks. Their ability to confine and manipulate electromagnetic fields at the nanoscale can be leveraged to create secure communication channels with reduced vulnerability to eavesdropping and interference. Overall, plasmonic metamaterials represent a promising avenue for advancing the performance and capabilities of 5G communication systems. As research in this area progresses, we can expect to see the integration of plasmonic metamaterials into various components of 5G infrastructure, unlocking new possibilities for high-speed, low-latency wireless communication.

2.2.2.5 Dielectric Metamaterials

Dielectric metamaterials manipulate electromagnetic waves through the use of dielectric materials with engineered properties. They can be employed to create lenses, waveguides, and other components that contribute to the miniaturization and efficiency of communication devices. Dielectric metamaterials offer intriguing opportunities for revolutionizing both 5G networks and laying the groundwork for future 6G technologies. In the context of 5G, dielectric metamaterials hold promise for addressing key challenges such as signal propagation, interference mitigation, and spectrum efficiency. These metamaterials, composed of engineered dielectric structures rather than metallic elements, provide unique electromagnetic properties that can be tailored to specific frequencies and applications.

In 5G networks, dielectric metamaterials can be employed in various ways to enhance performance. For instance, they can be integrated into antennas to achieve beamforming, allowing for precise directionality of signals and improved coverage. Dielectric metamaterials can also enable the development of compact, low-profile antennas suitable for deployment in urban environments where space is limited. Additionally, these metamaterials can assist in managing electromagnetic interference, optimizing signal quality, and increasing data transmission rates, all critical aspects of 5G communication systems. Looking ahead to 6G, dielectric metamaterials are poised to play an even more significant role in shaping the future of wireless communication. With the anticipated need for higher frequencies, wider bandwidths, and ultra-low latency in 6G networks, dielectric metamaterials offer solutions for addressing these requirements. Their ability to manipulate electromagnetic waves at the nanoscale enables the creation of advanced components for 6G systems, including highly efficient antennas, ultra-fast switches, and novel signal processing devices. Moreover, dielectric metamaterials hold promise for enabling new functionalities in 6G networks, such as terahertz communication, quantum communication, and wireless power transfer. These metamaterial-based technologies could revolutionize various industries, from telecommunications and healthcare to manufacturing and transportation, ushering in an era of unprecedented connectivity and innovation.

2.2.2.6 Nanostructured Metamaterials

Nanostructured metamaterials involve materials with structures at the nanoscale. These materials can offer unique electromagnetic properties and are explored for their potential in enhancing signal processing, sensing, and imaging capabilities in 5G and 6G systems. The development and application of metamaterials in 5G and future wireless communication technologies are areas of active research and innovation, and new types of metamaterials may emerge as the technology evolves [27, 28].

Nanostructured metamaterials offer immense potential for advancing both 5G networks and paving the way towards the development of 6G technologies. These metamaterials, composed of intricately designed nanostructures, possess unique electromagnetic properties that can be tailored to specific frequencies and applications. In the context of 5G, nanostructured metamaterials hold promise for addressing critical challenges such as signal propagation, spectrum efficiency, and interference mitigation. By leveraging their ability to manipulate electromagnetic waves at the nanoscale, these metamaterials enable the creation of highly efficient antennas, compact devices, and advanced signal processing components. In 5G networks, nanostructured metamaterials can play a crucial role in enhancing data transmission rates, improving coverage, and enabling innovative functionalities such as beamforming and massive MIMO (Multiple Input Multiple Output) systems. Looking towards 6G, nanostructure metamaterials are poised to become even more instrumental in shaping the future of wireless communication. With the anticipated requirements for ultra-high frequencies, ultra-wide bandwidths, and ultra-low latency in 6G networks, nanostructured metamaterials offer solutions for meeting these demanding specifications. They enable the development of next-generation components and devices capable of pushing the boundaries of speed, efficiency, and connectivity in wireless communication systems. Additionally, nanostructured metamaterials facilitate the exploration of emerging technologies such as terahertz communication, quantum communication, and intelligent reconfigurable surfaces, laying the foundation for transformative advancements in telecommunications and beyond.

2.3 Metamaterials in 5G Communication

Metamaterials represent a cutting-edge technology with profound implications for 5G communication systems. These artificially engineered materials possess unique electromagnetic properties that enable precise control over the behavior of electromagnetic waves. In the context of 5G, metamaterials offer innovative solutions to several key challenges. One area where metamaterials excel is in antenna design. By leveraging metamaterials, antennas can be made more compact, efficient, and versatile. This is particularly important in 5G networks, where the deployment of massive MIMO systems and small cells requires antennas to be smaller and more densely packed. Metamaterials also enable the development of reconfigurable antennas, allowing for dynamic adjustment of antenna properties to adapt to changing network conditions. Another application of metamaterials in 5G is in beamforming and beam-steering. Metamaterials can be used to create phased arrays capable of steering beams with high precision, enabling improved coverage, higher data rates, and reduced interference. This is essential for delivering the promised benefits of 5G, such as ultra-fast speeds and low latency. Furthermore, metamaterials offer solutions for managing signal interference in crowded spectrum environments. Frequency-selective surfaces (FSS) based on metamaterials can be used to selectively filter out unwanted signals while allowing desired signals to pass through. This helps improve signal quality and reliability in 5G networks, especially in urban areas where spectrum congestion is a significant issue.

Overall, metamaterials hold great promise for revolutionizing 5G communication systems by enabling more efficient antennas, advanced beamforming capabilities, and enhanced interference mitigation techniques. As research in this field continues to advance, we can expect to see metamaterials playing an increasingly important role in shaping the future of wireless communication.

2.3.1 Current Challenges in 5G

2.3.1.1 Bandwidth Limitations

Bandwidth limitations present a significant challenge in the context of 5G communication, and metamaterials offer potential solutions to address this issue. As 5G networks aim to support massive data rates, ultra-low latency, and a vast number of connected devices, the available spectrum becomes increasingly congested. Traditional communication technologies face limitations in bandwidth allocation, hindering the delivery of high-speed, reliable connectivity. Metamaterials, with their ability to manipulate electromagnetic waves at the nanoscale, hold promise for expanding available bandwidth in 5G communication systems. Researchers are exploring metamaterial-based solutions to enable efficient operation across a broader range of frequencies, thus alleviating bandwidth constraints. These solutions include the development of compact antennas with enhanced bandwidth capabilities, frequency-selective surfaces for interference mitigation, and reconfigurable metamaterial structures for dynamic spectrum allocation.

Despite the potential benefits, several challenges must be addressed to fully leverage metamaterials in overcoming bandwidth limitations in 5G communication. Fabrication processes for metamaterials often involve intricate nanostructures or microstructures, demanding advanced and costly techniques. Additionally, ensuring seamless integration of metamaterial-based components into existing communication infrastructure requires careful design considerations and compatibility testing. Moreover, optimizing the performance of metamaterials for specific 5G use cases and frequency bands is complex, requiring sophisticated modeling and simulation tools. Metamaterial performance may also be sensitive to environmental factors, necessitating robustness testing under varying operating conditions. Finally, cost-effectiveness is crucial to the practical deployment of metamaterial-based solutions in 5G networks, balancing performance benefits with production costs and scalability. Addressing these challenges will be essential to fully realize the potential of metamaterials in expanding bandwidth and unlocking the capabilities of 5G communication systems. Continued research and development efforts are necessary to overcome these hurdles and accelerate the adoption of metamaterials in the telecommunications industry.

2.3.1.2 Signal Interference

Signal interference poses a significant challenge in 5G communication systems, and metamaterials offer promising avenues to address this issue. Interference occurs when unwanted signals disrupt the transmission or reception of desired signals, leading to degradation in communication performance and reliability. Metamaterials can play a crucial role in mitigating signal interference through various mechanisms. One approach involves the use of metamaterial-based antennas with advanced beamforming capabilities. By precisely controlling the directionality of transmitted and received signals, these antennas can focus energy where it's needed while minimizing interference from other sources. Moreover, metamaterials can enable the development of reconfigurable electromagnetic environments, where the properties of the surrounding medium can be dynamically adjusted to adapt to changing interference conditions. This adaptability allows for real-time mitigation of interference by modifying the transmission environment to minimize the impact of unwanted signals. Additionally, frequency selective surfaces (FSS) based on metamaterials can be utilized to selectively filter out interfering signals while allowing desired signals to pass through. These surfaces can be integrated into communication devices or infrastructure to enhance signal quality and reduce the effects of interference. Despite the potential benefits, addressing signal interference with metamaterials presents challenges. Designing and implementing effective metamaterial-based solutions require consideration of factors such as frequency bands, signal propagation characteristics, and environmental conditions. Furthermore, ensuring compatibility and interoperability with existing communication systems is essential for the seamless integration of metamaterial technologies.

2.3.1.3 Latency Issues in 5G Networks

Latency, or the delay in transmitting data between devices over a network, is a critical challenge in 5G communication systems, and metamaterials can contribute to addressing this issue. In 5G networks, ultra-low latency is essential for supporting applications such as real-time gaming, autonomous vehicles, remote surgery, and industrial automation, where even milliseconds of delay can impact performance and safety. Metamaterials offer potential solutions to reduce latency in 5G networks through various means. One approach involves the development of metamaterial-based antennas and signal processing components with enhanced efficiency and speed. These components can help minimize transmission delays and processing times, thus reducing overall network latency.

2.3.2 Metamaterials Solutions for 5G

Metamaterials present innovative solutions to key challenges encountered in 5G communication systems. Through their unique electromagnetic properties, metamaterials offer a range of benefits, including enhanced antenna performance, beamforming capabilities, interference mitigation, and ultra-low latency. Metamaterial-based antennas enable the development of compact, high-performance antennas capable of operating across multiple frequency bands with improved efficiency and bandwidth, essential for supporting the high data rates and massive connectivity demands of 5G networks. Additionally, metamaterials facilitate advanced beamforming and beam-steering techniques, allowing for more efficient and targeted transmission of signals, which enhances coverage and reduces interference. Moreover, metamaterials, such as frequency selective surfaces (FSS), selectively filter out interfering signals while allowing desired signals to pass through, thereby improving signal quality and reliability. Furthermore, metamaterials enable the development of components and devices with enhanced processing capabilities and reduced signal propagation delays, contributing to lower latency in 5G networks. By optimizing signal paths and processing efficiency, metamaterial-based solutions minimize latency and improve the responsiveness of communication systems. Overall, metamaterials offer transformative solutions that address critical challenges in 5G communications, paving the way for higher data rates, lower latency, and improved spectral efficiency in wireless networks.

2.4 Towards 6G: Future Challenges and Metamaterials Integration

Numerous challenges are confronting 6G wireless communication at terahertz frequency bands, which require urgent attention to address practical and efficient services. Some of these challenges are categorized into four parts, as shown in Figure 2.2.

2.4.1 Anticipated Challenges in 6G

Anticipated challenges in the development and deployment of 6G communication systems encompass a spectrum of technical, regulatory, and societal considerations. As the demand for ultra-high-speed, ultra-low-latency connectivity continues to rise, finding and allocating sufficient

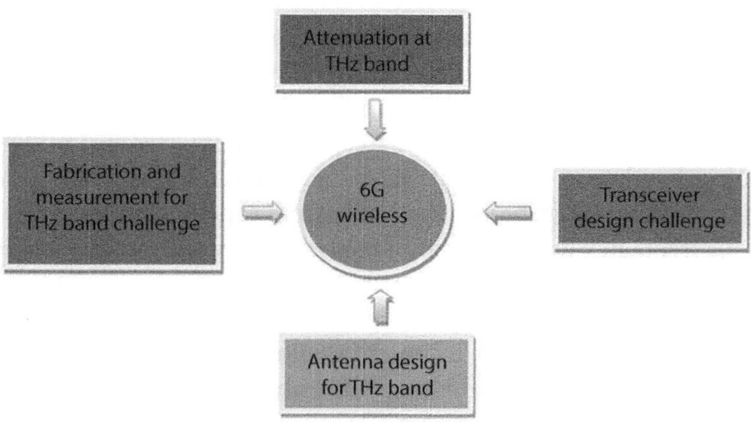

Figure 2.2 Some of the issues associated with the 6G wireless communication system.

spectrum for 6G networks will be a primary obstacle. Expanding into higher frequency bands, including terahertz frequencies, presents technical hurdles due to increased signal attenuation and shorter propagation distances. Achieving ultra-low latency, critical for real-time applications like autonomous vehicles and remote surgery, poses a significant challenge requiring breakthroughs in network architecture and signal processing. Furthermore, ensuring energy efficiency in 6G systems while meeting performance demands will demand innovative solutions and careful resource management. Security and privacy concerns loom large, requiring robust encryption mechanisms and defenses against cyber threats. Interference management and spectrum coexistence are vital for optimizing spectrum usage amidst the proliferation of wireless devices and technologies. Global standardization efforts must navigate diverse interests to enable interoperability and seamless connectivity worldwide. Cost considerations and infrastructure deployment challenges will also be significant, requiring substantial investments and equitable access strategies. Moreover, ethical and societal implications, including digital inclusion and data privacy, must be addressed to ensure that 6G technologies benefit society as a whole while mitigating potential risks and disparities. Addressing these multifaceted challenges will demand collaborative efforts from industry, governments, academia, and civil society to realize the full potential of 6G communication systems.

2.4.2 Metamaterials Innovations for 6G

The transition from 5G to 6G involves addressing new challenges and requirements, and metamaterials are expected to play a crucial role in shaping the capabilities of future communication systems. While specific developments may have occurred since my last update, here are some potential areas of innovation for metamaterials in the context of 6G [2, 8]. 6G is expected to explore terahertz (THz) frequencies for communication [9], which present both opportunities and challenges. Metamaterials can be designed to manipulate and control THz waves, enabling advanced communication technologies at these higher frequencies [5, 6, 12]. Metamaterials with properties optimized for ultra-broadband communication can be designed to support a wide range of frequencies. This could lead to improved spectral efficiency and flexibility in 6G networks [14]. Incorporating dynamic and reconfigurable metamaterials into 6G systems can enable adaptive control of electromagnetic waves. These materials can be adjusted in real time to optimize performance based on changing network conditions and communication requirements. Advanced metamaterial antennas and beamforming technologies can enhance the efficiency of communication links in 6G networks. Metasurfaces and metamaterial-based antennas could provide beam steering, beam shaping, and other capabilities for improved coverage and connectivity [10, 11]. Metamaterial-based smart surfaces, also known as reconfigurable intelligent surfaces (RIS), can be employed to control and manipulate signal propagation in 6G environments. This can lead to improved signal quality, reduced interference, and enhanced coverage. Integrating metamaterials into energy-harvesting technologies could be explored to power low-power devices and sensors in 6G networks. Harvesting ambient electromagnetic energy using metamaterials may contribute to the sustainability of future communication systems. Research in quantum metamaterials may lead to innovative applications in quantum communication and information processing, which could be relevant to the development of secure and efficient communication systems in 6G. Metamaterials can be applied to create advanced sensing and imaging devices, contributing to the development of intelligent and context-aware 6G networks. This could be beneficial for applications such as augmented reality, virtual reality, and autonomous systems. Nonlinear metamaterials may find applications in signal processing within 6G networks. These materials can enable the generation of new frequencies and nonlinear effects, potentially enhancing signal processing capabilities for communication and sensing. It's important to note that the field of 6G is still in its early stages, and ongoing research and development will shape the role of metamaterials in future communication systems. For the latest advancements and innovations in this field, it's recommended to refer to recent literature and research publications.

2.5 Case Studies and Applications

2.5.1 Practical Implementations in 5G Networks

Practical implementations in 5G networks cover a wide range of technologies and applications designed to leverage the capabilities offered by fifth-generation wireless technology. As of my last knowledge update in January 2022, here are some practical implementations in 5G networks. 5G provides significantly higher data rates compared to previous generations, enabling enhanced mobile broadband services. This includes faster download and upload speeds, improved streaming quality, and better overall user experiences for applications like video streaming, gaming, and multimedia content consumption. Massive MIMO involves the use of a large number of antennas at base stations to serve multiple users simultaneously. This technology enhances spectral efficiency, increases network capacity, and improves the overall performance of wireless communication systems [18, 19, 29]. URLLC is designed to support applications that require extremely low latency and high reliability, such as mission-critical communication in industrial automation, autonomous vehicles, and remote surgery. 5G's low-latency capabilities make it suitable for applications where real-time communication is crucial [20]. 5G is designed to efficiently connect a massive number of devices, making it well-suited for IoT deployments. This includes smart cities, smart homes, industrial IoT (IIoT), and other applications where a large number of devices need to communicate seamlessly [21]. Network slicing enables the creation of virtual networks tailored to specific use cases with different performance requirements. This allows operators to optimize network resources for diverse applications, such as enhanced mobile broadband, URLLC, and massive IoT, within the same infrastructure [22]. 5G networks support edge computing, bringing computing resources closer to the end-users. This is particularly beneficial for applications requiring low latency, such as augmented reality (AR), virtual reality (VR), and real-time analytics [23]. 5G FWA allows users to access high-speed broadband services using wireless connections instead of traditional wired infrastructure. This is particularly useful in areas with limited wired connectivity or as a high-speed alternative in urban environments [24]. Beamforming technology allows 5G networks to focus signals toward specific users or devices, improving the efficiency of data transmission. Beam tracking further enhances this by dynamically adjusting the direction of the beams based on the movement of users [25, 30, 31]. DSS allows the simultaneous operation of 4G and 5G technologies in the same frequency band. This facilitates a smoother transition to 5G by enabling operators to utilize existing spectrum resources efficiently [26]. 5G incorporates improved security features, such as enhanced encryption and authentication mechanisms, to address the evolving threat landscape associated with wireless networks. 5G networks utilize advanced radio technologies, including smart antennas, to enhance coverage, reduce interference, and improve overall network efficiency [11].

2.5.2 Envisioning 6G Applications

Envisioning 6G applications involves imagining a future where wireless communication technologies have evolved beyond the capabilities of 5G, enabling transformative advancements across various industries. While 6G is still in the early stages of conceptualization, some potential applications are being envisioned [7]. 6G is expected to leverage terahertz frequencies, enabling data rates far beyond what is achievable with existing technologies. High-frequency terahertz communication could facilitate ultra-fast and low-latency wireless connectivity, supporting applications such as real-time holographic communication and instantaneous data transfers. 6G is likely to revolutionize AR and VR experiences by providing seamless, high-fidelity interactions. Immersive applications could include holographic telepresence, virtual collaboration, and augmented environments that integrate seamlessly with the physical world. 6G is expected to further connect and interlink the Internet of Things (IoT) devices, forming the Internet of Everything (IoX). This could lead to a highly interconnected and intelligent network where devices, sensors, and machines communicate and collaborate autonomously, facilitating efficient resource management, smart cities, and advanced industrial automation. Advanced sensing technologies, possibly using metamaterials and other innovations, could enable ubiquitous and highly accurate environmental sensing. This could lead to applications such as precision agriculture, environmental monitoring, and enhanced situational awareness for disaster response. 6G could revolutionize healthcare by enabling high-resolution remote diagnostics and even remote surgery. Surgeons could operate on patients from different locations, leveraging real-time haptic feedback and high-fidelity visuals, leading to improved healthcare accessibility. The ultra-low latency promised by 6G could lead to breakthroughs in applications that require real-time responsiveness. This includes autonomous vehicles with instantaneous communication, enabling safer and more efficient transportation systems. 6G is likely to seamlessly integrate with artificial intelligence (AI) and edge computing, enabling faster and more efficient processing of data at the network edge. This could lead to enhanced AI applications, such as personalized services, predictive analytics, and intelligent automation. 6G could play a vital role in optimizing energy consumption and resource management. Smart grids, smart buildings, and energy-efficient systems could benefit from advanced communication capabilities, leading to a more sustainable and interconnected world. With increased data rates and low latency, 6G could offer personalized and immersive entertainment experiences. This includes high-fidelity streaming, interactive gaming, and augmented reality-enhanced content delivery. 6G aims to provide connectivity to even the most remote and underserved areas, bridging the digital divide. This could empower communities with access to education, healthcare, and economic opportunities on a global scale.

It's important to note that these envisioned applications are speculative, and the actual implementation of 6G technologies will depend on technological advancements, regulatory frameworks, and industry collaborations. As the development of 6G progresses, these applications will likely be refined and expanded upon.

2.6 Future Directions and Research Challenges

The future directions and research challenges of 5G and the emerging 6G networks encompass a wide range of technological, economic, and societal considerations. As of my last knowledge update in January 2022, below are some potential areas of focus and challenges for researchers and industry stakeholders [3, 4].

2.6.1 Future Directions

Future directions in both 5G and the emerging 6G technologies are shaped by ambitious goals and evolving demands for connectivity, speed, and reliability. In 5G, ongoing efforts are focused on optimizing network performance, enhancing spectral efficiency, and enabling new use cases such as the Internet of Things (IoT), smart cities, and augmented reality. This includes advancements in antenna technologies, network architecture, and edge computing to support the massive data rates and ultra-low latency requirements of emerging applications. Additionally, research is exploring the integration of artificial intelligence and machine learning to optimize network management and resource allocation, improving overall efficiency and user experience. Looking forward to 6G, research is guided by the vision of enabling even faster data rates, lower latency, and seamless connectivity across a wide range of devices and environments. This includes exploring new frequency bands, such as terahertz frequencies, and leveraging emerging technologies like quantum communication and computing to push the boundaries of what is possible in wireless communication. Moreover, future research will need to address challenges related to energy efficiency, security, and the ethical implications of ubiquitous connectivity, ensuring that 6G networks are not only faster and more reliable but also sustainable and inclusive. Overall, the future of both 5G and 6G is characterized by innovation, collaboration, and a relentless pursuit of pushing the limits of what wireless communication can achieve in the digital age.

2.6.2 Research Challenges

Research challenges in both 5G and 6G are multifaceted, spanning technical, regulatory, and societal domains. In 5G, ongoing research aims to address issues such as spectrum scarcity, network densification, and energy efficiency. Maximizing spectral efficiency while minimizing interference requires innovative approaches to spectrum sharing and dynamic spectrum management. Moreover, the deployment of small cells and massive MIMO (Multiple Input Multiple Output) systems poses challenges in terms of infrastructure deployment, backhaul connectivity, and power consumption. Additionally, ensuring the security and privacy of data transmitted over 5G networks is a critical research area, given the proliferation of connected devices and the potential for cyber threats. Looking towards 6G, research challenges extend beyond enhancing speed and latency to encompass fundamental questions about the feasibility of terahertz communication, quantum communication, and intelligent reconfigurable surfaces. Overcoming technical barriers related to signal propagation, hardware development, and protocol design is essential to realizing the vision of 6G networks. Furthermore, addressing regulatory and policy challenges, such as spectrum allocation and standardization, will be crucial for enabling global interoperability and seamless connectivity. Moreover, ethical considerations regarding data privacy, digital inclusion, and environmental sustainability must be integrated into the research and development of both 5G and 6G technologies to ensure that future wireless communication systems benefit society as a whole. Overall, addressing these research challenges requires interdisciplinary collaboration, innovative solutions, and a holistic approach to shaping the future of wireless communication.

2.7 Conclusion

Metamaterials hold great promise in the advancement of 5G and potential future generations, such as 6G. These engineered materials with unique electromagnetic properties have the potential to address various challenges and unlock new possibilities in wireless communication technologies. Metamaterials can enable the manipulation of electromagnetic waves, leading to increased bandwidth and spectral efficiency in communication systems. This is crucial for meeting the growing demands of data-intensive applications and services. Metamaterials play a pivotal role in antenna design and beamforming technologies. They allow for the creation of compact and efficient antennas, as well as the manipulation of signals for improved coverage, reduced interference, and enhanced data rates. Metamaterials, including electromagnetic bandgap structures and frequency-selective surfaces, enable precise control over the propagation and transmission of signals. This contributes to mitigating interference issues and optimizing the use of available spectrum. Reconfigurable metamaterials provide the ability to dynamically adjust their properties, allowing for adaptive response to changing network conditions. This adaptability is valuable in optimizing performance, especially in scenarios with varying communication requirements. Metamaterial-based smart surfaces, such as reconfigurable intelligent surfaces (RIS), have the potential to optimize signal propagation, reduce interference, and enhance overall network performance in 6G. Metamaterials may find applications in secure communication by enabling the development of secure communication channels and enhancing privacy. Additionally, they can be utilized in sensing applications, contributing to the development of intelligent and context-aware networks. While metamaterials offer exciting possibilities, challenges remain, including the need for cost-effective fabrication methods, integration complexities, and addressing potential health concerns. Ongoing research is essential to overcome these challenges and fully realize the potential of metamaterials in 5G and beyond. Metamaterials are at the forefront of technological advancements in wireless communication, offering solutions to challenges and opening avenues for innovations in bandwidth, antenna design, frequency control, and network optimization. As 6G continues to take shape, metamaterials are likely to play a crucial role in shaping the future of wireless communication technologies.

References

1. Pendry, J.B., Holden, A., Stewart, W., Youngs, I., Extremely low-frequency plasmons in metallic mesostructures. *Phys. Rev. Lett.*, 76, 4773, 1996.
2. Huang, T., Yang, W., Wu, J., Ma, J., Zhang, X., Zhang, D., A survey on green 6G network: Architecture and technologies. *IEEE Access*, 7, 175758–175768, 2019.
3. Lu, Y. and Zheng, X., 6G: A survey on technologies, scenarios, challenges, and the related issues. *J. Ind. Inf. Integr.*, 100158, 2020.
4. Nawaz, S.J., Sharma, S.K., Wyne, S., Patwary, M.N., Asaduzzaman, M., Quantum machine learning for 6G communication networks: State-of-the-art and vision for the future. *IEEE Access*, 7, 46317–46350, 2019.
5. Malhotra, I., Jha, K.R., Singh, G., Terahertz antenna technology for imaging applications: A technical review. *Int. J. Microwave Wireless Technolog.*, 10, 271–290, 2018.

6. Saeed, A., Gurbuz, O., Akkas, M.A., Terahertz communications at various atmospheric altitudes. *Phys. Commun.*, 41, 101113, 2020.
7. Wang, X., Huang, J., Wang, H., Gao, X., You, X., Hao, Y., 6G wireless channel measurements and models: Trends and challenges. *IEEE Veh. Technol. Mag.*, 15, 22–32, 2020.
8. Rappaport, T.S., Xing, Y., Kanhere, O., Ju, S., Madanayake, A., Mandal, S., *et al.*, Wireless communications and applications above 100 GHz: Opportunities and challenges for 6G and beyond. *IEEE Access*, 7, 78729–78757, 2019.
9. Tekbıyık, K., Ekti, A.R., Kurt, G.K., Görçin, A., Terahertz band communication systems: Challenges, novelties and standardization efforts. *Phys. Commun.*, 35, 100700, 2019.
10. Zhou, E., Cheng, Y., Chen, F., Luo, H., Wideband and high-gain patch antenna with reflective focusing metasurface. *AEU Int. J. Electron. Commun.*, 134, 153709, 2021.
11. Sa'don, S.N.H., Jamaluddin, M.H., Kamarudin, M.R., Ahmad, F., Yamada, Y., Kamardin, K., *et al.*, Analysis of graphene antenna properties for 5G applications. *Sensors*, 19, 4835, 2019.
12. He, Y., Chen, Y., Zhang, L., Wong, S., Chen, Z., An overview of terahertz antennas. *China Commun.*, 17, 7, 124–165, 2020.
13. Jamshed, M.A., Nauman, A., Abbasi, M.A.B., Kim, S.W., Antenna selection and designing for THz applications: suitability and performance evaluation: a survey. *IEEE Access*, 8, 113246–113261, 2020.
14. Hocini, M., Khedrouche, D., Zamani, M., Novel approach for the design and analysis of a terahertz microstrip patch antenna based on photonic crystals. *Photonics Nanostruct. Fundam. Appl.*, 36, 100723, 2019.
15. Zhang, W., Wu, Y., Ding, K., Li, R., Review of 3D printed millimeter-wave and terahertz passive devices. *Int. J. Antennas Propag.*, 2017, 2017.
16. Kim, S.W., Cho, I.K., Hong, S.Y., Design of transmitting coil for the wireless charging system to expand charging area for drone applications. *Microwave Opt. Technol. Lett.*, 60, 1179–1183, 2018.
17. Naghdehforushha, S.A. and Moradi, G., High directivity plasmonic graphene-based patch array antennas with tunable THz band communications. *Optik*, 168, 440–445, 2018.
18. Agrawal, T., High-Performance Circularly Polarized MIMO Antenna with Polarization Independent Metamaterial. *Wireless Pers. Commun.*, 116, 3205–3216, Kumar2021.
19. El-Nady, S., Zamel, H.M., Hendy, M., Zekry, A.A., Attiya, A., Gain enhancement of a millimeter wave antipodal Vivaldi antenna by epsilon-near-zero metamaterial. *Prog. Electromagn. Res. C*, 85, 105–116, 2018.
20. Yin, J., Wu, Q., Yu, C., Wang, H., Hong, W., Broadband endfire magnetoelectric dipole antenna array using SICL feeding network for 5G millimeter-wave applications. *IEEE Trans. Antennas Propag.*, 67, 4895–4900, 2019.
21. Huang, H., Li, X., Liu, Y., A novel vector synthetic dipole antenna and its common aperture array. *IEEE Trans. Antennas Propag.*, 66, 3183–3188, 2018.

22. Liang, Y., Zhang, J., Liu, Q., Li, X., High-power dual-branch helical antenna. *IEEE Antennas Wirel. Propag. Lett.*, 17, 472–475, 2018.
23. Dixit, S. and Kumar, S., The enhanced gain and cost- effective antipodal Vivaldi antenna for 5G communication applications. *Microwave Opt. Technol. Lett.*, 62, 2365–2374, 2020.
24. Bhadoria and Kumar, S., A novel omnidirectional triangular patch antenna array using Dolph Chebyshev current distribution for C-band applications. *Prog. Electromagn. Res. M*, 71, 75–84, 2018.
25. Ghosh, S., Das, S., Samantaray, D., Bhattacharyya, S., Meander-line-based defected ground microstrip antenna slotted with split-ring resonator for terahertz range. *Eng. Rep.*, 2, e12088, 2020.
26. Krzysztofik, W.J. and Cao, T.N., Metamaterials in application to improve antenna parameters. *Metamater. Metasurfaces*, 12, 63–85, 2018.
27. Krzysztofik, W.J., Antenna properties improvement using modern technology, in: *2014 20th International Conference on Microwaves, Radar and Wireless Communications (MIKON)*, pp. 1–4, 2014.
28. Krzysztofik, W.J., Fractal Geometry in Electromagnetics Applications – from Antenna to Metamaterials. *Microwave Rev.*, 19, 2013.
29. Jiang, H., Si, L.-M., Hu, W., Lv, X., A symmetrical dual-beam bowtie antenna with gain enhancement using metamaterial for 5G MIMO applications. *IEEE Photonics J.*, 11, 1–9, 2019.
30. Li, J., Zeng, Q., Liu, R., Denidni, T.A., Beam-tilting antenna with negative refractive index metamaterial loading. *IEEE Antennas Wirel. Propag. Lett.*, 16, 2030–2033, 2017.
31. Shevada, L., Raut, H.D., Malekar, R., Kumar, S., Comparative Study of different beamforming techniques for 5G: A Review. *Inventive Commun. Comput. Technol.*, 589–595, 2021.
32. Dakhla, S., Rmili, H., Floc'h, J.M., Sheikh, M., Dobie, A., Mahdjoubi, K., *et al.*, Printed multiband metamaterial- inspired antennas. *Microwave Opt. Technol. Lett.*, 58, 1281–1289, 2016.
33. Cao, T.N. and Krzysztofik, W.J., *Fractal antenna of MIMO system WLAN*, 2018.
34. Shalini, M. and Madhan, M.G., Design and analysis of a dual-polarized graphene-based microstrip patch antenna for terahertz applications. *Optik*, 194, 163050, 2019.
35. Tao, H., Padilla, W.J., Zhang, X., Averitt, R.D., Recent progress in electromagnetic metamaterial devices for terahertz applications. *IEEE J. Sel. Top. Quantum Electron.*, 17, 92–101, 2010.

3

Optimization of Time-Modulated Circular Antenna Array for MIMO Systems through Evolutionary Algorithms

Satish Kumar*, **Gopi Ram, Durbadal Mandal and Rajib Kar**

Department of Electronics and Communication Engineering, National Institute of Technology Durgapur, Durgapur, India

Abstract

This article introduces innovative methodologies, namely Differential Evolution (DE), Particle Swarm Optimization (PSO), and Novel Particle Swarm Optimization (NPSO), for the design of a 12-element time-modulated asymmetric circular antenna array (TMASCAA). The primary objective is to minimize sidelobe levels and mitigate interference, enhancing the array's overall performance. The novel particle swarm optimization technique achieves ultra-low sidelobe levels by determining an optimal switch-ON time sequence and progressive phase delay. This study compares the effectiveness of novel particle swarm optimization to the conventional PSO and DE methods, highlighting the superior performance of novel particle swarm optimization in diverse applications. The implications of this research extend beyond antenna design, with potential applications in improving the efficiency and performance of Multiple Input, Multiple Output (MIMO) systems. Based on these findings, the investigation assesses the array's directivity, gain, feed network efficiency, and sideband levels within MIMO systems. These performances of TMASCAAs have been compared with uniform circular Antenna Array (UCAA) configurations. One of the disadvantages of UCAA is that the amplitude excitation of each array element serves as the only control parameter. Furthermore, the UCAA has a large dynamic range ratio (DRR) between the highest and lowest optimal current excitations. Devices with high amplitude patterns and dynamic range ratios face significant development challenges. The comparative analysis emphasizes the potential of a TMASCAA as an alternative that addresses these challenges, showcasing its efficiency and adaptability in

**Corresponding author*: sk.ece.nitdgp@gmail.com

Dilip Kumar Choudhary, Indrasen Singh, Manoj Kumar Singh and Amit Kumar Jain (eds.) Compact and Flexible Microwave Devices, (49–64) © 2025 Scrivener Publishing LLC

real-world applications. The practical application of the TMASCAA is considered at the fundamental frequency f_0=2.4 GHz, ensuring the relevance and applicability of the proposed methodologies in contemporary communication standards. The research findings highlight the potential of DE, PSO, and NPSO techniques in advancing antenna array design, particularly optimizing performance metrics crucial for MIMO systems.

Keywords: MIMO, time-modulated circular antenna array, sidelobe level, sideband level, feed network efficiency, novel particle swarm optimization

3.1 Introduction

Cellular infrastructure evolved with 1G analog systems in the 1980s and 2G digital systems like GSM. In contemporary 3G and 4G networks, dispersed architectures replaced traditional setups, situating radio modules atop antenna towers to enhance link gain. Thick, low-loss coaxial cables linked baseband and radio modules, compensating for power loss, while fiber front hauls transmitted digital data in scattered networks. Baseband processing centralizes in 4.5G and 5G, while remote radio units integrate with numerous antenna components, enabling the MIMO scheme for effective wireless communication and data transmission. Recent theoretical research focuses on various aspects of MIMO systems, underscoring their significant potential in meeting the demanding needs of 5G networks, ushering in a new era of high-speed, high-capacity wireless communication to cater to evolving digital landscapes. Because adapting to this advancement is difficult, enhancing capacity, improving efficiency, and reducing interference becomes critical. In theory, satisfying these criteria requires using antennas with essential characteristics such as strong directivity and real-time beam steering [1]. These qualities improve spectral efficiency and gain while minimizing the effects of multipath propagation. For this application, employing a time modulation switching approach is a viable option in antenna arrays. Shanks and Bickmore pioneered using a fourth dimension, "Time," in antenna array design [2]. The word "Time" is added as an extra parameter for controlling the radiation pattern of antenna arrays [3]. Unlike standard techniques, this strategy can potentially improve radiation patterns [4]. The computation entails calculating Switch-ON time sequences for a time-modulated antenna array to obtain the required radiation pattern. Despite the benefits, one significant disadvantage to the time-modulation technique is that some electromagnetic energy is redirected to sideband signals [5]. To solve this issue, sideband levels (SBLs) are frequently evaluated throughout the optimization process [6]. An evolutionary optimization approach can efficiently resolve a precisely built objective function that includes the primary design objectives while decreasing sideband levels (SBLs) [7].

This study primarily computes the side lobe level (SLL), sideband level (SBLs), feed network efficiency (FNE), and directivity (DIR) of circular antenna arrays. Utilizing a 12-element array arranged uniformly in a circular configuration facilitated this analysis.

The portions of this study are detailed as follows: Section 3.2 describes the overall structure of the mathematical model for the time-modulated Asymmetric Circular Antenna Array (TMASCAA). Section 3.3 briefly describes the DE, PSO, and NPSO techniques notable for their simplicity and efficacy in global search. Section 3.4 focuses on the construction of cost functions. Section 3.5, "Numerical Results," looks at the radiation pattern and Optimized Switch-ON time sequence graph. Section 3.6 describes the convergence plot of 12-elements TMASCAA. Section 3.7 summarizes the paper's contributions.

3.2 Design Equations

In an X-Y plane, 'N' components are uniformly spaced at 'd' (where, $d=\lambda/2$) along the Z-axis in a circular arrangement.

When considering isotropic sources with the element's current I_n and angular position φ_n in the MIMO system, the array factor (AF) of the CAA indicates the pattern [8]. The Array Factor (AF) is given by (3.1).

$$AF(\phi) = \sum_{n=1}^{N} I_n.e^{j.\left(ka.\cos(\varphi-\varphi_n)+\psi_n\right)} \tag{3.1}$$

where 'r' is the circle's radius given by (3.2).

$$r = \frac{N * d}{2\pi} \tag{3.2}$$

$$\phi_n = \frac{2\pi r}{\lambda}\sum_{i=1}^{n} d_i \tag{3.3}$$

The distance between consecutive elements, d_i, is the arc length. The main beam pattern can be steered in the direction φ_o by applying a progressive phase delay to the nth element in the MIMO system as equation (3.4).

$$\psi_n = -kr.\cos\,(\phi_o - \phi_n) \tag{3.4}$$

from equations (3.2) and (3.4), the array factor is written as follows equation (3.5).

$$AF(\phi) = \sum_{n=1}^{N} e^{j.kr.(\cos(\phi-\phi_n)-\cos(\phi_o-\phi_n))} \tag{3.5}$$

Figure 3.1 shows an array in the X-Y plane with a dipole positioned in the Z-axis. In equation (3.5), apply time modulation technique, the AF can be expressed as [9].

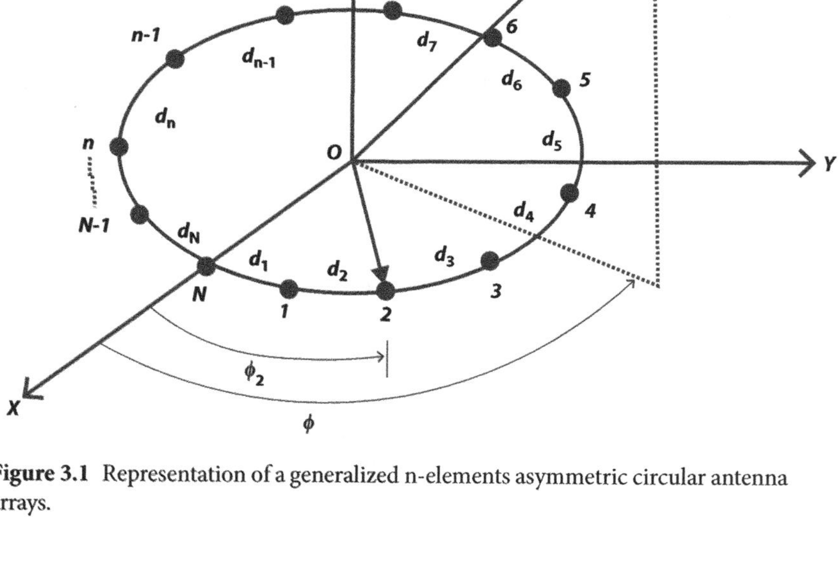

Figure 3.1 Representation of a generalized n-elements asymmetric circular antenna arrays.

$$AF(\varphi,t) = e^{j2\pi f_0 t}\sum_{n=1}^{n} I_n.U_n(t)\exp\{j.k[\cos(\varphi-\varphi_n)-\cos(\phi_o-\phi_n)]\} \tag{3.6}$$

$U_n(t)$ is the nth periodic switch ON time sequence. The element of the antenna array is switched ON for the period T_p. λ is the operational wavelength. $F_p = 1/T_p$ is the time modulation frequency. The switch ON periodic sequence in the frequency domain may be separated into FS, as given by

$$U_n(t) = \sum_{m=-\infty}^{\infty} i_{mn} e^{j2\pi m F_p t} \tag{3.7}$$

where,

$m = 0, \pm 1, \pm 2, \ldots\ldots, \pm\infty$.= harmonic frequency components,

m=0 stands for the operating frequency. i_{mn} shows the excitation amplitude value of nth elements for the mth harmonic in equation (3.7).

The AF of a far-field pattern antenna array can be expressed into a Fourier series (FS) from equations (3. 6) and (3.7) and given by equations (3.8) and (3.9).

$$\begin{aligned} AF(\varphi,t) = {} & \sum_{m=-\infty}^{\infty}\sum_{n=1}^{N} \frac{I_n\tau_n}{T_p}\sin c(\pi m F_p \tau_n) e^{-j\pi m F_p \tau_n} \\ & \times \exp\{j[kr\cos(\varphi-\varphi_n)+\beta_n]\} e^{j2\pi(f_0+m.F_p)t} \end{aligned} \tag{3.8}$$

$$\begin{aligned} AF_m(\varphi,t) = {} & e^{j2\pi(f_0+m.F_p)t}\sum_{n=1}^{N} \frac{I_n\tau_n}{T_p}\sin c(\pi m F_p \tau_n) e^{-j\pi m F_p \tau_n} \\ & \times \exp\{j[kr\cos(\varphi-\varphi_n)+\beta_n]\} \end{aligned} \tag{3.9}$$

f_0 is the operating frequency of the carrier wave. The pattern multiplication approach is used to construct the aforementioned geometry in real antenna arrays. This method entails multiplying the radiation patterns of practical antenna elements by the AF of an isotropic antenna array.

The element pattern of the dipole by [10] is as follows.

$$EP(\theta)=\frac{\cos\left(\frac{KL}{2}\cos\theta\right)-\cos\left(\frac{KL}{2}\right)}{\sin\theta} \tag{3.10}$$

For the dipole element, $L=\lambda/2$, the element pattern for an antenna array is provided by (3.11).

$$EP(\theta)=\frac{\cos\left(\frac{\pi}{2}\cos\theta\right)}{\sin\theta} \tag{3.11}$$

where, θ is angle formed by the dipole's axis and the line of sight. Equation (3.12) shows the total pattern of antenna array.

$$AF_{Total}(\theta,\phi)=EP\times AF \tag{3.12}$$

FNE is the feed network efficiency which is explained by equation (3.13).

$$FNE(\%)=\frac{\sum_{n=1}^{N}\tau_n}{N-N_0} \tag{3.13}$$

where, N_0 represents the count of antenna elements that are active for less than 20 % of the period T_0 during the optimization process. The directivity of CAAs is described in [11] as given in equation (3.14).

$$DIR=\frac{P(\theta,\varphi)}{\frac{1}{4\pi}\int_{4\pi}^{\infty}P(\theta,\varphi)\,d\Omega} \tag{3.14}$$

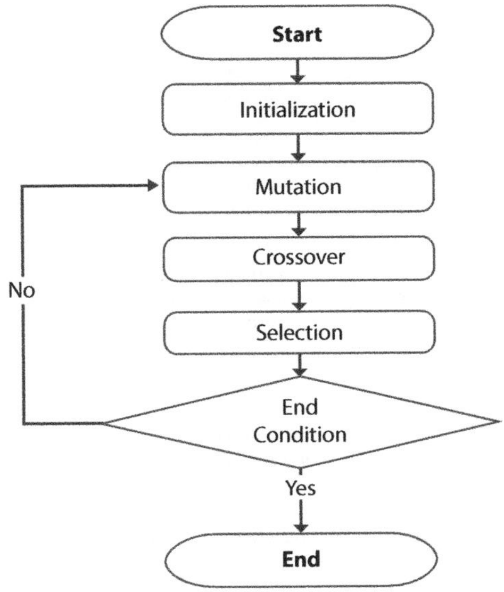

Figure 3.2 Flow chart of DE technique.

3.3 Evolutionary Optimization Method Used

DE, and NPSO technique have been briefly discussed in [12] and [13], respectively. This is a modified technique of PSO [13]. The flow chart of DE and NPSO techniques have been shown in Figure 3.2 and Figure 3.3, respectively.

3.4 Cost Function Formulation

In this study, the switching time sequences and progressive phase delays are the optimizing variables for circular array. The feeding current coefficient is kept constant and distance between elements is 0.5λ. Control parameter values of DE, PSO, and NPSO for 12-elements has been discussed in Table 3.1. The cost function (CF) is given in equation (3.15).

$$CF = W_1 \times \left| \frac{\prod_{\varphi=-180^\circ}^{180^\circ} \left|AF(\varphi_{SLL}, I_n)\right|}{\left|AF(\varphi_o, I_n)\right|_{\max}} \right|_{f_o} + W_2 \times \left| \frac{\prod_{\varphi=-180^\circ}^{180^\circ} \left|AF(\varphi_{SBL}, I_n)\right|}{\left|AF(\varphi_o, I_n)\right|_{\max}} \right|_{f_o + mF_p}$$

$$+ W_3 \times FNE + W_4 \times \frac{1}{DIR} \tag{3.15}$$

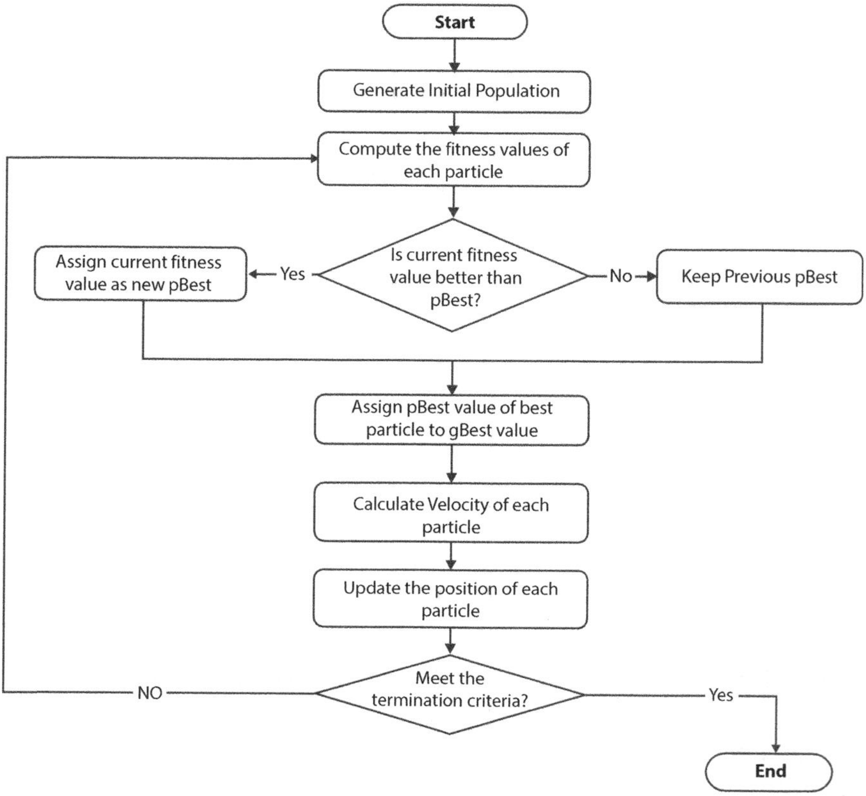

Figure 3.3 Flow chart of NPSO technique.

where, W_1, W_2, W_3, and W_4 are the weight coefficient with different values that are chosen such like the optimal values of SLL and SBL continue to be more imposing than ideal values of first null beamwidth and CF never be negative. FNE and DIR is the feed network efficiency and the maximum directivity, respectively.

3.5 Computational Result

The proposed 12-element of TMASCAA design's numerical results and a thorough analysis are presented in this part, where DE, PSO, and NPSO techniques have been applied to optimize the switch-ON time sequence and progressive phase delay of the array as given in Table 3.2 to achieve the ultra-low SLL and SBL at same time. Using DE technique, the values of SLL, SBL at first harmonic frequency (SBL_1), SBL at second harmonic

Table 3.1 Control parameter values for 12-elements antenna array.

Parameters	Values for 12-elements		
	DE	**PSO**	**NPSO**
Swarm Size	120	120	120
Iteration Cycles	300	300	300
Local acceleration of the particle	NR	1.85	1.6
Global acceleration of the particle	NR	1.85	1.6
Scaling Factor	0.5	NR	NR
Crossover Rate	0.9	NR	NR
W_1	0.4	0.65	0.5
W_2	0.75	0.5	0.45
W_3	0.6	0.3	0.3
W_4	0.6	0.7	0.6

NR* = Not Required

frequency (SBL_2), FNE, DRR, and DIR are -29.33 dB, -7.90 dB, -15.12 dB, 71.6825%, 1, and 4.4235 dB respectively. Using PSO technique, the values of SLL, SBL at first harmonic frequency (SBL_1), SBL at second harmonic frequency (SBL_2), FNE, DRR, and DIR are -30.75 dB, -6.13 dB, -18.34 dB, 65.0375%, 1, and 4.2843 dB respectively. Using NPSO technique, the values of SLL, SBL at first harmonic frequency (SBL_1), SBL at second harmonic frequency (SBL_2), FNE, DRR, and DIR are -36.83 dB, -9.08 dB, -16.10 dB, 72.8167%, 1, and 5.7603 dB respectively. DRR value is 1, after considering the feeding currents of TMASCAA are uniform ($I_n = 1$). As a result, the issue of large DRRs is resolved, which means the TMASCAA design may accomplish a considerably simplified array feed network driven by high-speed RF switches. TMASCAA also outperforms conventional CAA for achieving ultra-low SLLs Using DE, PSO, and NPSO techniques, as shown in Figure 3.4, Figure 3.5, and Figure 3.6. Optimized Switch-ON time sequences and Progressive phase delay are represented in Figure 3.7 and Figure 3.8, respectively.

Table 3.2 Optimized value for N=12 elements using DE, PSO, and NPSO algorithm.

Algorithm	SLL (dB)	SBL_1 (dB)	SBL_2 (dB)	FNE (%)	DIR (dB)	Optimized Switch-ON time sequence	Optimized progressive phase delay
DE	-29.33	-7.90	-15.12	71.6825	4.4235	0.5990 0.0893 0.6408 0.0635 0.6298 0.8553 0.6228 0.0651 0.6309 0.0616 0.6159 0.8606	-2.1190 0.3245 1.6698 -3.0667 -0.9225 -1.0958 -0.9037 -3.7721 1.6504 0.4538 -8.4202 4.4009
PSO	-30.75	-6.13	-18.34	65.0375	4.2843	0.5435 0.0694 0.5624 0.0506 0.5773 0.7771 0.5749 0.0774 0.5689 0.0399 0.5723 0.7893	1.5631 4.4819 -0.9891 -6.1678 -3.5575 2.5604 2.7401 0.0121 -1.0150 -2.4711 1.5539 1.7543
NPSO	-36.83	-9.08	-16.10	72.8167	5.7603	0.6422 0.2547 0.5563 0.1546 0.7717 0.9645 0.6211 0.1913	0.1590 4.3700 -2.2222 2.3922 1.4440 1.2720
						0.5844 0.0924 0.7681 0.9522	7.4556 -1.3621 -2.2832 2.0576 0.4500 0.3409

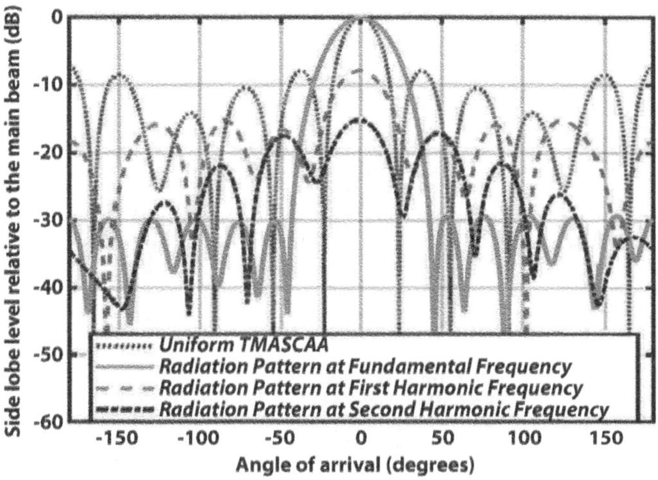

Figure 3.4 Radiation pattern of 12-elements TMASCAA using DE.

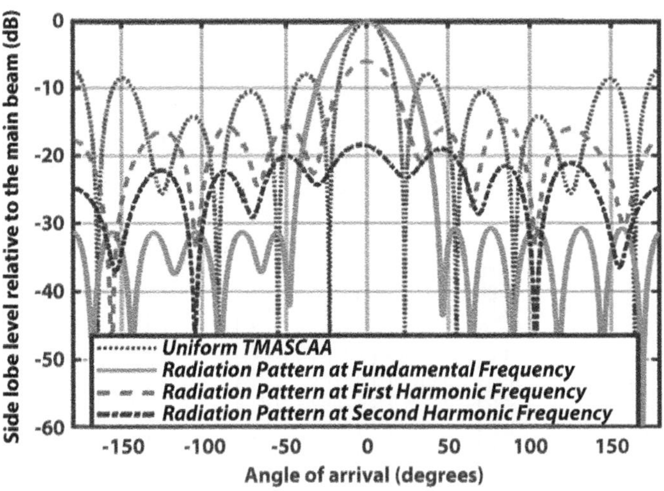

Figure 3.5 Radiation pattern of 12-elements TMASCAA using PSO.

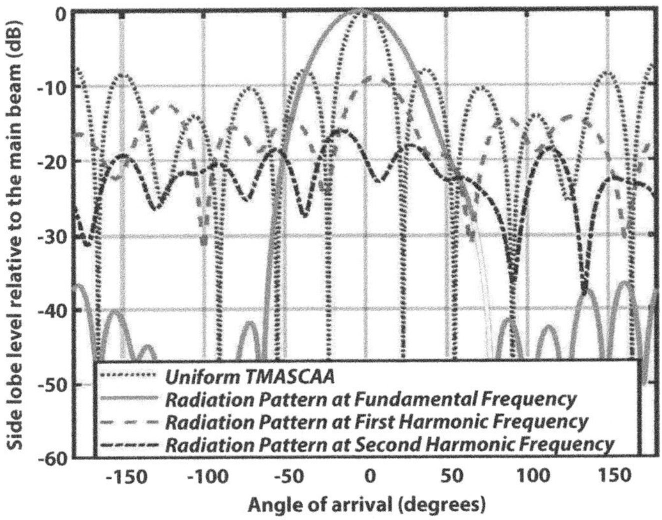

Figure 3.6 Radiation pattern of 12-elements TMASCAA using NPSO.

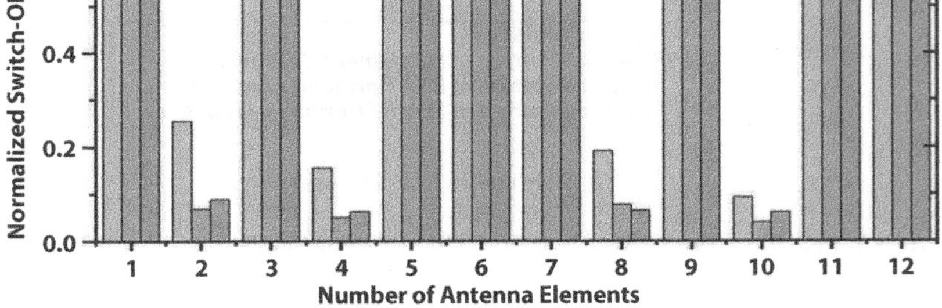

Figure 3.7 Switch-ON time sequence for 12-element TMASCAA using evolutionary algorithms.

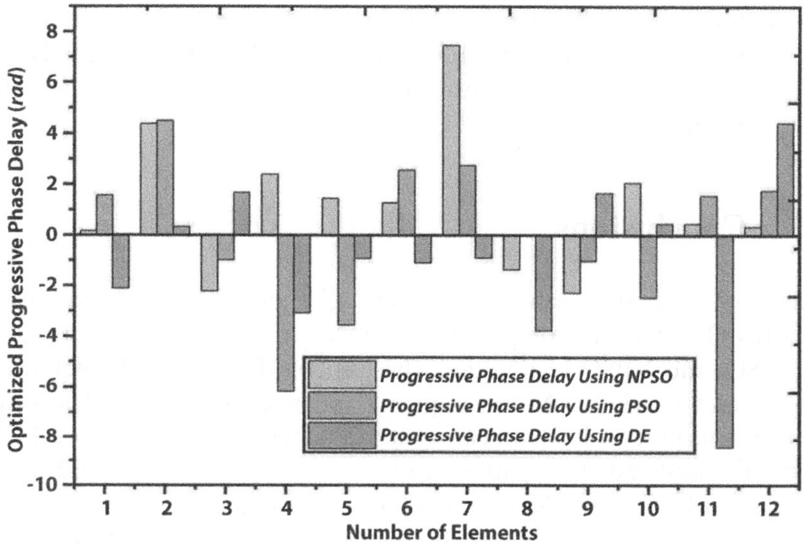

Figure 3.8 Progressive phase delay for 12-element TMASCAA using evolutionary algorithms.

3.6 The Convergence Curves of DE, PSO, and NPSO

Figure 3.9 shows convergence profile of 12-elements TMASCAA using DE, PSO, and NPSO which swiftly exploits the potential places as it eventually

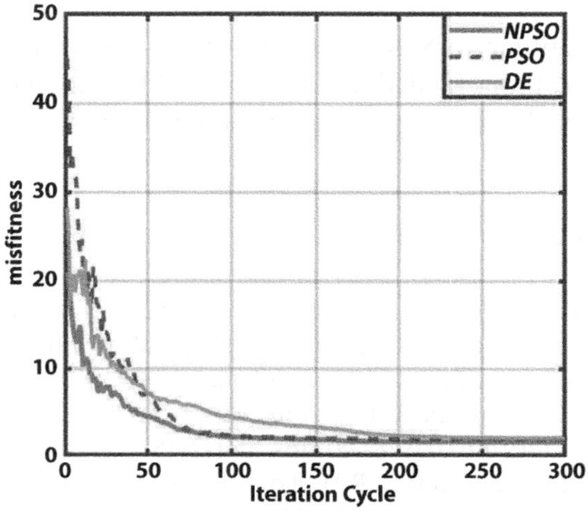

Figure 3.9 Convergence curve for 12-elements TMASCAA.

converges to the global optimal position. The lowest fitness values reach the constant value 2.2835 after 100 iterations for TMASCAA using NPSO. Using this graph, it can be analyzed that the NPSO technique is the fastest technique in place of DE, and PSO.

3.7 Conclusions

This research demonstrates that TMASCAA modelling enhanced the SLL for MIMO systems as compared to a conventional approach by using the DE, PSO, and NPSO techniques. These methods successfully determine the ideal set of switch-ON time sequence and progressive phase delays for a 12-elements practical antenna array at fundamental frequency f_0= 2.4 GHz to get the best radiation pattern with the highest directivity and higher feed network efficiency. NPSO technique is the best technique to get lowest SLL, high directivity, and high feed network efficiency of TMASCAA for MIMO systems as compared to DE, and PSO techniques. Simulations are done in MATLAB 2022b version.

Future studies will include designing various geometries such as hexagonal and concentric circular structures. Additionally, efforts will focus on minimizing the side lobe level and first null beamwidth (FNBW) using diverse evolutionary algorithms.

Acknowledgement

We express gratitude to SERB, Department of Science and Technology, Government of India (Sanction Order No: EEQ/2021/000700; Dated 4 March 2022) for the funding essential to conduct this research.

References

1. Chakraborty, A., Ram, G., Mandal, D., Electronic beam steering in timed antenna Array by controlling the harmonic patterns with optimally derived pulse-shifted switching sequence. *International Conference on Innovative Computing and Communications: Proceedings of ICICC 2021*, vol. 3, pp. 205–216, 2022, DOI:10.1007/978-981-16- 3071-2-18.
2. Shanks, H.E. and Bickmore, R.W., Four-dimensional electromagnetic radiators. *Can. J. Phys.*, 37, 3, 263–275, March 1959.

3. Haupt, R.L., Antenna Arrays in the time domain: an introduction to timed arrays. *IEEE Antennas Propag. Mag.*, 59, 3, 33–41, 2017.
4. Yang, S., Gan, Y.B., Khiang, T.P., A new technique for power pattern synthesis in time-modulated linear arrays. *IEEE Antennas Wireless Propag. Lett.*, 2, 285–287, 2003.
5. Aksoy, E. and Afacan, E., Thinned nonuniform amplitude time-modulated linear arrays. *IEEE Antennas Wireless Propag. Lett.*, 9, 514–517, 2010.
6. Poli, L., Rocca, P., Manica, L., Massa, A., Handling sideband radiations in time-modulated arrays through particle swarm optimization. *IEEE Trans. Antennas Propag.*, 58, 4, 1408–1411, Apr. 2010.
7. Zheng, L., Yang, S., Nie, Z., Pattern synthesis with specified broad nulls in time-modulated circular antenna arrays. *Electromagnetics*, 31, 5, 355–367, 2011.
8. Kumar, S., Ram, G., Kar, R., Mandal, D., Radiation Pattern Comparison of Circular Antenna Arrays Using GA and PSO. *IEEE International Symposium on Smart Electronic Systems (ISES)*, Warangal, India, pp. 164–168, 2022, DOI: 10.1109/iSES54909.2022.00042.
9. Kumar, S., Ram, G., Mandal, D., Kar, R., Optimal Design of Time-Modulated Linear and Circular Antenna Array for Feed Network Efficiency Using PSO. *International Conference on Recent Advances in Electrical, Electronics, Ubiquitous Communication, and Computational Intelligence (RAEEUCCI)*, 2023, DOI: 10.1109/RAEEUCCI57140.2023.10134328.
10. Schlieter, H. and Eigenbrod, H., Method for the formation of radiated beams in direction finder systems, Patent US 6021096 A, Feb. 1, 2000.
11. Bach, H., Directivity of basic linear arrays. *IEEE Trans. Antennas Propag. Lett.*, 18, 107–110, 1970, DOI: 10.1109/TAP.1970.1139620.
12. Kumar, S., Ram, G., Kar, R., Mandal, D., Far Field Radiation Pattern Synthesis of Circular Antenna Arrays Using NPSO. *IEEE Microwaves, Antennas, and Propagation Conference (MAPCON)*, pp. 676–680, 2022, DOI: 10.1109/MAPCON56011.2022.10047493.
13. Kumar, S., Ram, G., Kar, R., Mandal, D., Analysis of Feed Network Efficiency in Time-Modulated Linear and Circular Array. *IEEE Wireless, Antenna, and Microwave Symposium (WAMS)*, 2023, DOI: 10.1109/WAMS57261.2023.10242809.

4

Fractal Antenna MIMO Arrays: A Promising Multiband Solution for Modern 5G Wireless Automotive Applications

Gurmeet Singh[1]*, Ashish Kumar[2] and Amar Partap Singh Pharwaha[3]

[1]*School of Computing Science and Engineering, Galgotias University, Uttar Pradesh, India*
[2]*Chitkara University Institute of Engineering and Technology, Chitkara University, Punjab, India*
[3]*Department of Electronics and Communication Engineering, Sant Longowal Institute of Engineering and Technology, Longowal, Punjab, India*

Abstract
The rapid advancements in modern integrating circuit technology have led to a continuous reduction in the dimensions of electronic products, such as mobile handsets, in response to user demands. This trend has necessitated the integration of the RF-part (wireless interfaces) into a single antenna, while simultaneously requiring systems that can perform efficiently over multiple frequency bands and adapt to changing demands. Moreover, high data rate, uninterrupted signal, reliable connection and low free space path loss are also some of the features that have been very significant in ensuring efficient 5G and beyond communication. Multi-input-multi-output (MIMO) antenna systems and fractal antenna structures have emerged as a promising solution to address the aforementioned features due to their potential for miniaturization and enhanced performance. Natural patterns have served as an inspiration for fractal antennas, which are defined by their innate self-similarity in geometrical structure. The field of fractal electrodynamics has combined fractal geometry with electromagnetic theory, leading to the exploration of new methods of radiation and propagation problems. Also, a MIMO antenna provides enhanced capacity of the system when antennas are arranged in application specific configuration. However, the main challenge is to reduce the mutual coupling between the closely packed elements. This chapter will focus on

**Corresponding author*: ergurmeet96@gmail.com

Dilip Kumar Choudhary, Indrasen Singh, Manoj Kumar Singh and Amit Kumar Jain (eds.) Compact and Flexible Microwave Devices, (65–96) © 2025 Scrivener Publishing LLC

the various aspects and challenges of the fractal antenna arrays and MIMO configuration for recent sub-6 GHz and mm wave frequencies dedicated for modern 5G wireless communications. Moreover, by leveraging the unique properties of fractal geometries, fractal antenna arrays achieve multi-band characteristics, minimum side lobe levels, systematic approaches to low profiling, and rapid beam-forming algorithms. These arrays exhibit fractional dimensions derived from the generating short array used to recursively create them. The investigation of fractal antenna arrays presents significant potential for enhancing antenna engineering in various applications. The ability to achieve miniaturization and multi-band performance without sacrificing efficiency offers new opportunities for wireless communication systems and electronic devices. The study of fractal antenna arrays opens up avenues for innovative and efficient antenna design, addressing the growing demand for compact, high-performance solutions in modern wireless communication networks. Moreover, this chapter also focuses on some of the aspects of beam-forming and phased array antennas which will facilitate covering more dead spots in rural areas and also while travelling. These fractal MIMO antenna array can also be integrated in the plastic parts of the modern passenger car which would be hidden and enhance the aesthetic appearance of the car. However, the plastic or glass material of the car will affect the performance parameters of the antenna arrays. All these effects have been studied in this chapter with examples. Overall, this chapter will provide insight about fractal structure antenna arrays for various 5G mobile automotive wireless communications.

***Keywords*:** Fractal, automotive, antennas, wireless, frequency, defected ground structure, feed, microstrip patch

4.1 Introduction

Wireless communication has experienced rapid growth and advancements due to growing user demand, which has further led to multiple components on a single chip in the form of circuit integration and miniaturization. These developments have made moveable radio equipment smaller, more affordable, and highly reliable. Antennas are one of the significant components for reliable and efficient wireless communication. The antennas are the means of transmitting and receiving radio waves which can act as a bridge between guided device and free space [1, 2]. The antennas can be categorized on the basis of operating frequency, material used, application specific, performance parameters specific, etc. Moreover, for some applications, a single unit cell of the antenna is sufficient while for complex application a group of antennas known as antenna array can be utilized with proper design considerations. Based on the various parameters, these antennas can be as straightforward as a loop, dipole, or monopole, or they can be as intricate as a parabolic reflector antenna. However, when specific requirements demand more gain, more directive patterns, main beam scanning, or other attributes that cannot be achieved with single-element antenna, an array of antennas becomes more significant. In an array of antennas, multiple elements are excited and arranged simultaneously to increase the field strength in preferred directions. This arrangement allows for better coverage, increased gain, and control over the radiation pattern. While non-uniform radiation patterns may be preferred in many broadcast services, they may not be suitable for point-to-point communication. There are various types of antenna arrays used in various commercial, and military applications, each employing different elements such as dipoles, loops, apertures, microstrips, horns, reflectors, etc. One common configuration is the sectoral array, where each four-element array on each side of the triangle covers an angular sector of 120 degrees. An example of a classic sectoral array of dipoles is the Yagi-Uda array as shown in Figure 4.1, which finds application in TV and amateur radio. Another dipole-based array, the log-periodic antenna as shown in Figure 4.2, offers larger bandwidth than the Yagi-Uda array but minimum directivity and is commonly used for TV reception. Additionally, there are arrays utilizing microstrips as elements, as shown in Figure 4.3. Overall, antenna arrays play a crucial role in enhancing wireless communication systems, and their design and selection depend on the specific application's requirements and performance objectives. In recent years, the dimensions of electronic products, such as mobile handsets, have been continuously shrinking to meet user needs, thanks to advancements in modern integrating circuit technology.

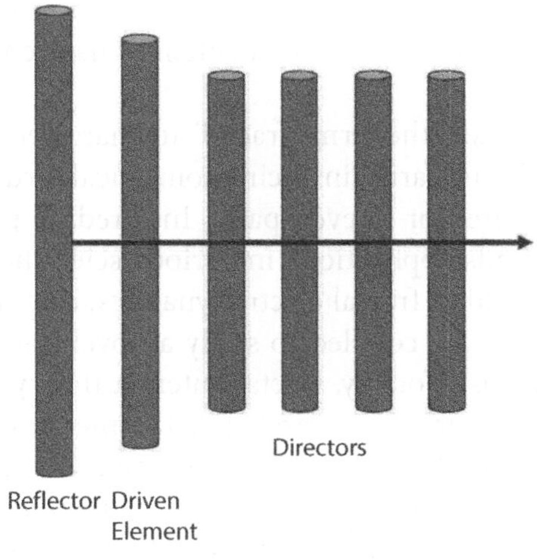

Figure 4.1 Yagi-Uda antenna array configuration [2].

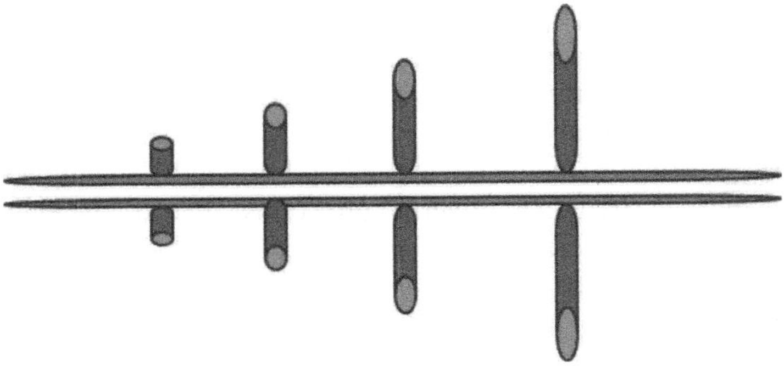

Figure 4.2 Log periodic dipole array [2].

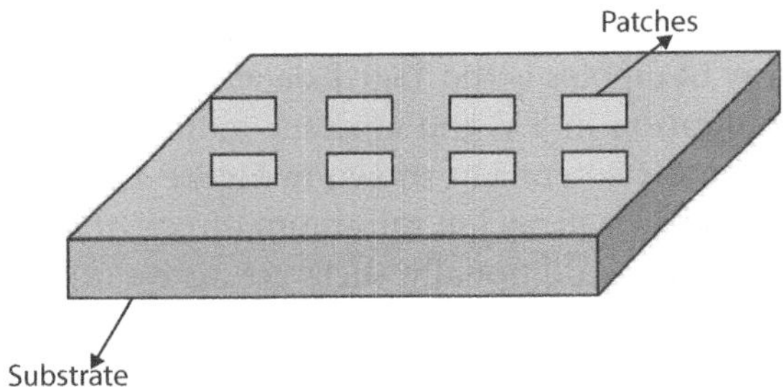

Figure 4.3 Microstrip patch array [2].

As a result, there is a growing need to integrate the RF-part (wireless interfaces) into a single antenna. Additionally, operators are seeking systems that can perform over multiple frequency bands for different applications. To address these requirements, fractal antennas have emerged as a promising solution.

Mandelbrot first used the term "fractal" to characterize complex structures that have self-similarity in their geometrical structure. The phrase now refers to fractured or uneven parts. Inspired by patterns in nature, fractal geometry finds applications in various scientific and engineering fields. Within the field of fractal electrodynamics, electromagnetic theory and fractal geometry are coupled to study a novel class of radiation and propagation problems. Notably, fractal antenna theory has gained attention as a relatively new area of research. Fractal antennas offer the potential for miniaturization, particularly in wire antennas like dipoles and loops. They can serve as multiband solutions and small-sized antennas without sacrificing performance [3]. To achieve directivity and gain in an antenna without increasing its size, researchers turn to antenna arrays. Antenna arrays are systems that combine radiations from a group of similar antennas through wave interference. These arrays consist of spaced and properly phased radiators, referred to as elements, which can take various shapes based on the requirements [4, 5]. The focus of this chapter is on recent developments in fractal antenna engineering, with particular emphasis on fractal arrays. Fractal arrays possess notable properties, such as multiband characteristics, low side lobe levels, and systematic approaches to low profiling by exploiting the recursive nature of fractals. These arrays exhibit fractional dimensions derived from the generating subarray used to recursively create them [5]. In conclusion, fractal antennas and fractal arrays represent promising advancements in antenna engineering, offering miniaturization possibilities and enhanced performance across multiple frequency bands. The utilization of fractal geometries has opened up new avenues for research and design, paving the way for innovative and efficient antenna solutions.

4.2 Various Forms of Antenna Array

Antennas can be configured in various shapes, such as straight lines, circles, triangles, rectangles, and more. However, only a limited number of antenna arrays find practical use. In a multi-element array, the elements are typically $\lambda/2$ dipole antennas, although these elements may differ from the standard dipole antenna [6]. This concise and straightforward paragraph conveys two essential points related to antennas and antenna arrays. It mentions that antennas can be placed in different configurations, which gives the reader an idea of their versatility. However, it emphasizes that only a limited number of these configurations are practically useful, hinting at the importance of selecting appropriate array designs based on specific applications. Additionally, it mentions that in multi-element arrays, the commonly used elements are $\lambda/2$ dipole antennas, but these elements can vary from the standard dipole antenna. This implies that there is room for flexibility and customization in the design of antenna arrays. Overall, the paragraph effectively conveys the key information without unnecessary elaboration.

4.2.1 Array of Two-Point Sources

In the realm of arrays of isotropic point sources, the simplest scenario involves two-point sources assumed to be separated by a certain distance and sharing the same polarization. In the theory of antenna arrays, when these sources are superimposed at a significant distance, their fields combine through amplitudes and phases. Hence array of two isotropic point sources deals with different cases like Equal and Unequal amplitudes and Phases.

(a) Arrays of two-point sources with same amplitude and phase: Two isotropic point sources symmetrically situated with reference to origin is shown in Figure 4.4 [6]

Total field at a distant point from the origin have been calculated. Waves from the source 1 reaches at a point p at a later time than from source 2, so path difference between two waves is given by [6]

$$\text{Path Difference} = \left(\frac{d}{2}\cos\theta + \frac{d}{2}\cos\theta\right) \tag{4.1}$$

$$= \frac{d}{\lambda}\cos\theta \tag{4.2}$$

Then phase angle is given by

$$\text{Phase angle } (\Psi) = 2\pi\left(\frac{d}{\lambda}\cos\theta\right) \tag{4.3}$$

$$\Psi = kd\cos\theta \tag{4.4}$$

where Ψ is the phase angle difference between the fields of the two-source measured at angle θ. Then total far field at distant point is given by

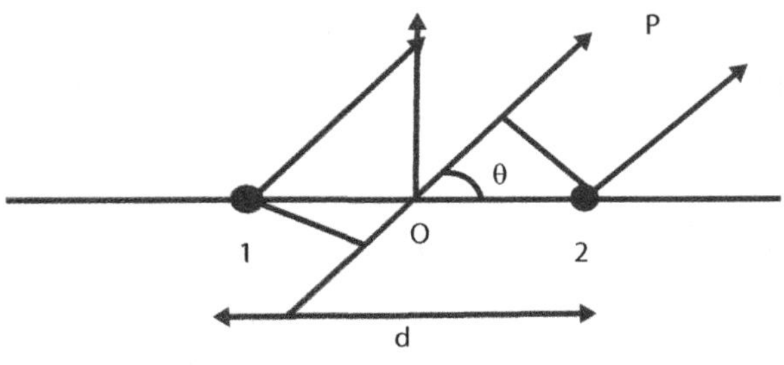

Figure 4.4 Array of two-point source [6].

$$E = E_1 e^{-j\frac{\psi}{2}} + E_2 e^{+j\frac{\psi}{2}} \tag{4.5}$$

Due to equal amplitude and phase far field pattern of two isotropic point sources is given by

$$E = 2E_o \cos\frac{\Psi}{2} \tag{4.6}$$

(b) Arrays of two-point sources with same amplitude and opposite phase: In this case, point source 1 is out of phase or opposite phase to source 2, i.e., when there is maximum occur in source 1 minima occurs in source 2 at that instant. So total far field is given by [6]

$$E = -E_1 e^{-j\frac{\Psi}{2}} + E_2 e^{+j\frac{\Psi}{2}} \tag{4.7}$$

Since the reference point is at the origin and amplitude is equal

$$E_o = E_1 = E_2$$

$$E = 2jE_o \sin\frac{\Psi}{2} \tag{4.8}$$

(c) Arrays of two-point sources with different amplitude and phase: In this case, amplitudes of two-point sources are not equal and hence any phase difference says β, E_1 is greater than E_2 so total phase difference between the radiations of two-point sources is given by

$$\Psi = kd\cos\theta + \beta \tag{4.9}$$

where β is the phase angle how source 2's current surpasses source 1's current. If $\beta = 0°, 180°$ and $E_1 = E_2 = E_o$ then it is same as the above two cases.

4.2.2 Broadside Array

The broadside array is a crucial and commonly used antenna configuration in practical applications. It consists of multiple identical parallel antennas arranged along a line perpendicular to their individual axes as shown in Figure 4.5. These antennas are evenly spaced and fed with currents of equal magnitude and in the same phase. Consequently, this arrangement radiates in the broadside direction, resulting in a bidirectional radiation pattern [6]. In numerous applications, achieving maximum radiation directed normal to the array's axis (broadside, $\theta=90°$) is highly desirable. To achieve an optimized design, it is essential for both the single element and the array factor to direct their maxima toward $\theta_o=90°$. The requirements for the single elements can be fulfilled by carefully selecting appropriate radiators, while those for the array factor involve the reasonable separation and feeding of individual radiators. In this section, we will explore and develop the specific requirements that enable the array factor to efficiently radiate in the broadside direction, enhancing the overall performance of the broadside array. The first maximum of the array factor is given by

$$\varphi = kd\cos\theta + \beta = 0 \tag{4.10}$$

For first maximum directed toward then $\theta_o = 90°$, then

$$\varphi = kd\cos\theta + \beta = 0 \,|_{\theta=90°} = \beta = 0 \tag{4.11}$$

Hence, in addition to having the same amplitude excitation, every element in a uniform linear array must have the same phase excitation in order for the array factor to reach its maximum, which is pointed broadside to the array's axis. Any value can be assigned to the distance between the items. In order to prevent main maxima, also known as grating lobes, from

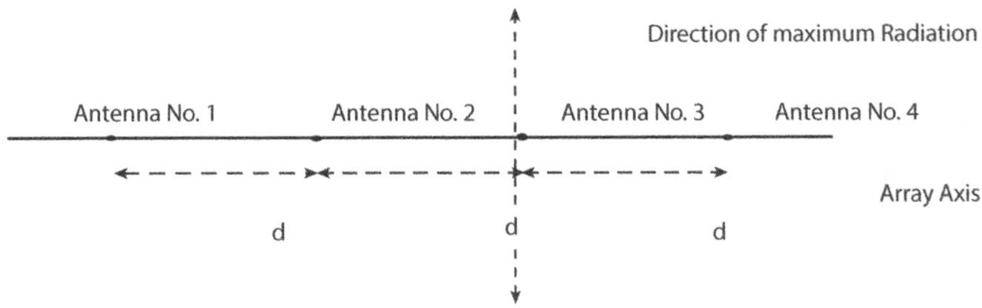

Figure 4.5 Broadside array arrangement [6].

existing in other directions, the distance between the elements shouldn't equal multiples of a wavelength. ($d \neq n\lambda$, $n = 1, 2, 3 \ldots$) when $\beta = 0$. If $d = n\lambda$, $n = 1, 2, 3, \ldots$ and $\beta = 0$, then

$$\varphi = kd\cos\theta + \beta \Big|_{\substack{d=n\lambda \\ \beta=0 \\ n=1,2,3,\ldots}} = 2\pi n \cos\theta \Big|_{\theta=0^\circ,180^\circ} = \pm 2n\pi \tag{4.12}$$

As a result, for a uniform array with $\beta = 0$ and $d=n\lambda$, there are extra maxima directed along the array's axis (θ=0°,180°) (endfire radiation) in addition to the maxima of the array factor oriented broadside (θ=90°) to the array's axis. Avoiding additional maxima—also known as grating lobes—in addition to the primary maximum is one of the goals in many designs. Choosing the greatest distance between the elements without any grating lobes may often be necessary. The maximum distance between the elements should be smaller than one wavelength in order to prevent any grating lobes ($d_{max} < \lambda$) [1].

4.2.3 End-Fire Array

The end-fire array shares similarities with the broadside array, but with a key distinction—the individual elements are fed out of phase (180°). Instead of maximizing radiation in the broadside direction, the end-fire array is designed to direct its maximum radiation along the axis of the array, as depicted in Figure 4.6. In the end-fire array, multiple identical elements are equally spaced along a line, but the phases vary progressively with currents of equal magnitude. This unique arrangement ensures that the principal direction of radiation aligns precisely with the direction of the array axis. In fact, the design is tailored in such a way that the array radiates towards a specific direction, and only one direction. By controlling the phase differences among the elements, the end-fire array achieves a highly focused radiation pattern, making it ideal for applications where targeted and directional transmission is essential. The ability to concentrate radiation in a specific direction allows for enhanced signal strength and reception in the desired area of interest. To direct the first maximum toward ($\theta_o = 0°$)

$$kd\cos\theta + \beta = 0 \,|_{\theta=0^\circ} = kd + \beta = 0; \beta = -kd \tag{4.13}$$

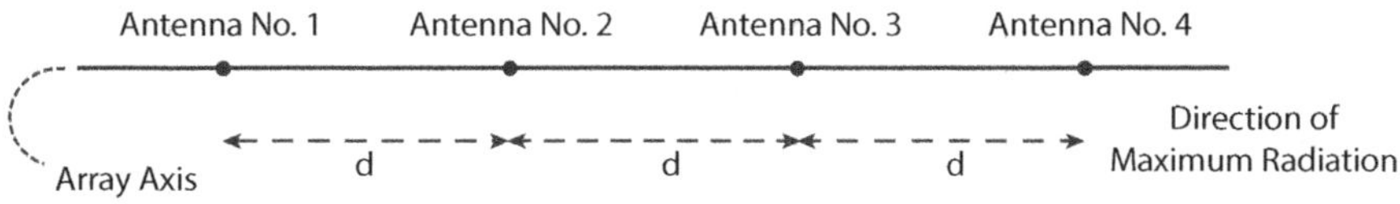

Figure 4.6 Arrangement of antennas in end fire configuration.

If the first maximum is desired toward $(\theta_o = 180°)$ then

$$kd\cos\theta + \beta = 0\,|_{\theta=180°} = -kd + \beta = 0; \beta = kd \qquad (4.14)$$

Thus end-fire radiation is completed when $\beta = -kd\ (\text{for}\ \theta_o = 0°)$ or $\beta = kd$ (for $\theta_o = 180°$). If the element distance is $d = \lambda/2$, end-fire radiation occurs concurrently in both directions ($\theta_o = 0°$ or $\theta_o = 180°$) and if the element spacing is a multiple of a wavelength ($d = n\lambda$, n = 1, 2, 3, . .) then there are maxima in the broadside directions in addition to end-fire radiation in both directions. Thus for $d = n\lambda$, n = 1, 2, 3, . . there exist four maxima; two along the array's axis and two in the broadside directions. In order to prevent any grating lobes and to have only one end-fire maximum, the maximum spacing between the elements should be smaller than $d_{max} < \lambda/2$ [2].

4.2.4 Parasitic Array

To address the challenge posed by fed lines in antenna arrays, a solution often employed is the concept of parasitic feeding. In this approach, specific elements of the array are fed parasitically rather than directly through a transmission line. The driven element is the one directly supplied power from the transmission line, while the adjacent elements receive power parasitically and are termed parasitic elements. These parasitic elements draw power from the nearby driven element through electromagnetic coupling. The simplest configuration of a parasitic array involves just two elements: one driven element and one parasitic element. However, in more complex scenarios, multi-element parasitic arrays consist of multiple parasitic elements along with at least one driven element to introduce power into the array [6]. By utilizing parasitic elements, the need for individual transmission lines to each element is reduced, resulting in a more streamlined and efficient antenna array design. This technique enhances the directivity and gain of the array, offering improved performance in various applications, such as communication systems, radar, and satellite communication. The electromagnetic coupling between elements enables power transfer, leading to a well-coordinated and coherent radiation pattern from the entire array. The versatility and effectiveness of parasitic feeding make it a valuable tool in modern antenna engineering.

4.3 Feed Networks for Antenna Array

Arrays play a highly versatile role, serving multiple purposes in antenna engineering. One of their key applications is the synthesis of radiation patterns that cannot be achieved with a single element alone. Additionally, arrays enable beam scanning in antenna systems, leading to increased directivity and various other functionalities that would be challenging to achieve using a single element. To power the elements in an array, two distinct feed methods are commonly employed. Figure 4.7(a) illustrates the use of a single feed line, known as a series-feed network. On the other hand, Figure 4.7(b) demonstrates a feed network arrangement where multiple lines are utilized, referred to as a corporate-feed network [2]. The choice between series-feed and corporate-feed networks depends on specific design considerations and performance objectives. These feeding techniques significantly impact the array's ability to produce desired radiation patterns and cater to diverse communication and radar requirements. In conclusion, the versatility and functionality of arrays make them indispensable tools in modern antenna engineering, enabling the efficient realization of complex radiation patterns and enhancing the overall performance of antenna systems.

4.3.1 Corporate Feed Network

Power splits of 2^n are provided by corporate-feed networks (i.e., n = 2, 4, 8, 16, 32, etc.). This can be achieved via quarter wavelength impedance transformers or tapered lines, as in Figure 4.7(b), to match 100-ohm patch components to a 50-ohm input.

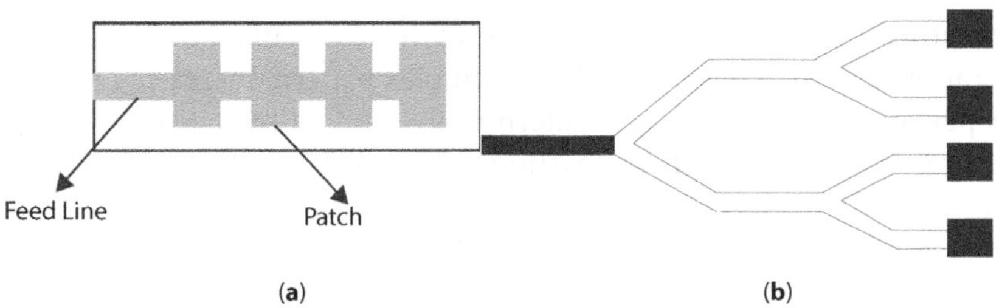

Figure 4.7 (a) Series fed. (b) Corporate fed.

4.3.2 Series Fed

Series-fed arrays offer a convenient fabrication process using photolithography for overall antenna. This technique proves effective for arrays with fixed beams or those scanned by varying the frequency. Moreover, it is suitable for linear and planar arrays with single or dual polarization. However, there are certain limitations and considerations that need to be addressed in the design process. Any modifications or changes to one element or feed line can have a significant impact on the performance of the entire array. As a result, it becomes crucial to account for various effects, including mutual coupling and internal reflections, during the design phase. Careful consideration of these factors ensures optimal array performance and helps overcome potential challenges. By understanding and managing these effects, designers can create high-performing and efficient series-fed arrays, tailored to meet specific radiation pattern requirements and communication objectives.

4.4 Fractal Geometries

Fractal-shaped antennas have demonstrated unique characteristics, closely related to the geometrical properties of fractals. Their self-similarity property makes them particularly suitable for designing multifrequency antennas. Some existing fractal geometries are worth exploring, such as the Koch curve. The Koch curve fractal is intriguing because of its resemblance to certain fractals found in nature, resembling coastlines of continents or islands. Unlike smooth, straight lines, coastlines exhibit intricate details at various scales. The Koch curve begins with a simple pattern—a line divided into three equal parts. The middle segment is erased and replaced with an upside-down "V" shape, resulting in four-line segments. This process is repeated recursively. Each of the four lines is divided into thirds, and the middle segment is replaced with a "V," resulting in a total of 16-line segments. Fractals perpetuate never-ending patterns by iteratively repeating the same concept. In the case of the Koch curve, each subsequent iteration leads to a more jagged and complex pattern, increasing its length or perimeter. Eventually, the pattern evolves into a fractal that resembles natural formations, such as coastlines or snowflakes. Drawing the Koch curve fractal involves using a pencil to replace each segment with a smaller version of the starting pattern. This requires dividing each line segment into thirds and substituting the middle segment with the "V" shape repeatedly, creating a pattern that becomes 1/3 of the original size with four times as many of them [6]. The Koch curve fractal exemplifies the captivating world of fractals and their potential application in designing antennas with multifrequency capabilities. Its resemblance to natural formations further emphasizes the significance of fractal geometries in various scientific and engineering disciplines.

(a) **Koch Fractal Geometry:** The Koch monopole stands as a remarkable exemplar showcasing the remarkable potential of fractals in enhancing the characteristics of traditional Euclidean shapes. With its distinctive attributes, the Koch curve unfolds into a captivating nonrectifiable curve, its length progressively growing at each iteration as depicted in Figure 4.8. Strikingly, this curve defies the realm of piecewise continuity and differentiation, rendering it nowhere differentiable. Its form emerges as intricately rough and

Figure 4.8 Koch curve fractal for various iteration.

uneven, presenting itself as a promising contender to assume the role of an efficient radiator [3, 9]. In the world of antennas and radiators, the Koch monopole boldly asserts the transformative influence of fractals, unlocking new avenues for innovation in the design and performance of wireless communication systems. Its nontraditional and irregular nature challenges the conventional norms, offering an exciting frontier to explore in the quest for advanced, high-performance radiating structures. As the realm of fractals continues to captivate researchers and engineers alike, the Koch monopole stands resolute, symbolizing the profound impact of fractal geometries in reshaping the landscape of modern antenna engineering.

(b) Koch Snowflake: This is another naturally occurring fractal that can be constructed using the Koch curve. Three copies of the Koch curve, rotated and combined as in Figure 4.9, yield an object that is sixfold symmetric and resembles a snowflake. Snowflakes multiply by branching repeatedly and spreading outward from the center. While the method is not exactly the same as that of the Koch curve, they are both created by repeatedly performing a basic action. Complex shapes originate from simple repetition, just like all fractals do [6].

(c) Sierpinski Gasket: An exemplary instance of a self-similar shape lies in the mesmerizing Sierpinski triangle, also known as the Sierpinski gasket. This captivating fractal bears the name of the renowned Polish mathematician Waclaw Sierpinski,

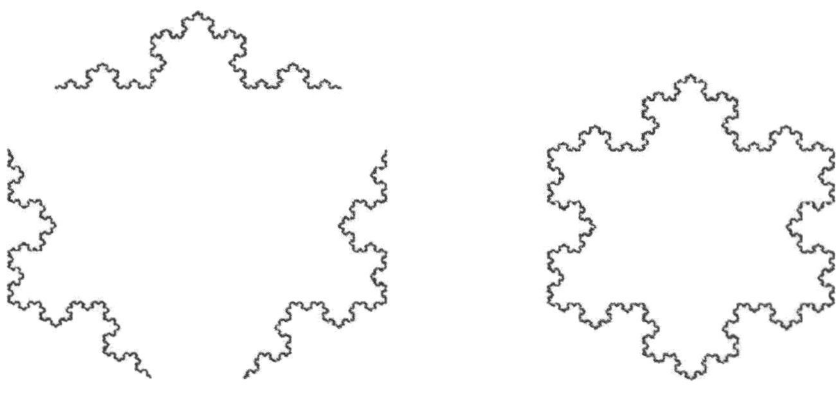

Figure 4.9 Koch snowflake fractal structure.

who introduced it to the world in 1916. The Sierpinski triangle is generated through a remarkable process involving three iterations, employing the decomposition algorithm. To construct this fractal, an equilateral triangle is taken as the starting point. By connecting the midpoints of each side of the triangle and subsequently removing the central inverted triangle from the parent triangle, three half-scaled triangles emerge. This process is then iteratively repeated on each of the three smaller triangles, and this cascade continues through three iterations, as depicted in Figure 4.10 [7, 8]. The enchanting Sierpinski triangle exemplifies the infinite beauty and complexity of self-similar structures, resonating deeply with the intricate patterns found in nature. As it continues to captivate the imagination of mathematicians, artists, and researchers alike, the Sierpinski fractal stands as an enduring testament to the captivating realm of fractal geometry and its profound influence across various scientific and creative disciplines.

(d) Sierpinski Carpet: In recent times, the Sierpinski carpet antenna has garnered significant attention as a remarkable

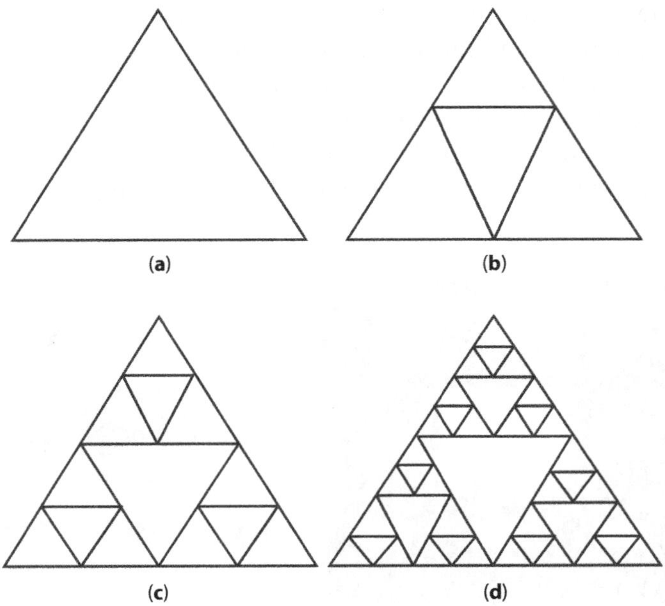

Figure 4.10 Sierpinski gasket fractal antenna [7].

extension of the Sierpinski gasket, primarily due to its captivating multiband behavior [10]. This novel low-profile microstrip antenna exhibits a remarkable capability to operate in not just one but three distinct frequency bands, with resonant frequencies of f1, 3f1, and 9f1, respectively. This remarkable feature sets it apart from traditional multiband antennas, making it a highly sought-after choice for various communication applications. Moreover, the Sierpinski carpet antenna stands out for its simplicity in structure and cost-effectiveness, presenting an attractive solution for modern communication systems. The implementation of the Sierpinski carpet antenna can be achieved in two ways: a positive configuration and a negative configuration, each with its own unique attributes. In the positive configuration, the antenna takes the form of a planar surface adorned with square holes, while in the negative configuration, individual squares are skillfully grouped together. The distinction between these configurations can be seen in Figure 4.11, where black represents metal elements and white signifies the dielectric material. Notably, the positive configuration is produced in a manner similar to how the Sierpinski gasket is created, showcasing the fascinating interplay of fractal geometry in antenna engineering [10]. The versatility and multiband capabilities of the Sierpinski carpet antenna have unlocked exciting opportunities in modern communication technologies. As this antenna continues to captivate researchers and engineers, it holds the promise of revolutionizing the field of antenna design, offering innovative

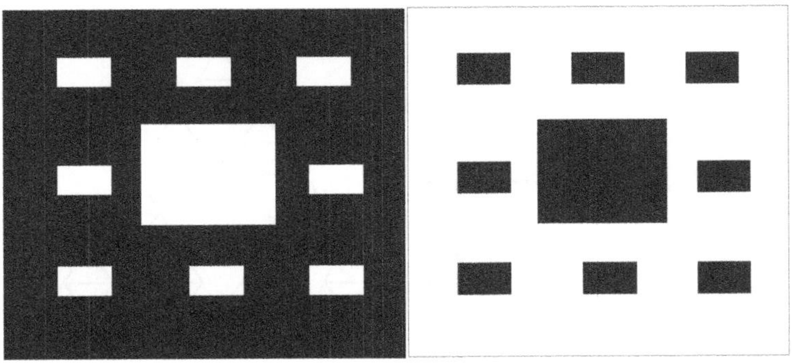

Figure 4.11 Sierpinski carpet configurations up to 2nd iteration [14].

solutions for efficient and cost-effective wireless communication systems.

(e) **Minkowski curve:** The initiator and generator principles that gave birth to the Koch curve possess the remarkable capacity for generalization, enabling the creation of a diverse array of meandering curves. By applying the generator concept to the Minkowski curve, a fascinating transformation unfolds, wherein a straight-line segment, spanning four segments in length, is replaced with a curvilinear path extending eight segments in length, which can be visualized in Figure 4.12. The growth of the Minkowski curve's length accelerates more rapidly between each stage of construction compared to the Koch curve [11]. The profound implications of these generalization principles unveil a mesmerizing world of complex and ever-evolving curves, akin to the intricacies found in nature's most captivating patterns. The Minkowski curve stands as a striking exemplar of this phenomenon, mesmerizing mathematicians, scientists, and creative minds alike with its innate ability to metamorphose and expand at an accelerated pace. As researchers delve deeper into the realm of fractal geometry and its applications, the captivating potential of these meandering curves continues to spark

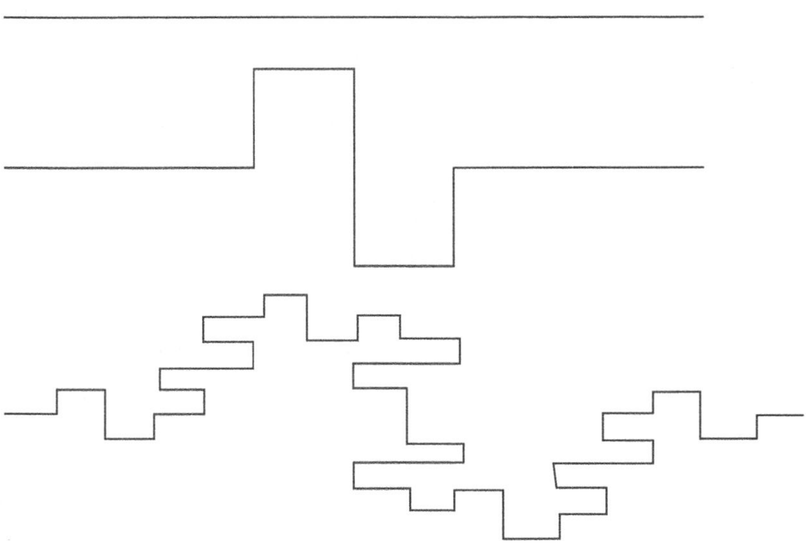

Figure 4.12 Minkowski curve up to 2nd iteration [11].

inspiration and drive the exploration of new frontiers in diverse scientific and artistic disciplines.

4.5 Fractal Antenna Arrays

In the mid-1980s, a groundbreaking idea emerged, suggesting the use of fractal geometry to complement traditional Euclidean methods for element placement in linear arrays. The objective was to merge the desirable low side lobes of periodic arrays with the robustness in element excitation and placement seen in random arrays, achieved through the application of random fractals [12]. The quest for effective array design emphasized the need to consider mutual coupling, particularly as arrays were packed more tightly to increase scan angles in phased array systems. One approach to controlling mutual coupling involved miniaturizing the array elements. This reduction in element size minimized coupling by increasing the spacing between elements, thereby enhancing overall array performance [13]. To achieve miniaturization, fractal geometries proved to be instrumental. These geometries were also employed in defining the distribution of elements within the arrays. Recently, fractal arrays have gained attention, mainly to introduce self-similar features in radiation patterns, enabling multiband frequency usage of the array. The array factor, representing the pattern of an array of isotropic point sources, plays a crucial role in array design. This factor is obtained by multiplying the individual source patterns and the pattern of an array of isotropic point sources, each situated at the phase center of the respective individual sources, with relative phase and amplitude [6]. In the pursuit of refined array performance, understanding the array factors for an arbitrary row of symmetric elements along the z-axis holds significant importance [5]. These intricate considerations and advancements in array design, empowered by fractal geometry and mutual coupling control, promise to revolutionize antenna technology and enable unprecedented capabilities in modern communication systems.

$$\text{Array Factor}(\varphi) = \begin{cases} a_o + 2\sum_{m=1}^{M} a_m cos\left[m\varphi\right], odd\, no.of\ elements\left(2M+1\right) \\ \\ 2\sum_{m=1}^{M} a_m cos\left[\left(m-1/2\right)\varphi\right], even no.of\ elements\left(2M\right) \end{cases} \tag{4.15}$$

where M = number of element

$$a_m = \begin{cases} 1 = element\ turned\ on\ or\ connected\ to\ feed\ network \\ 0 = element\ turned\ off\ or\ connected\ to\ matched\ load \end{cases}$$

$\varphi = kdu_o$

$k = 2\pi / \lambda$

λ = wavelength

d = constant spacing between the elements

$$u_o = \cos\theta - \cos\theta_o$$

$\theta = angle\ of\ incidence\ of\ electromagnetic\ plane\ wave$

$\theta_o = direction\ of\ main\ beam$

Element weights are either 1 or 0 and indicate whether or not the individual elements contribute to the total radiation pattern of the array.

4.5.1 Deterministic Fractal Arrays

Within the realm of antenna engineering, a fascinating class of fractal arrays emerges, intricately crafted through a recursive process involving a generating subarray. This subarray serves as the foundation at scale one (P = 1), forming the building blocks for larger arrays at higher scales (P > 1). The generating subarray exhibits a clever arrangement, with specific elements turned on and off in a prescribed pattern. By adhering to a precise formula for copying, scaling, and translation of the generating subarray, a captivating fractal array is brought to life. These fractal arrays, born from the iterative application of the generating subarray, boast an enchanting feature: a sequence of self-similar subarrays. In essence, they manifest as arrays of arrays, with each level retaining the characteristic attributes of the parent subarray. This delightful phenomenon allows for the creation of sophisticated and multifaceted antenna structures, exuding elegance and efficiency in their design [5, 13]. As antenna technology continues to evolve, the allure of fractal arrays holds the promise of unlocking new possibilities and pushing the boundaries of what is achievable. This approach not only facilitates the construction of intricately detailed arrays but also presents a fertile ground for innovation in communication systems, radar technology, and other scientific endeavors. By embracing the beauty of self-similarity and recursive patterns, fractal arrays showcase the marvels of fractal geometry in the world of modern antenna engineering. The array factor for a fractal array of this type may be expressed in the general form

$$AF_p(\varphi) = \prod_{p=1}^{P} GA\left(\delta^{p-1}\varphi\right) \tag{4.16}$$

where $GA(\varphi)$ represents the array factor associated with the generating subarray. The parameter δ serves as a pivotal scale or expansion factor, dictating the size of the array as the generating subarray is applied recursively. In Equation (4.16), the fractal array factor is elegantly expressed as the product of scaled versions of the generating subarray factor. This formulation allows us to perceive Equation (4.16) as a formal manifestation of the pattern multiplication theorem for fractal arrays. In essence, this theorem articulates the captivating phenomenon wherein the intricate pattern of a fractal array emerges through the multiplication of scaled and repeated subarrays. As we explore the rich landscape of fractal geometry within antenna engineering, this theorem assumes profound significance, guiding the design and analysis of fractal arrays. Its ability to capture the essence of self-similarity and repetition in the formation of fractal arrays unveils a world of innovation and possibilities, inspiring researchers and engineers alike to delve further into the realm of fractal antenna design. By leveraging the insights gained from the pattern multiplication theorem, fractal arrays hold the potential to revolutionize the capabilities of modern communication systems and usher in a new era of antenna engineering excellence.

4.5.2 Cantor Linear Array

Figure 4.13 depicts a linear array comprising isotropic elements, uniformly arranged along the z-axis with a constant spacing of distance d. The array factor associated with this linear configuration is elegantly expressed, as discussed in equation (4.16) [14]. In this simple yet powerful representation, the array factor encapsulates the intricate interplay of the isotropic elements and their spatial distribution, enabling a comprehensive understanding of the array's radiation pattern. By delving into the equation, antenna engineers and researchers gain valuable insights into the array's directivity, radiation efficiency, and other critical performance parameters.

The linear array of isotropic elements, coupled with the robust analytical framework provided by equation (4.16), serves as a fundamental building block for more sophisticated and specialized antenna systems. As we delve further into the realm of array design and optimization, this expression stands as a guiding beacon, driving the exploration of innovative antenna configurations and heralding a new era of antenna engineering excellence.

These arrays take on fractal-like characteristics through the strategic manipulation of elements, involving the selective turning off or removal of specific components. As a result, the fractal arrays generated through this process fall into a distinct category known as thinned arrays. A noteworthy example of a fractal linear array arises from the renowned Cantor set, with its potential for low-sidelobe array design being extensively studied [4, 15]. At its core, the basic triadic Cantor array begins with a three-element generating subarray, where the center element is turned off or removed (i.e., 101). Subsequently, this generating subarray undergoes iterative application over P scales of growth, resulting in the recursive replacement of 1 with 101 and 0 with 000 at each stage of construction as illustrated in Table 4.1. This ingenious process gives rise to the mesmerizing triadic Cantor array, a prime illustration of the captivating interplay between fractal geometry and antenna engineering. The construction of fractal arrays in this manner presents an exciting avenue for antenna engineers and researchers, offering innovative solutions in the quest for enhanced radiation patterns, reduced sidelobes, and improved performance across a broad range of applications. As the exploration of fractal arrays continues to captivate the imagination of the

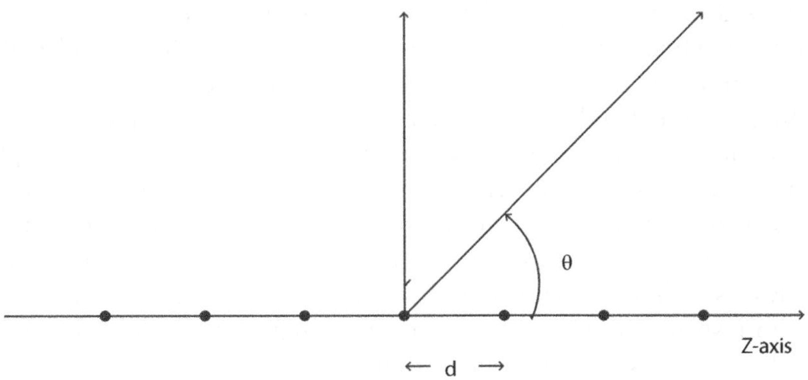

Figure 4.13 Linear array of uniformly spaced isotropic sources [14].

Table 4.1 Element distribution for fractal linear arrays for even elements.

S. no	Element pattern	Active elements	Total elements
1	1010	2	4
2	1010000010100000	4	16
3	1010000010100000000000 000000000101000001010 00000000000000000000	8	64

scientific community, the Cantor set remains a beacon of inspiration, guiding the way towards new frontiers in antenna design and array optimization.

The array factor of the four elements generating subarray with the representation 1010 is, from equation (4.17)

$$2\sum_{m=1}^{M}\cos(n-\frac{1}{2})\varphi, \mathit{for}\, 2M$$

$$\text{Array Factor} = 2\cos(\varphi/2) \tag{4.17}$$

The captivating world of fractal linear antenna arrays unravels an intriguing phenomenon: arrays with an even number of elements exhibit remarkable multiband characteristics. This multiband behavior represents a truly remarkable feat, wherein the side-lobe ratio and radiation pattern characteristics display striking similarities across multiple frequency bands. In essence, the fractal linear antenna array unveils its versatility and adaptability, effortlessly accommodating a wide spectrum of frequencies while maintaining consistent and desirable radiation patterns. This exceptional feature holds immense promise in modern communication systems, enabling the design of compact and efficient antenna arrays that can seamlessly operate across various frequency bands. As researchers and engineers continue to explore the boundless possibilities of fractal antenna arrays, the multiband behavior stands as a testament to the remarkable potential of fractal geometry in reshaping the landscape of antenna engineering. With its capacity to achieve impressive performance in diverse frequency ranges, the fractal linear antenna array emerges as a formidable contender in the quest for advanced, high-performance communication solutions.

4.5.3 Sierpinski Carpet Arrays

The fascinating application of fractal geometric concepts to thinned linear arrays has been explored earlier. Now, we extend the concept to embrace the more versatile realm of fractal planar arrays. The focus now shifts to a symmetric planar array, comprising isotropic sources arranged with uniform spacing along both the x and y directions at distances d_x and d_y, respectively. Renowned in the field, the array factor for this distinctive planar array configuration is elegantly expressed in the following manner [5]. As we delve deeper into the realm of fractal planar arrays, the possibilities for innovative antenna designs and advanced communication solutions are boundless. These fractal-based techniques offer an alluring blend of symmetry, efficiency, and adaptability, captivating the minds of antenna engineers and researchers alike. By embracing the power of fractal geometry in planar arrays, we set the stage for unprecedented advancements in antenna technology. The quest to optimize radiation patterns, enhance directivity, and achieve multiband operation becomes a captivating journey, guided by the intricate principles of fractal design. As we uncover the vast potential of fractal planar arrays, we usher in a new era of antenna engineering excellence, laying the foundation for the communication systems of the future.

$$AF(\varphi_x,\varphi_y)=\begin{Bmatrix} I_{11}+2\sum_{m=2}^{M} I_{m1}\cos[m\varphi_x]+I_{1m}\cos[m\varphi_y]+ \\ 4\sum_{n=2}^{M}\sum_{m=2}^{M} I_{mn}\cos[m\varphi_x]\cos[n\varphi_y],\ for\,(2M-1)^2\,elements \\ 4\sum_{n=1}^{M}\sum_{m=1}^{M} I_{mn}\cos[(m-1/2)\varphi_x]\cos[(n-1/2)\varphi_y],\ for\,(2M)^2\,elements \end{Bmatrix} \tag{4.18}$$

where

$$\varphi_x = kd_x[\sin\theta\cos\varnothing - \sin\theta_o\cos\varnothing_o]$$

$$\varphi_y = kd_y[\sin\theta\cos\varnothing - \sin\theta_o\cos\varnothing_o]$$

where

$$I_{mn} = \begin{Bmatrix} 1, if\ elements(m,n) is\ turned\ on \\ 0, if\ elements(m,n) is\ turned\ off \end{Bmatrix}$$

A two-dimensional cantor set is called a Sierpinski carpet, and it can be used in a similar way to thin planar arrays. Take a look at the straightforward generating subarray that is

$$\begin{matrix} 1 & 1 & 1 \\ 1 & 0 & 1 \\ 1 & 1 & 1 \end{matrix}$$

The normalized array factor associated with this generating subarray, for $d_x = d_y = \lambda/2$, is given by

$$GA(u_x, u_y) = \frac{1}{4}\left[\cos(\pi u_x) + \cos(\pi u_y) + 2\cos(\pi u_x)\cos(\pi u_y)\right] \tag{4.19}$$

where

$$u_x = \sin\theta \cos\varnothing - \sin\theta_o \cos\varnothing_o\ and\ u_y = \sin\theta \sin\varphi - \sin\theta_o \sin\varnothing_o$$

Substitute Equation (4.19), into equation (4.15) with an expansion factor of $\delta = 3$ yields the following expression for the fractal array factor at stage P

$$AF_p(u_x, u_y) = \frac{1}{4^P}\prod_{p=1}^{P}[\cos(3^{P-1}\pi u_x) + \cos(3^{P-1}\pi u_y) + 2\cos(3^{P-1}\pi u_x)\cos(3^{P-1}\pi u_y)] \tag{4.20}$$

The above Equation gives the array factor for Sierpinski carpet array generated using subarray. So, the above array factor has been used for radiation plot for various stages of growth.

4.6 Recent Trends in the Fractal Antenna Arrays

As discussed in the above sections, there are numerous modifications in the conventional fractal geometries and their array structures have been discussed in the form of MIMO or using different feeding techniques. In such attempts, a sub 6 GHz 5G MIMO antenna systems have been presented with the utilization of defected ground structure (DGS) [16]. Various performance parameters have been evaluated to verify the diversity of MIMO antennas. In this [17], a circular fractal array with DGS has been presented for 4.6 GHz to 16.8 GHz operating in C-band and satellite/radar imaging applications. In [18], an 8-element antenna array has been designed for 5G smartphone applications. The proposed design provides the required efficiency and channel capacity for the 5G NR frequency bands. In [19], a periodic fractal antenna with DGS has been implemented for cross polarization suppression for the C-band applications. A two-element fractal array structure is designed in the form of MIMO operating in 5.45 GHz-5.72 GHz frequency band. The proposed design shows excellent performance in terms of Diversity gain and correlation coefficients [20]. MIMO arrays of antennas with measured high isolation (>50 dB) and inter-element separation of 0.2 mm (0.023~ at 35 GHz) are reported. Radiating patch is modified in terms of slot length and size to enhance isolation within the 28–37.5 GHz impedance bandwidth. The suggested self-isolation method is validated using parametric analysis, current distributions. Significant improvement in bandwidth (>29%), efficiency (>90%), minimal ECC (<0.005) and gain (>9.5 dB) noticed, throughout the intended bandwidth [21]. The uniform linear antenna array presented in this research satisfies requirements of the DSRC band in terms of performance. A Wilkinson power divider is used to provide feed network to the antenna elements. In this work, a novel technology is introduced by etching the square's four corners utilizing the Koch-snowflake method. Furthermore, a flaw has developed in the ground plane. The suggested array has a CP bandwidth of 58.00 MHz [22]. The suggested antenna array reduces mutual coupling S_{12} to below -30dB by incorporating fractal architecture. Nonetheless, the antenna performs well in two frequency bands, with S_{11} less than -10dB at 3.78GHz and 8.24GHz. The antenna's dimension is highly miniaturized without compromising mutual coupling. The antenna array's radiation patterns are broadside toward boresight direction [23]. A 2.4-2.7GHz two element MIMO system with good gain and a spiral type EBG structure is suggested. First, a divider stub is placed between the two parts to improve isolation; this results in -17dB isolation. Using the EBG structure, greater isolation is finally reached to -25.864dB, along with improved radiation properties. 6.29dBi is the gain at the intended frequency of 2.6 GHz [24]. This work presents a circular antenna with an inner round slot and a rectangular slot along the length edge to enable resonance of the suggested design at 5.57 GHz, which is specifically, designated for 5G communication applications. Array arrangement is used to obtain the needed gain, improving the bore side gain from 6.66 dB to 12.4 dB [25]. For use in the production of next-generation mobile phones, hexagonal shaped radiator fractal antenna array (HFAA) with MIMO configuration has been conceived and built. Radiation properties at both lower and higher frequencies and return loss have somewhat improved with this arrangement. Better impedance matching is achieved by the radiating patch with defected ground structure (DGS). The first iteration of the simulated radiation characteristics shows that at 2.52 GHz, it has bandwidth of 1.58%. With a 620 MHz bandwidth of 10 dB (1.26%), the transceiver's simulated return loss was found to be 29 dB and 26 dB at 2.6 GHz and 3.5 GHz [26]. This study has presented a hybrid fractal antenna array with high-gain, showing resonance at 4.17 and 5.97 GHz, as well as dual-band, low-profile features. The original design of the single-element antenna made use of two distinct substrates: FR4 and Rogers TMM. A Wilkinson power divider was also constructed to feed the fractal antenna array, ensuring an equal and wide band power split among four array elements [27]. This study introduces a two-port MIMO array, with high isolation less than -35 dB. To increase bandwidth, circle-shaped slotted patch array elements are composed. To enable the 5G MMW, the antenna operates between 27 and 40 GHz. There is a high degree of agreement between the measurement and simulation results. It exhibits a good TARC (<30dB) performance. Additionally, the DG is getting close to 10 dB, the ECC is less than 0.004, and the MEG is less than -6 dB [28]. In order to meet the criteria for high performance 5G MIMO communication systems, a unique antenna array is designed. The array's functionality has been confirmed through experimentation. Every radiating component consists of three rows of connected square ring resonators with a matching stub [29]. This publication presents a two-port MIMO antenna with stub loaded ground plane for 5G wireless applications. Performance of suggested antenna is compared with various DGS and it is discovered that the alteration in ground plane enhances the impedance bandwidth, 20 (1. 0 to 21. 4GHz) and (23. 9 to 30GHz) [30]. The performance parameters of all the discussed fractal antenna array is discussed in Table 4.2.

Table 4.2 Detailed analysis of recent research papers regarding fractal antenna array.

References	Design	Antenna size (mm^2)	Operating frequency (GHz)	Gain (dB)	Mutual coupling (dB)	Application
[16]	Sierpinski Triangle MIMO Array	30 × 40	2-5.2	6.3	-20	Sub-6 GHz 5G
[17]	Circular Fractal	34×68.7	4.6-16.8	4.57	-23.24	4G WLAN
[18]	Inverted-L	103.8× 68	3.1-6	N.A.	-10	Smartphone
[19]	U-shaped and arc shaped DGS	30 × 30	2.5-3.75	N.A.	-20	Commercial
[20]	Sierpinski Gasket MIMO	136 × 136	4.5-5.7	DG=9.9	-10	Wireless applications
[21]	Printed Patch MIMO	19 × 12	28-37.5	9.6	-35	Mm wave 5G
[22]	Eight flower-shaped etched Array	151 × 43	5.92	11.98	-28	Vehicular Communication
[23]	Bended Sierpinski Fractal Array	50 × 30	3.78 and 8.24	N.A.	-20	MIMO applications
[24]	Meander Line Array	130×80	2.4-2.7	6.29	-25.8	LTE

(Continued)

Table 4.2 Detailed analysis of recent research papers regarding fractal antenna array. (*Continued*)

References	Design	Antenna size (mm^2)	Operating frequency (GHz)	Gain (dB)	Mutual coupling (dB)	Application
[25]	Circular Shaped Antenna	160×70	5.6-5.67	12.4	-30	Mobile Phones
[26]	Hexagonal MIMO Fractal Array	44.6×79.9	2.52, 3.5	4.2	N.A.	5G smartphone
[27]	Combined Minkowski–Sierpinski Carpet Antenna	240×240	4.17 and 5.97	9.61	-40	WLAN and Wi-Fi
[28]	2-element Fractal Array	55.27×27.63	28 and 38	10	-30	5G applications
[29]	Fractal Antenna with Matching Stubs	80×80	3.5-5.0	11.25	-27	Sub-6 GHz 5G
[30]	Hybrid Fractal MIMO	75×40	1-30	14	-20-50	5G NR and LTE

4.7 Conclusion

In conclusion, this chapter has explored the fascinating world of fractal antenna arrays, revealing their immense potential as a multiband solution with promising miniaturization capabilities. Fractal geometry has proven to be a powerful tool in antenna engineering, enabling the design of arrays that exhibit self-similar patterns, efficient radiation characteristics, and the ability to operate across multiple frequency bands. Through the study of various fractal geometries such as the Koch curve, Sierpinski triangle, Minkowski curve, Cantor set, and more, we have witnessed the emergence of fractal antenna arrays that surpass the limitations of traditional Euclidean approaches. These arrays, constructed using recursive generating subarrays, have opened new frontiers in array design, offering enhanced directivity, reduced sidelobes, and improved radiation efficiency. The miniaturization potential of fractal arrays has been particularly noteworthy, driving advancements in compact and low-profile antenna systems. The use of fractal geometries has facilitated the creation of multifunctional antennas capable of operating across different frequency bands, making them indispensable in modern communication applications. As we continue to explore the fascinating possibilities of fractal antenna arrays, it becomes evident that this research field holds tremendous promise for the evolution of communication systems. The unique attributes of fractal geometry, combined with the ability to achieve multiband behavior and miniaturization, offer a paradigm shift in antenna engineering. In the future, further research and experimentation will undoubtedly lead to even more innovative fractal antenna designs, catering to the evolving demands of wireless communication, satellite systems, and beyond. By harnessing the power of fractals, we unlock a world of possibilities in antenna technology, shaping the trajectory of communication systems and paving the way for a connected and efficient future.

References

1. Mandelbrot, B.B., *The Fractal Geometry of Nature*, W. H. Freeman, New York, 1983.
2. Balanis, C.A., *Antenna Theory: Analysis and Design*, John Wiley & Sons, New York, 2005.
3. Baliarda, C.P., Romeu, J., Cardama, A., The Koch Monopole: A Small Fractal Antenna. *IEEE Trans. Antennas Propag.*, 48, 11, 2000.

4. Puente Baliarda, C. and Pous, R., Fractal Design of Multiband and Low Side-lobe Arrays. *IEEE Trans. Antennas Propag.*, 44, 730–739, 1996.
5. Werner, D.H. and Haupt, R.L., Fractal Constructions of Linear and Planar Arrays. *IEEE Antennas and Propagation Society International Symposium*, vol. 3, pp. 1968–1971, 1997.
6. Prasad, K.D., *Antenna and Wave Propagation*, Satya Parkashan, New Delhi, 2009.
7. Jaggard, D.L. and Jaggard, A.D., Fractal ring arrays. Elsevier science/*Wave Motion*, 34, 281–299, 2001.
8. Werner, D.H., Haup, R.L., Werner, P.L., Fractal Antenna Engineering: The Theory and Design of Fractal Antenna Array. *IEEE Antennas Propag. Mag.*, 41, 5, 37–59, I999.
9. Yadav, S., Choudhary, R., Soni, U., Peswani, B., Sharma, M.M., Koch curve fractal antenna for Wi-MAX and C-Band wireless applications. *2014 5th International Conference - Confluence. Next Generation Information Technology Summit (Confluence)*, Noida, India, pp. 490–494, 2014, doi: 10.1109/CONFLUENCE.2014.6949356.
10. Gianvittorio, J.P. and Rahmat-Sami, Y., Fractal Elements in Array Antennas: Investigating Reduced Mutual Coupling and Tighter Packing. *IEEE Antennas and Propagation Society International Symposium*, 2000.
11. Vinoy, K.J. and Pal, A., Dual-Frequency Characteristics of Minkowski-Square Ring Antennas. *IET Antennas Propag.*, 4, 2, 219–224, 2010.
12. Ma, M.T., *Theory and Application of Antenna Arrays*, John Wiley and Sons, 1974.
13. Kumar, A. and Singh, A.P., Design of micro-machined modified Sierpinski gasket fractal antenna for satellite communications. *Int. J. RF Microwave Comput. Aided Eng.*, 28, 8, 2019.
14. Na, Y. and Xiao-wei, S., Analysis of the Multiband Behavior on Sierpinski Carpet Fractal Antennas. *IEEE APMC Proceedings*, 2005.
15. Choukiker, Y., Sharma, S.K., Behera, S.K., Hybrid Fractal Shape Planar Monopole Antenna Covering Multiband Wireless Communications with MIMO Implementation for Handheld Mobile Devices. *Antennas Propag. IEEE Trans.*, 62, 1483–1488, 2014, 10.1109/TAP.2013.2295213.
16. Alibakhshikenari, M., *et al.*, An innovative antenna array with high inter element isolation for sub-6 GHz 5G MIMO communication systems. *Sci. Rep.*, 12, 1, 7907, May 2022.
17. Sidhu, A.K. and Sivia, J.S., Design of Wideband Fractal MIMO Antenna using Minkowski and Koch Hybrid Curves on Half Octagonal Radiating Patch with High Isolation and Gain for 5G Applications. *Adv. Electromagn.*, 12, 1, 58–69, Mar. 2023.
18. Hassan Ghadeer, S., *et al.*, An innovative fractal monopole MIMO antenna for modern 5G applications. *AEU Int. J. Electron. Commun.*, 159, 154480, Feb. 2023.

19. Sohi, A.K. and Kaur, A., UWB aperture coupled circular fractal MIMO antenna with a complementary rectangular spiral defected ground structure (DGS) for 4G/WLAN/radar/satellite/international space station (ISS) communication systems. *J. Electromagn. Waves Appl.*, 34, 17, 2317–2338, Nov. 2020.
20. Sim, C.-Y.-D., Liu, H.-Y., Huang, C.-J., Wideband MIMO Antenna Array Design for Future Mobile Devices Operating in the 5G NR Frequency Bands n77/n78/n79 and LTE Band 46. *IEEE Antennas Wirel. Propag. Lett.*, 19, 1, 74–78, Jan. 2020.
21. Zhang, Z.L., Wei, K., Xie, J., Li, J.Y., Wang, L., The MIMO Antenna Array with Mutual Coupling Reduction and Cross-polarization Suppression by Defected Ground Structures. *Radioengineering*, 27, 4, 969–975, Sep. 2018.
22. Sudhashree, S. and Chitra, S., Design and Development of Improved Fractal Mimo Antenna. *Telecommun. Radio Eng.*, 78, 15, 1377–1387, 2019.
23. Sokunbi, O., Attia, H., Hamza, A., Shamim, A., Yu, Y., Kishk, A.A., New Self-Isolated Wideband MIMO Antenna System for 5G mm-Wave Applications Using Slot Characteristics. *IEEE Open J. Antennas Propag.*, 4, 81–90, 2023.
24. Patanvariya, D.G., Chatterjee, A., Kola, K.S., High-Gain and Circularly Polarized Fractal Antenna Array for Dedicated Short Range Communication Systems. *Prog. Electromagn. Res. C*, 101, 133–146, 2020.
25. Al-Dulaimi, Z., Elwi, T.A., Atilla, D.C., Aydin, C., Design of Fractal Based Monopole Antenna Array with Ultra-Mutual Coupling Reduction for MIMO Applications, in: *2018 18th Mediterranean Microwave Symposium (MMS)*, pp. 39–42, 2018.
26. Das, D., Thiripurasundari, D., Poonkuzhali, R., MIMO antenna array at LTE for portable devices, in: *2017 International Conference on Innovations in Information, Embedded and Communication Systems (ICIIECS)*, pp. 1–4, 2017.
27. Khan, J., Ullah, S., Tahir, F.A., Tubbal, F., Raad, R., A Sub-6 GHz MIMO Antenna Array for 5G Wireless Terminals. *Electronics*, 10, 24, 3062, Dec. 2021.
28. Palanisamy, S., Thangaraju, B., Khalaf, O.I., Alotaibi, Y., Alghamdi, S., Alassery, F., A Novel Approach of Design and Analysis of a Hexagonal Fractal Antenna Array (HFAA) for Next-Generation Wireless Communication. *Energies*, 14, 19, 6204, Sep. 2021.
29. Vallappil, A.K., Khawaja, B.A., Rahim, M.K.A., Uzair, M., Jamil, M., Awais, Q., Minkowski–Sierpinski Fractal Structure-Inspired 2 × 2 Antenna Array for Use in Next-Generation Wireless Systems. *Fractal Fract.*, 7, 2, 158, Feb. 2023.
30. Megahed, A.A., Abdelhay, E.H., Abdelazim, M., Soliman, H.Y.M., 5G millimeter wave wideband MIMO antenna arrays with high isolation. *EURASIP J. Wireless Commun. Netw.*, 2023, 1, 61, Jul. 2023.

5

Multiband Fractal Antenna: A Novel Miniaturization Technique

Ruchi Kadwane

Electronics and Telecommunication Engineering Department, G H Raisoni University Amravati, Maharashtra, India

Abstract

Fractal antenna engineering represents a relatively new field of research that combines attributes of fractal geometry with antenna theory. Fractals are space-filling geometries that can be used as antennas to effectively fit long electrical lengths into small areas. Iterative function schemes represent an extremely versatile method for conveniently generating a wide variety of usual fractal structures. The demand for antennas which provide wide and multiband characteristics with high gain is increasing for both civilians and military applications. This drives the research in the field of antennas in many different directions; one such emerging field is the design of a microstrip antenna element using fractals. An antenna design engineer has to face the task of optimizing the design for meeting the varied requirements of the application at hand. In many cases the criteria that need to be satisfied are in conflict with each other. Some of the common requirements are small size, high gain, wide or multiple bandwidths, high radiation efficiency, high directivity, etc. This chapter focuses on design and performance analysis of low-profile multiband fractal patch antenna for GHz applications. New space filling rectangular fractal microstrip patch antenna design is presented in this chapter for multiple frequency band performance. Fractal geometry, in terms of the addition of smaller and smaller rectangles in a step-by-step iterative process, improves the radiation properties in terms of return loss, directivity, surface current distribution, gain, beamwidth and radiation pattern. This proposed antenna assures simplicity in design and fabrication. Since the antenna exhibits good multiband characteristics, it has found various applications in wireless communication at GHz frequency.

Email: kadwaneruchi09@gmail.com

Dilip Kumar Choudhary, Indrasen Singh, Manoj Kumar Singh and Amit Kumar Jain (eds.) Compact and Flexible Microwave Devices, (97–124) © 2025 Scrivener Publishing LLC

Keywords: Band width, beamwidth, directivity, fractal, radiation pattern, return loss, VSWR

5.1 Introduction

Nowadays, owing to growth in multimedia applications, demand for antennas that could cover joint bands has arisen. These antennas are useful for a number of applications where several bandwidths are required in conjunction with directivity and a modest level of gain. They are sometimes used over the HF portion of the spectrum and as per requirement they also use lower bands of frequency spectrum. They can be used at VHF and UHF for a variety of applications.

Today's antenna system must be flexible and unobtrusive. Many applications require antennas to be as small as possible. Wireless communication systems usually require smaller devices to achieve smaller circuit sizes and lower costs. Miniaturization of antennas is very important in wireless communications and it is advantageous to miniaturize antennas while achieving performance comparable to large antennas. Although there is a lower bound on antenna size for a given resonant frequency, other important metrics such as gain and bandwidth have a greater impact on small antennas. So, the initiative is a trade-off between antenna gain and size [1].

Fractals have played a well-known role in reducing the size of antennas at the expense of additional parameters such as bandwidth and efficiency. Therefore, antenna miniaturization techniques must strike a balance between relevant parameters and size. Recently, research efforts have been made to reduce the size of antennas in order to reduce the surface area used while maintaining performance.

The demand for high-performance multi-standard communication systems has led to the study and research of this interesting subject matter. Therefore, it is essential to study the basic concepts of multiband fractal antenna systems, devices that bring the world of wireless communication into a brand new era.

5.2 Fractal Designs

The latest developments in communication systems require antennas with high bandwidth and small dimensions. The small size, low manufacturing complexity and low cost of such antennas are increasing demand for both military and commercial applications. If the size of the conventional antenna is less than a quarter wavelength, the radiation bandwidth and efficiency will be reduced. This problem is solved by using fractal geometry in the design of the antenna.

Fractal is a concept that is implemented in a microstrip antenna. The word fractal is derived from the Latin word "fractus," meaning broken, uneven, any of a variety of extremely irregular curves or shapes that repeat themselves at whatever scale they are examined. Using a fractal in an antenna maximizes the length or increases the circumference (on internal parts or external structure) of material that can receive or emit electromagnetic radiation within a given total surface or volume.

In fractal antennas, the self-similarity and plane-filling nature of fractal geometries are often quantitatively linked to its frequency characteristics. Fractals are geometric shapes that are similar to each other, repeating themselves at different scales. Geometry fractals are important because the effective length of fractal antennas can be increased while maintaining the same total area. The shape of the fractal antenna can be created by an iterative mathematical process called an Iterative Function Scheme (IFS). There are different types of fractals that reveal this when we zoom in on the image at finer and finer scales; the same pattern reappears, making it virtually impossible to know what level we are looking at [2].

Fractal geometry is important because the effective length of the fractal antenna can be increased while maintaining the total area same. Fractal antenna design has two things:

1) *Initiator (0th stage)*: It is basic shape of the geometry. It can be any shape either triangle, rectangle or any other quadrilateral.
2) *Generator*: It is the shape which is obtained by scaling the initiator and will be repeated either inside or outside on the initiator to obtain subsequent stages to reach final fractal geometry. The generator is obtained from the initiator itself.

Figure 5.1 shows a type of fractal geometry known as *Sierpinski gasket* which is derived by taking a triangular geometry as initiator and repeating a down-scaled version of initiator called a generator inside it to obtain subsequent stages of the gasket [3]. There are many features of fractal antennas that make them useful for many applications. Some of them are listed in the following Table 5.1.

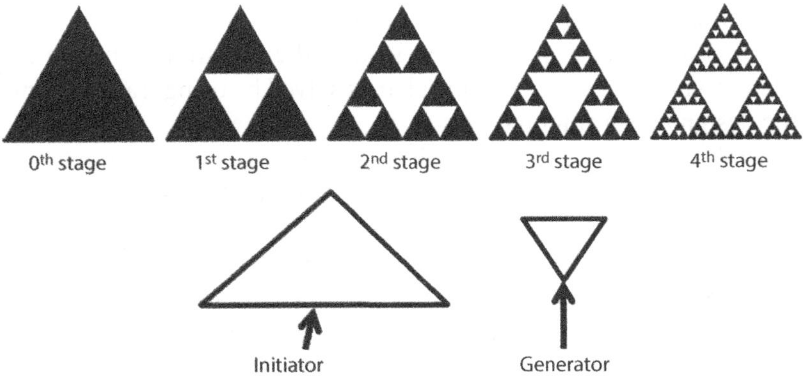

Figure 5.1 Sierpinski gasket with subsequent stages showing initiator and generator.

Table 5.1 Features of fractal antennas.

Self-Similarity	Useful in designing multi-band antenna.
Small Dimension	Useful to design electrically small antennas.
Space-Filling quality	Useful for miniaturization of an antenna, it increases electrical length in compact physical volume.
Increasing number of Iterations	Useful to decrease the resonant frequency while electrical length increases.
Sharp Edges, Corners and Discontinuities	Helps to make antenna to radiate efficiently.

Some important features:

- They have no characteristic shape.
- They have an infinite range of scales within them; a structure that consists of an infinite number of clusters that are equal to the whole shape but on a smaller scale.
- They are highly coiled and have irregular shapes.
- Characteristic magnitudes must be avoided when designing a frequency-independent antenna, or at least the antenna structure must include many characteristic magnitudes to allow multi-wavelength operation, and a fractal antenna

must have this property to become a good candidate to became frequency independent.

- Fractals are an infinitely complex structure that is similar to itself. This means that as the structure is zoomed in, the structure is repeated. This property could be used to design antennas that can operate at multiple frequencies.
- A fractal can fill the space occupied by an antenna more efficiently than a traditional antenna with Euclidean geometry. This can lead to more power being coupled from the transmission lines into free space in a smaller volume. It has a large number of irregularities, resulting in a virtually infinite physical length.

5.2.1 Classes of Fractals

The different classes of fractals are described in flow chart form in Figure 5.2. Basically, there are two classes, deterministic and non-deterministic. Our point of discussion in this chapter is deterministic fractals, which are again characterized as linear and non-linear geometries. Linear geometry is derived using the Iterative Function System (IFS), which is the main topic of discussion in this chapter. Under linear geometry, there are many curves called fractal curves such as Koch curve, Cantor curve, Minkowski curve, Sierpinski seal and many others.

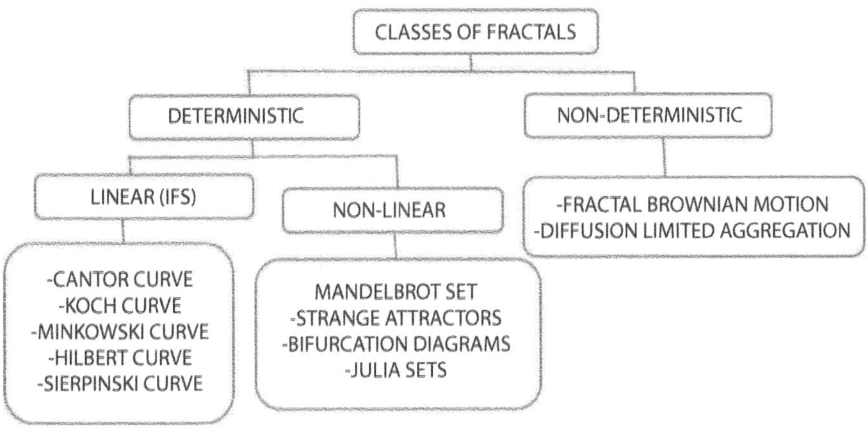

Figure 5.2 Classes of fractals.

5.2.2 Fractal Dimensions

Generally, we can think of objects that are zero dimensional (0-D), i.e., points, 1-D, i.e., lines, 2-D, i.e., planes and 3-D, i.e., solids. We are familiar with zero, one, two and three dimensions. But for fractal antenna, we will talk about fractal dimensions, i.e., non-integer dimensions, such as 2.12D, 1.14D, 3.79D, etc. There are many fractal dimensions; some of them will be discussed here.

A few of the fractal dimensions are *Similarity dimension* (DS), *the Hausdorff dimension* (DH), *Box-counting dimension* (DB), etc. We will mostly concentrate on similarity dimension, to characterize the construction of regular fractal objects. Fractals are characterized by their dimension. It is the key structural parameter describing the fractal and is defined by partitioning the volume where the fractal lies into boxes of side [4].

5.2.2.1 Similarity Dimension

The concept of dimension is closely associated with that of scaling. Consider a line is divided into N smaller self-similar segments, each d in length, then d is in the scaling ratio. Thus,

For unit line	$L = N\delta = 1$
For unit area	$L = N\delta^2 = 1$
For unit volume	$L = N\delta^3 = 1$

Therefore, we see that the exponent of d in each case is a measure of the dimension of the object. Thus,

$$N\delta^{DS} = 1$$

Therefore, $$DS = \frac{\log N}{\log\left(\frac{1}{\delta}\right)}$$

where, DS denotes the similarity dimension.

For Cantor Set, there are two such identical copies of the set contained within the set.

Hence, N=2 and $\delta = \frac{1}{3}$

$$DS = \frac{log2}{log3} = 0.6309$$

So, for Cantor Set, 0< DS< 1, that is it has a non-integer similarity dimension of 0.6309; due to fractal structure of the object.

5.3 Iterative Function System

Iterative function schemes represent an extremely versatile method for conveniently generating a wide variety of useful fractal structures. These iterated function systems are based on the application of a series of affine transformations, w, defined by

$$w\begin{pmatrix} x \\ y \end{pmatrix} = \begin{pmatrix} a & b \\ c & d \end{pmatrix}\begin{pmatrix} x \\ y \end{pmatrix} + \begin{pmatrix} e \\ f \end{pmatrix}$$

Or w(x,y)=(ax+by+e,cx+dy+f)

where a, b, c, d, e and f are real numbers. Hence, the affine transformations, w, is represented by six parameters

$$\left(\begin{array}{cc|c} a & b & e \\ c & d & f \end{array}\right)$$

where a, b, c, and d control rotation and scaling, while e and f control linear translation. Now, suppose we consider w_1, w_2, ..., w_N as a set of affine linear transformations and let A be the initial geometry. Then a new geometry, produced by applying the set of transformations to the original geometry, A, and collecting the results from $w_1(A)$, $w_2(A)$,......, $w_N(A)$, can be represented by

$$W(A) = U_{n=1}^{N} w_n(A)$$

where W is known as the Hutchinson operator.

A fractal geometry can be obtained by repeatedly applying W to the previous geometry. For example, if the set A_0 represents the initial geometry, then we will have

$$A_1 = W(A_0);\ A_2 = W(A_1); \ldots\ldots\ldots\ldots\ldots;A_{K+1} = W(A_K);$$

An iterated function system generates a sequence that converges to a final image, A_∞, in such a way that

$$W(A_\infty) = A_\infty$$

This image is called attractor of the iterated function system, and represents a "fixed point" of W.

5.4 Advantages and Limitations of Fractal Geometry in Antennas

The advantages and disadvantages of fractals in microstrip antennas are countless; some of them are discussed as follows:

Advantages:

- Miniaturization: Smaller size for multibandperformance
- Frequency independent and provides multi- frequency performance
- More design and use versatility
- Added inductance and capacitance withoutcomponents
- Consistent performance over huge frequency range
- Close packing of antennas
- Designed for harshest conditions
- Powerful solutions possible
- Use one antenna instead of many for wideband or multi-band purpose
- Lowers cost and enhances desirability
- Enables small, efficient, reliable antennas
- Greater versatility, new packaging options
- Small arrays with excellent steer ability with reduced mutual coupling

- In use by military and commercial customers
- Low profile: smaller in size, lighter in weight and lower in cost
- Good impedance matching
- Use of fewer components
- Provides space filling, self-similarity and scaling properties
- Provides increased bandwidth
- Provides enhanced gain and directivity
- Uses the essential combination of inductanceand capacitance providing multiple resonances for the similar structures.

Limitations

- Loss of gain in some cases
- Complex structure and complexity in modeling the antenna
- Numerical analysis limitations: mathematical limitations
- The benefits begin to diminish after first few iterations
- Not so beneficial in size after first few iterations.

5.5 Compact Printed Multiband Fractal Antenna: Novel Design Approach

In this section design of a low-profile compact printed fractal antenna for fixed bands is presented. The proposed fractal antenna (Figure 5.3) consists of a main patch, a ground plane and a 50Ω feed line. This proposed antenna generates five frequency bands, at 6.89, 8.13, 10.03, 16.11 and 17.81 GHz, with good performance. The dielectric material selected for the design is Epoxy FR4 which has dielectric constant of 4.4 and height of the substrate is 1.57 mm. The antenna is occupying an area of 20X24 mm^2 for the ground plane.

$$\text{Total Volume} = 20X24X1.57\ mm^3$$

For this fixed-frequency design, the five individual frequency bands can be adjusted and set independently over the wide ranges. The fixed design is studied using computer simulation. For verification of simulation results, the design is fabricated and the prototypes are measured. Fractals exhibit similar patterns at increasingly smaller scales, a property called self-similarity, also known as expanding symmetry or unfolding symmetry; if this replication

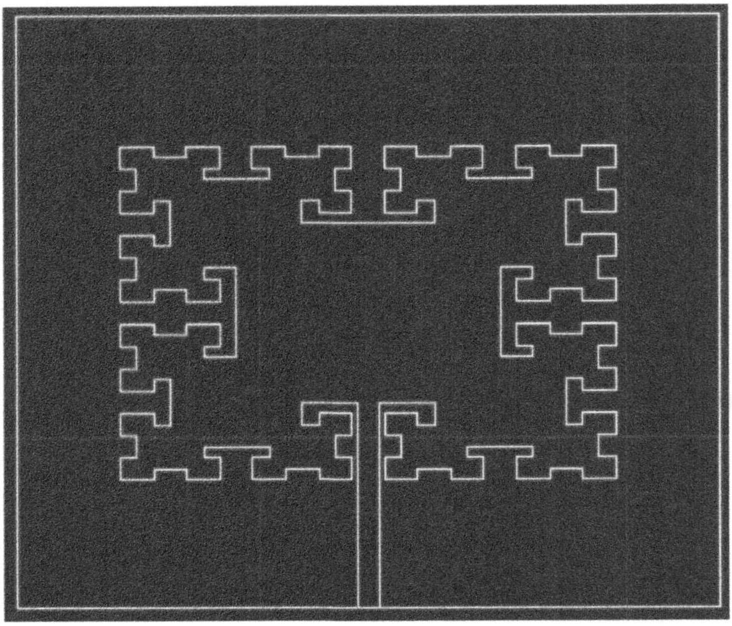

Figure 5.3 Structure of proposed antenna.

is exactly the same at every scale, as in the Menger sponge, it is called affine self-similar.

The fractal geometry is the best suited for its self-similar structures. This iterative geometry can be best conveyed pictorially; the antenna design starts with single rectangle patch as main radiator in first iteration as shown in Figure 5.4(a). Further iteration is carried out by adding smaller and smaller rectangles to the previously obtained rectangle, which produces the design of the second iteration which is shown in Figure 5.4(b).

Similarly, the third iteration is obtained by adding further rectangles to each corner of the previously obtained iteration which is shown in Figure 5.4(c). The fourth iteration is carried out by adding still more rectangles to the previously obtained rectangle geometry which is shown in Figure 5.4(d).

In the designed rectangle-shape fractal, surface of the radiating patch increases with increase in the number of iterations, i.e., with increase in the iteration, size (area) of the radiating patch increases.

The analysis and experimental results of various graphs based on different iterations are obtained, which are discussed as follows. A parametric study of the proposed patch was carried out to achieve multiband

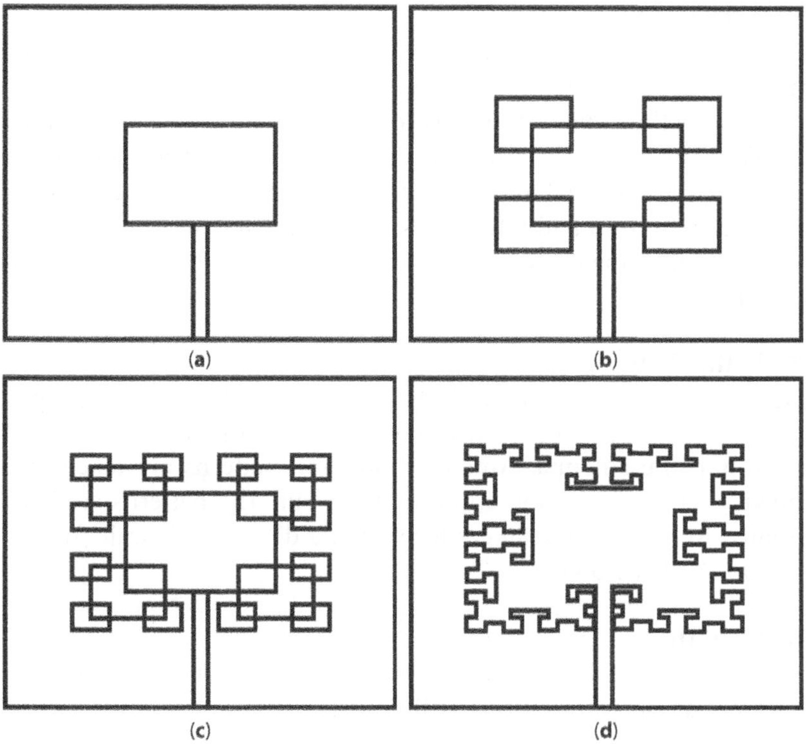

Figure 5.4 Iterative geometry. (a) Main radiator, (b) Main radiator with 4 sub-patches, (c) Main radiator with 12 sub-patches and (d) Main radiator with 36 sub-patches.

performance. The effects of different iterations of rectangle-shape fractal have been investigated based on the antenna performance.

The first iteration is done by adding four rectangles in the main rectangle; the second iteration is done by addition of twelve rectangles again. Similarly, the next iteration is done by addition of thirty-six smaller size rectangles in previously obtained geometry.

5.5.1 Parametric Analysis

1. Return Loss

Return loss is a measure of the reflected energy from a transmitted signal. It is a logarithmic ratio measured in dB (decibel) which compares the power reflected by the antenna with the power fed to the antenna from the transmission line. The larger the return loss value, the smaller it is reflected the energy reflected. For good impedance matching resonant frequency must lie below -10 dB [6].

2. VSWR

VSWR stands for Voltage Standing Wave Ratio. The parameter VSWR is a measure that numerically describes how well the antenna is impedance matched with the radio or transmission line it is connected to. The smaller the VSWR the better the antenna matched to the transmission line and more power is delivered to the antenna. For perfect matching VSWR = 1, there is no reflection and return loss. In the real system it is very hard to achieve a perfect match, so it is defined that have VSWR < 2 is still good matching system [5].

3. Radiation Pattern

A radiation pattern is a graphical representation of the relative field power emitted from or received by the antenna. It is a measurement of radiation around the antenna. Antenna radiation patterns are taken at one frequency, one polarization and one plane cut. The patterns are usually presented in polar or rectilinear form with a dB strength scale for $\varphi = 0°$, $90°$, $180°$, $270°$ and $360°$.

4. Bandwidth

Bandwidth is defined as the range between upper cut of frequency at 10 dB and lower cut of frequency at 10 dB.

$$BW = f_H - f_L$$

Bandwidth indicates range of frequency for which an antenna provides satisfactory operation. Proposed design has five bands of operations with narrow bandwidths.

5. Directivity

Directivity of an antenna is a measure of the concentration of radiated power in a certain direction. It can be considered as the ability of the antenna to direct the radiated power in a given direction. It is usually the ratio of the radiation intensity in a given direction to the average radiation intensity.

6. Gain

The gain of an antenna is the ability of the antenna to radiate more or less in any direction compared to the theoretical antenna. Gain is calculated by comparing the measured power transmitted or received by the antenna in a specific direction to the power transmitted or received by a hypothetical ideal antenna in the same situation [7].

7. Beamwidth

Beamwidth is the angle from which the majority of the antenna's power, on the radiation pattern's main lobe, radiates. It may be measured in the horizontal or vertical planes and is the distance between two points where the power is less than half of the maximum [8].

8. Surface Current Distribution

Surface current is a current flowing in a plane and has units of charge per unit time per unit length, measured in the direction in the same plane but perpendicular to the flow direction. In metallic antennas, the surface current is an actual electric current that is induced by an applied electromagnetic field [9].

5.5.2 Results and Discussion

In the design of multiband antennas, it is desirable to have the ability to set the frequency bands independently from each other, but achieving this is very challenging. Very often, when some parameters are adjusted to set a band to a particular frequency, the frequencies of all other bands are affected, and so the antenna has to be redesigned. A fractal is a geometric object that is similar to itself on all scales. If we zoom in on a fractal object it will look similar or exactly like the original shape. This property is called self-similarity. A parametric study of the proposed fractal patch antenna is carried out to achieve multiband performance. The effects of addition of self-similar shapes with smaller dimensions in step-by-step iterative process have been investigated based on the antenna performance. The design steps can be described as follows:

Step 1: The main radiator is designed to generate single band and its dimensions are optimized in phrases of minimizing the reflection coefficient across the band through simulation. It appears at 9.55GHz instead of maximum at 10GHz may be caused by some resonance effect. Figure 5.5 shows return loss Vs frequency plot for the main radiator, at 9.55 GHz, S_{11}=-11.45dB.

Step 2: In second step, we reduce the size of ground plane and analyze its effect on S parameter. It improves return loss parameter and gives two more resonant frequency bands, but resonant frequency at 9.55GHz get collapse. Figure 5.6 shows return loss Vs frequency plot. Simulated

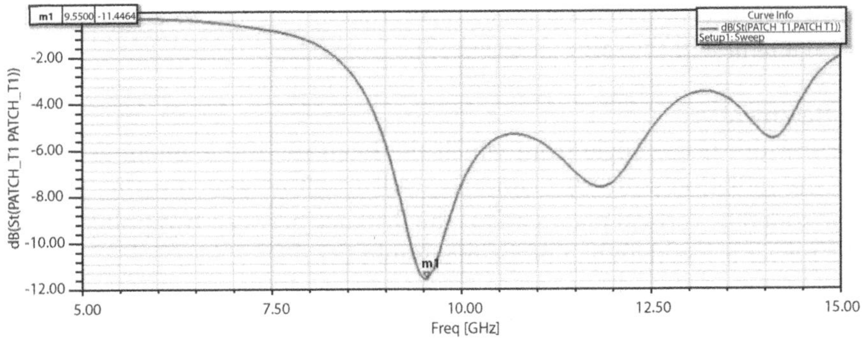

Figure 5.5 S_{11} parameter of main patch.

result presents two resonant frequencies at 15.63GHz and 19.05GHz with S_{11}=-15.14 and -18.04dB respectively.

Step 3: Now, we start design of fractal geometry with iterative process. Four sub-patches with same shape but smaller dimensions are added to the main radiator. It results in frequency band at 19.05GHz getting shifted to 17.91GHz, and one more band generates at 7.84GHz frequency. This new geometry generates resonant frequency for three bands at 7.84, 15.25 and 17.91 GHz with S_{11}=-28.03, -12.52 and -21.61dB respectively. Figure 5.7 shows return loss Vs frequency plot for first iteration.

Step 4: Now, twelve sub-patches with same shapes and smaller dimensions are added to each corner of the patch geometry achieved in the third step. This generates the resonant frequency for four bands. Frequency bands generated in step III shifted from 7.84GHz to 7.27GHz, 15.15GHz to 15.53GHz and from 17.72GHz to 17.34GHz. Fourth band at 18.58GHz frequency is generated with -20.77dB return loss. Thus, in step IV four

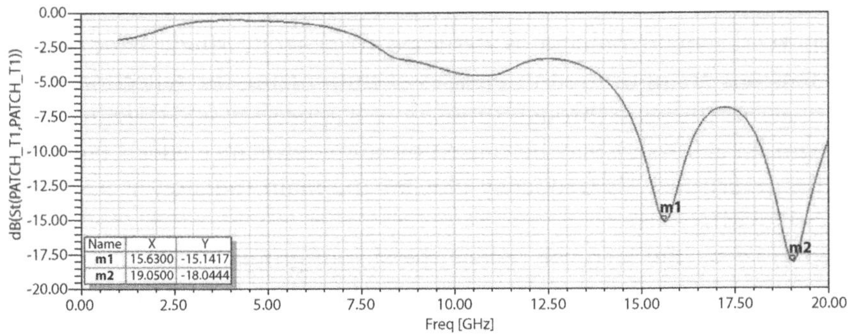

Figure 5.6 S_{11} parameter of main patch with reduced ground structure.

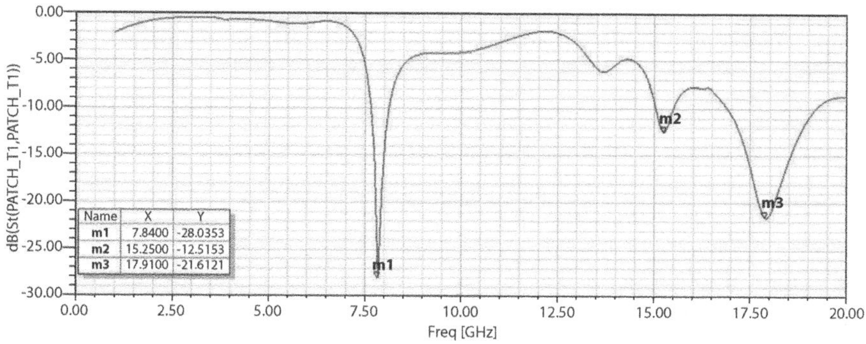

Figure 5.7 S_{11} parameter vs frequency: I iteration.

resonant frequency bands are achieved at 7.27, 15.54, 17.34 and 18.58 GHz with S_{11}=-18.56, -15.23, -16.39 and -20.77dB respectively. Figure 5.8 shows return loss Vs frequency plot for second iteration.

Step 5: To continue this iterative process thirty-six sub-patches with same shapes and smaller dimensions are added to the patch geometry achieved in previous step, in similar manner. Frequency bands generated in step IV slightly detuned and new bands are generated. It generates the resonant frequency for five bands at 6.89, 8.13, 10.03, 16.11 and 17.82 GHz with S_{11}=-19.69, -24.95, -25.11, -17.29 and -19.35dB respectively. Figure 5.9 shows return loss Vs frequency plot for fifth step, III iteration.

VSWR, 3D polar plot for directivity, radiation pattern, beamwidth, surface current distribution plot and gain plot for proposed final fractal antenna geometry are shown in Figures 5.10–5.15 respectively.

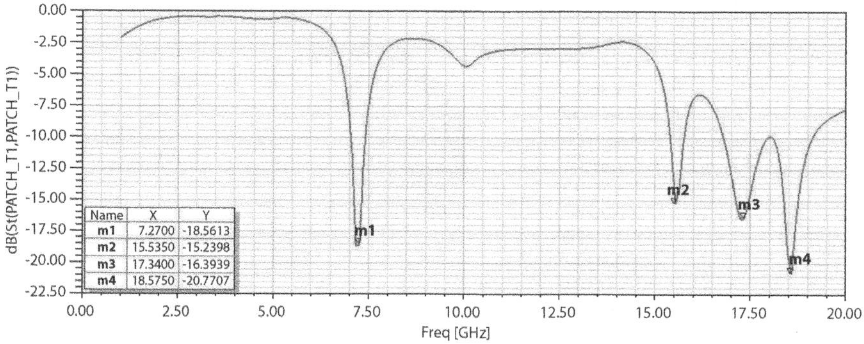

Figure 5.8 S_{11} parameter vs frequency plot: II iteration.

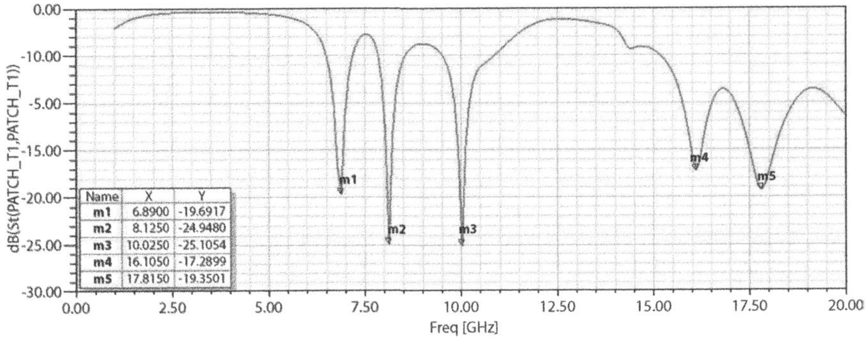

Figure 5.9 S_{11} parameter vs frequency plot: III iteration.

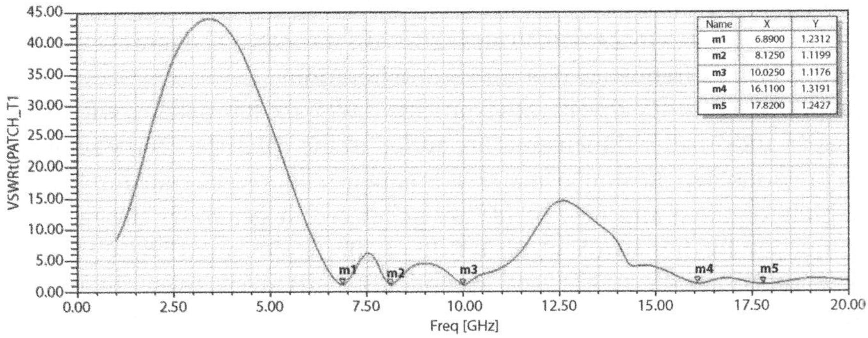

Figure 5.10 VSWR curve.

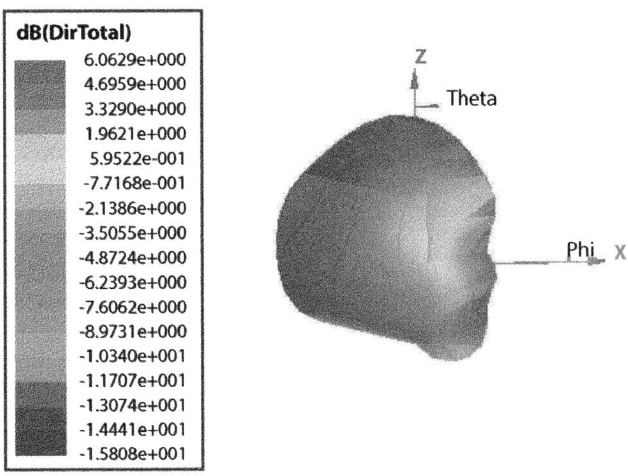

Figure 5.11 3D polar plot for directivity.

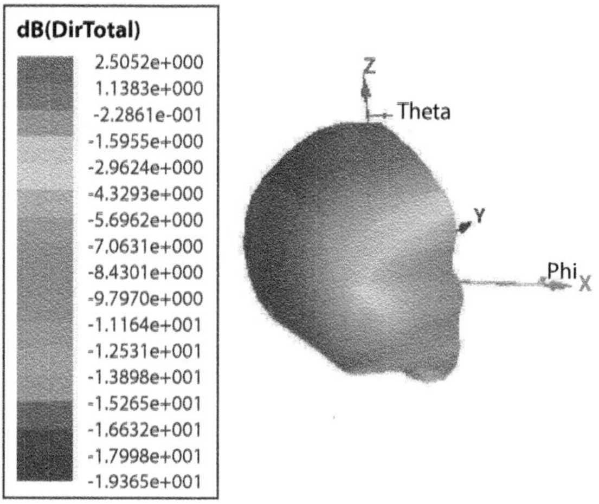

Figure 5.12 3D polar plot for gain.

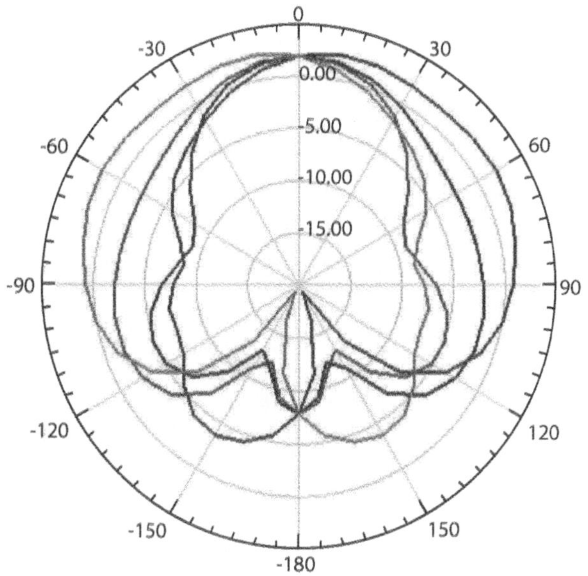

Figure 5.13 Radiation pattern curve.

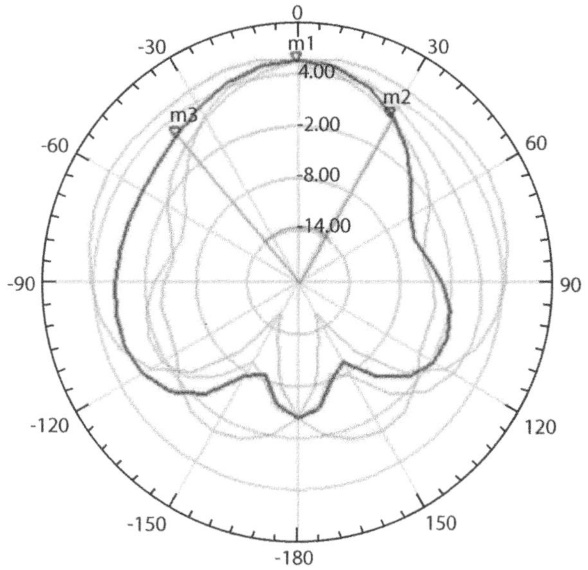

Figure 5.14 Beamwidth curve.

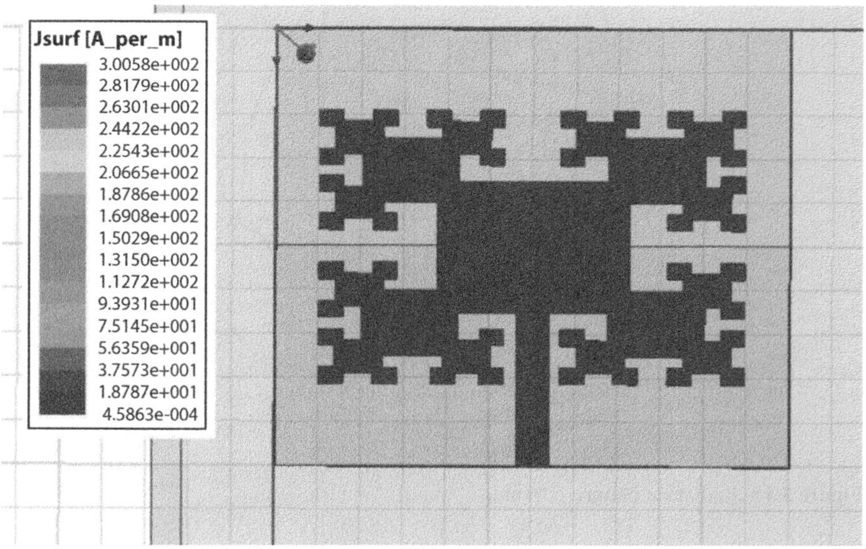

Figure 5.15 Surface current distribution.

Table 5.2 Result summary after simulation.

Frequency	Return loss(S_{11})	VSWR	Bandwidth
6.89GHz	-19.69dB	1.23	300 MHz
8.13 GHz	-24.95dB	1.12	281 MHz
10.03 GHz	-25.11dB	1.12	380 MHz
16.11 GHz	-17.29dB	1.32	855 MHz
17.82 GHz	-19.35dB	1.24	1520 MHz

The overall gain and directivity achieved by the antenna is 2.50dB and 6.06dB respectively. VSWR curve of proposed antenna shows that VSWR obtained for all five bands at 6.89GHz, 8.13GHz, 10.03GHz, 16.11GHz and 17.82GHz are 1.23, 1.12, 1.12, 1.32 and 1.24 respectively; which are between 1-2 range. All frequency bands having less than -10 dB return loss with 300, 281, 380, 855 and 1520MHz bandwidth respectively. Beamwidth is 70°. Table 5.2 summarizes values of Return Loss (S_{11}) in dB and their VSWR at all resonant frequencies.

In the study, it is identified that the current paths are responsible for radiation at different resonant frequencies. Thus, we can change those antenna parameters, which in turn alter the lengths of the current paths and set the resonant frequencies independently.

Variation in feedline position varies some parameters. S11, VSWR, directivity, gain, radiation parameter and beamwidth plot for new feedline position are shown in Figures 5.16–5.21.

The overall gain and directivity achieved by the antenna is 2.55dB and 6.15dB respectively. VSWR curve of proposed antenna shows that VSWR obtained for all five bands at 6.89GHz, 8.13GHz, 10.03GHz, 16.11GHz and 17.82GHz are 1.23, 1.12, 1.12, 1.32 and 1.24 respectively; which are between 1-1.5 range. All frequency bands having less than -10 dB return loss with 285, 291, 345, 735 and 1425MHz bandwidth respectively. Beamwidth is 70°.

Table 5.3 summarizes values of Return Loss (S_{11}) in dB and their VSWR at all resonant frequencies.

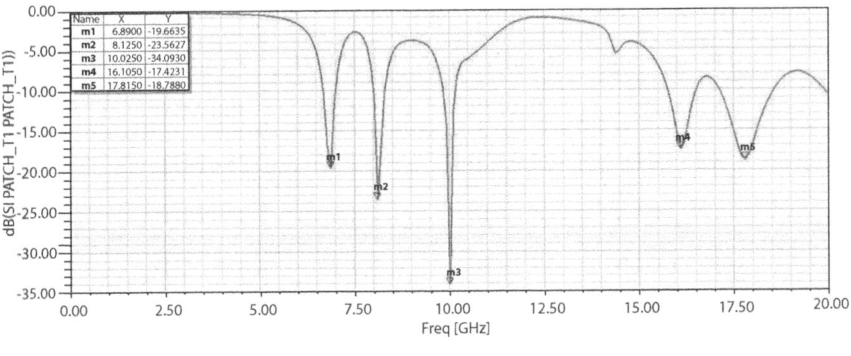

Figure 5.16 S_{11} parameter vs frequency plot.

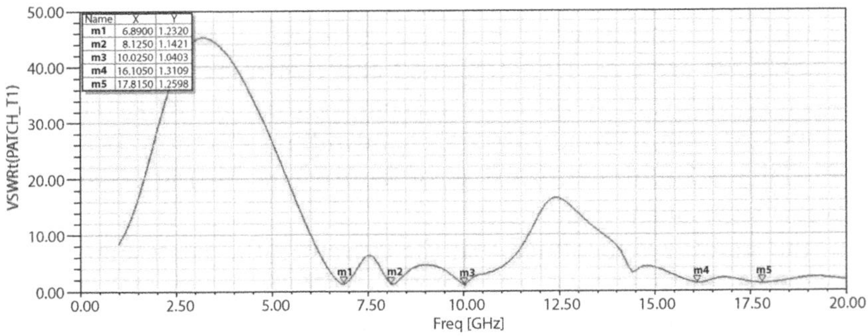

Figure 5.17 VSWR vs frequency plot.

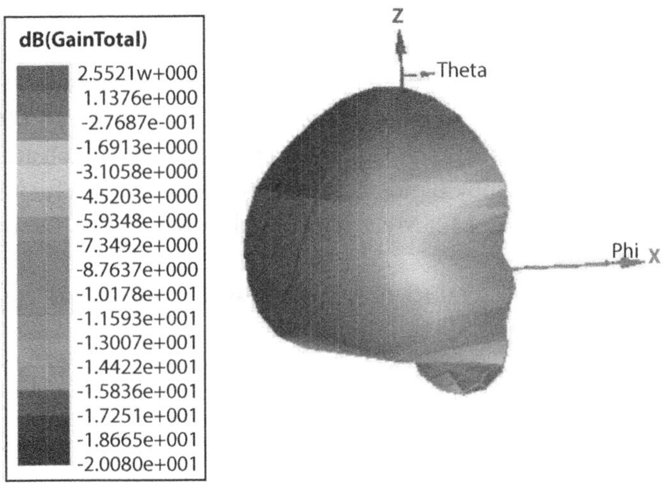

Figure 5.18 3D polar plot for directivity.

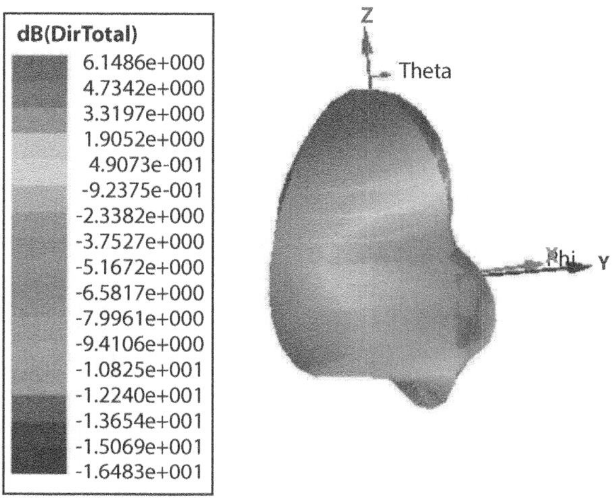

Figure 5.19 3D polar plot for gain.

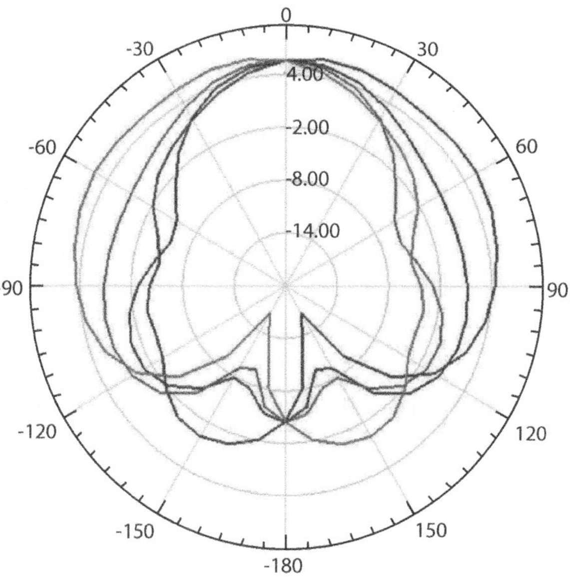

Figure 5.20 Radiation pattern curve.

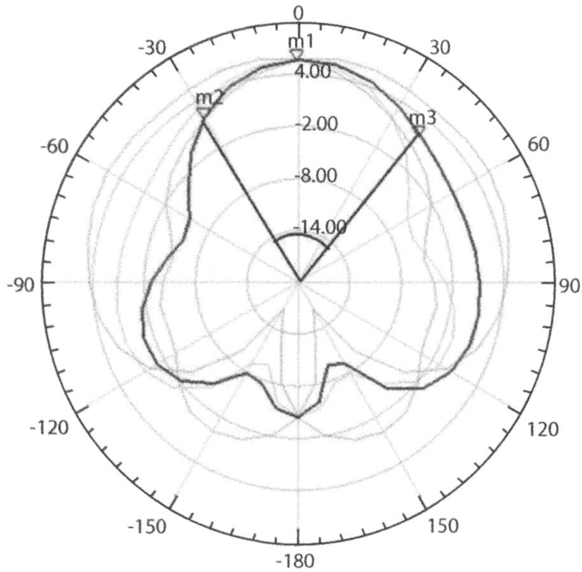

Figure 5.21 Beamwidth curve.

Table 5.3 Result summary after simulation.

Frequency	Return loss(S_{11})	VSWR	Bandwidth
6.89GHz	-19.66dB	1.23	285 MHz
8.13 GHz	-23.56dB	1.14	290.5 MHz
10.03 GHz	-34.09dB	1.04	345MHz
16.11 GHz	-17.42dB	1.31	735MHz
17.82 GHz	-18.78dB	1.26	1425MHz

The proposed fractal antenna geometry is fabricated on FR4 substrate which has the dielectric constant 4.4 and height of the substrate is 1.6mm. This antenna geometry is tested for some parameters with the help of Vector Network Analyzer (VNA) and anechoic chamber in lab. Return loss (s11) and VSWR measurement of fabricated as well as simulated proposed antenna is shown in figures.

In order to show the performance of the antenna, simulated results are compared through measurements in this section. Antenna parameters for proposed design are studied by simulation and measurements. Figures 5.22 and 5.23 show the measured Vs simulated plot for the proposed antenna. It suggests that measured result almost matches the simulated one. The slight

(a) Return loss

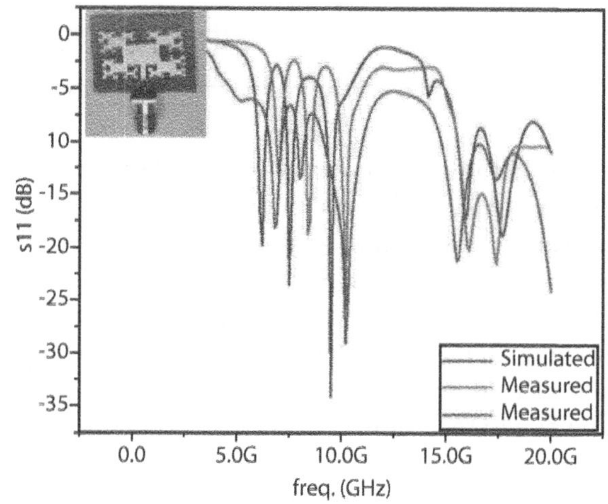

Figure 5.22 Return loss comparison between simulated and tested results.

(b) VSWR

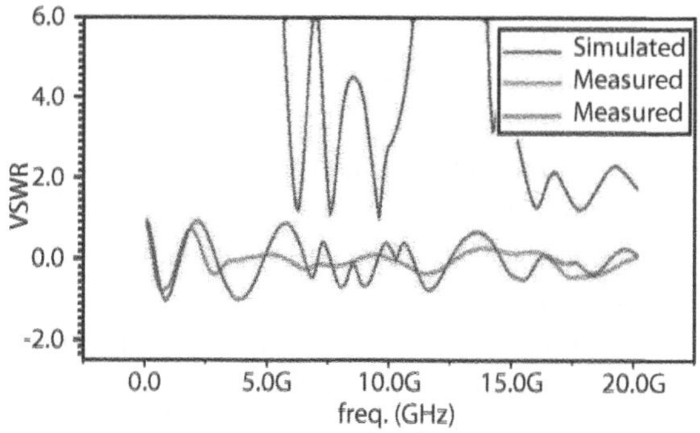

Figure 5.23 VSWR comparison between simulated and tested results.

Table 5.4 Comparison between simulated and measured results.

Frequency	S1 simulated	S11 measured	VSWR simulated	VSWR measured
6.89GHz	-19.66dB	-12.66 dB	1.23	1.56
8.13 GHz	-23.56dB	-20.20 dB	1.14	1.21
10.03 GHz	-34.09dB	-24.66 dB	1.04	1.10
16.11 GHz	-17.42dB	-20.00 dB	1.31	1.41
17.82 GHz	-18.78dB	-20.70 dB	1.26	1.22

variation occurs due to the uncertainty of the relative permittivity of our low cost FR4 substrate for high frequency.

The comparison between simulated and measured results is given in Table 5.4 above for proposed the design.

Fabrication and testing of the proposed antenna are done and it is observed that some shifts have occurred in the simulated and measured antenna results. The differences between the simulated and measured results might be due to the following reasons:

i) The loss of the FR-4 material used varies with frequency, but, in simulation, a hard and fast tangent loss became assumed in any respect frequencies.
ii) The cable and connector were used in measurements, while they were not taken into account in simulation.
iii) The fabrication tolerance in the prototype would also affect the measured results.
iv) There would be tolerances in the measurement system.

Use of fractals in an antenna maximizes the length or increases the perimeter of the material that can receive or transmit electromagnetic radiations within a given total surface area or volume. Fractal geometry in terms of addition of smaller and smaller rectangles in step-by-step iterative process, improve the radiation properties in terms of return loss, directivity, surface current distribution, gain, beamwidth and radiation pattern. The design has specific characteristics and operates at different bands. Some important points of the proposed geometry are as follows:

a) The characteristics, i.e., fractal geometry and multiband behavior of the antenna in rectangular patch have been successfully achieved.
b) Significant improvement in the number of operating frequency bands is achieved by created iterated fractals (rectangular). It also increases the total perimeter (electrical length) of patch antenna.
c) With modification in the ground plane, multiband characteristics have been successfully achieved with reduced dimensions.
d) Theoretical and simulated values of different parameters of antenna are verified by measurement. The measured results are found to be well matched to the simulated results.
e) Proposed antenna geometry has return loss less than -10dB and VSWR <1.8 for all the frequencies.
f) The proposed antenna is highly suitable for C, X, Ku band applications. It can be used for WLAN, Wi-MAX, WLL and other wireless applications.

The presented design is simulated using Ansoft HFSS software. It has given enough good results to satisfy our requirements to fabricate the antenna on hardware which can be used wherever needed. The prototype of the proposed compact size fractal patch antenna is fabricated using FR4 substrate having dielectric constant 4.4 and height of 1.6mm. Microstrip feedline of 50Ω is used in the design. The small frequency drift, seen in the measured results, is produced by the error in manufacturing and measurement.

5.6 Conclusion

Wireless communication systems are operated in different frequency bands. In recent years, amazing demands for an antenna with many facilities like miniaturization, multiband and wideband performance with excessive gain and low profile structure for modern communication services and applications have increased. Additionally, it will be much conformable and convenient for the single device (antenna) of small size to be able to cover multiple frequency bands. Design of multiband antennas is very challenging, because very often when some parameters are adjusted to set a band to a particular frequency, the frequencies of all other bands are affected and so the antenna has to be redesigned. Antenna technology needs to be revised to fulfil demands imposed by wireless systems, due to the fact conventional antenna technology cannot meet destiny demanding situations. Fractal antenna paves the way for those requirements. This chapter attempts to study and review the existing fractal antennas designs and to propose a unique structure with a simple geometrical shape and low-profile structure for fulfilling the demands of modern wireless communications systems [6].

A compact size novel fractal antenna geometry for fixed frequency bands is presented in this chapter for multiband performance. It has been demonstrated by HFSS simulation software that the proposed fractal design is suitable for five frequency bands of operation. The chapter provides a detailed study of various parameters of multiband antenna and explains how to design and fabricate fractal microstrip patch antenna using Ansoft HFSS software. Studies have been undertaken covering requirement of multiband antenna, fractal geometries, types and parameters, analysis methods and radiation mechanism. The properties of antenna such as bandwidth, S-Parameter, VSWR, directivity, beamwidth, gain, surface current distribution, are analysed for proposed geometry. The simulated fractal antenna is fabricated and tested using VNA and anechoic chamber for the various parameters.

References

1. Pozar, D.M., *Microwave Engineering*, 3rd, John Wiley & Sons, 2005.
2. Balanis, C.A., *Antenna Theory Analysis and Design*, 3rd, John Wiley & Sons, 2005.
3. Al-Shattel, M.K., Patch Antenna, https://www.scribd.com/document/73177048/Patch-Antenna.
4. Orban, D. and Moernaut, G.J.K., The Basics of Patch Antennas, https://www.rfglobalnet.com/doc/the-basics-of-patch-antennas-0002.
5. Kadwane, R. and Gohokar, V., Design and Characteristics Investigation of Multiband Microstrip Patch Antenna for Wireless Application. *Int. J. Emerging Eng. Res. Technol.*, 2, 3, 61–66, June 2014, ISSN 2349-4395 (Print) & ISSN 2349-4409.
6. Werner, D.H. and Ganguly, S., An overview of fractal antenna engineering research in. *IEEE Antennas Propag. Mag.*, 45, 1, 38–57, Feb. 2003.
7. Kadwane, R. and Singh, J., Compact Printed Multiband Fractal Antenna for C, X and Ku band Applications: Design & Analysis, in: *Proceedings of Trends in Electronics and Health Informatics*, Lecture Notes in Networks and Systems.

8. Deka, P. and De, A., Design of Fractal Antenna for Multiband Operation in Communication and Healthcare. *2nd Global Conference for Advancement in Technology (GCAT)*, Bangalore, India, pp. 1–4, 2021.
9. Werner, D.H. and Mittra, R., The Theory and Design of Fractal Antenna Arrays, in: *Frontiers in Electromagnetics*, pp. 94–203, IEEE, 2000.

6

Applications of Metasurfaces for Modern Planar Antenna Design

V. Bharathi[1], Parthasarathy Ramanujam[2*] and Krishnamurthy Ramanujam[1]

[1]Department of ECE, Indian Institute of Information and Technology, Tiruchirappalli, India
[2]Department of ECE, National Institute of Technology, Tiruchirappalli, India

Abstract

Metasurfaces (MSs) have drawn a lot of interest recently due to their controllable electromagnetic properties. MS are 2-D planar structures that are easy to fabricate with low profile and reduced losses. MS can increase the gain, efficiency of the antenna and change the polarization of the wave. The fundamental modes of the metasurface can be analysed using characteristics mode analysis (CMA) to achieve circular polarization (CP) by selecting orthogonal modes and giving excitation with 90° phase difference. The MS-based antenna operates in wideband since it is capable of generating additional resonances from the MS structures. These antennas are also known as a class of leaky wave (LW) antennas since the surface wave (SW) energy gradually radiates when it propagates on an impedance boundary condition (BC) plane. Because of the surface impedance interaction, the radiative LW is created, allowing for precise control over its amplitude and polarization. The fundamental idea of MS antennas is to impose the arbitrarily designed impedance BC perceived by the SW. Boundary conditions are optimised to achieve the desired radiation characteristics while maintaining the profile of the antenna. MS antenna design has proliferated and undergone substantial evolution, emerging as a major advancement in the field.

Another technology that can be used to improve the performance of the antenna is Frequency Selective Surfaces (FSS). FSS offers directional control over the signal being transmitted or received while suppressing the undesired radiation. In addition to performance improvement, FSS also aids antenna to achieve circular polarization and reduces its Radar signature. FSS structures can be loaded as a superstrate or beneath the planar antenna to realize this performance.

**Corresponding author*: parthasarathy@nitt.edu

Dilip Kumar Choudhary, Indrasen Singh, Manoj Kumar Singh and Amit Kumar Jain (eds.) Compact and Flexible Microwave Devices, (125–150) © 2025 Scrivener Publishing LLC

By incorporating FSS into antenna designs, beam steering, gain enhancement and frequency band selection can be accomplished. Antenna with reduced RCS and high gain are used widely in stealth technology. FSS-based structures have the ability to create reconfigurable and multifunctional antennas that are much in demand for real-time applications.

Both MS and FSS can be used to supress the coupling between the radiating elements in Multiple Input and Multiple output (MIMO) CP antenna without degrading the corresponding radiation and impedance parameters. The mutual coupling effect can be reduced greatly by incorporating two FSS structures that is placed orthogonally or side by side to the source antenna. Thus the MS, FSS-based CP antenna design considerations, methodology, advantages and examples with a wide range of applications are discussed in this chapter. This chapter is organized as the sections listed below.

a. Metasurfaces - Introduction and characteristics relationship
b. Characteristics mode analysis (CMA)
c. Realization and evaluations of MS-based antenna models
d. Frequency Selective Surfaces and its types
e. Relationship between Mutual Coupling reduction and FSS superstrate in CP-MIMO antennas
f. Conclusion

***Keywords*:** Metasurfaces characteristic mode analysis, MS based antenna, frequency selective surfaces, circular polarization, FSS as superstrate, MIMO, mutual coupling reduction, leaky wave antennas

6.1 Metasurfaces – Introduction and Characteristics Relationship

The word "meta" means "beyond" in Greek, which indicates that metamaterial means material with characteristics beyond the natural available form. Metamaterials are the artificially manufactured composite materials with distinctive qualities that come from their intrinsic microstructures. By engineering the arrangement of atoms in metamaterials into particular form, unique properties and functionalities can be achieved [1].

The functionalities of the material depend greatly on the chemical composition and structural arrangement of the atoms, either a periodic or aperiodic structures. This provides great flexibility in creating new materials that are not available in nature. Two fundamental parameters—electric permittivity (ε) and magnetic permeability (μ)—are used to classify the

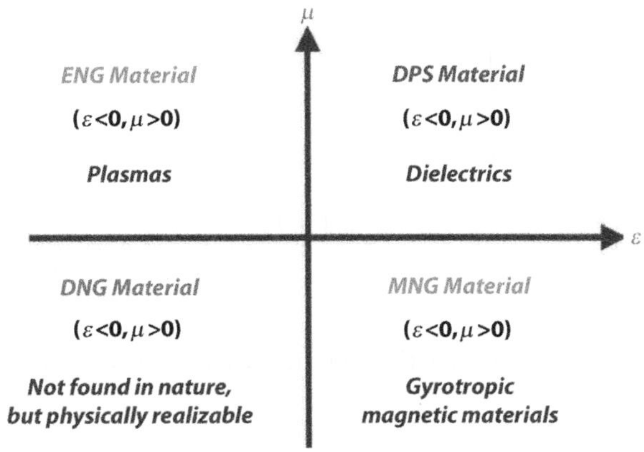

Figure 6.1 Classification of materials based on their properties.

qualities of materials. Dr. Veselago considered that these constitutive values of a homogeneous material can have negative values due to which the natural behaviour of the materials is changed drastically [2]. The refractive index of any material is related to μ and ε as $n=\sqrt{\varepsilon_r\mu_r}$, where $\varepsilon=\varepsilon_0\varepsilon_r$ and $\mu=\mu_0\mu_r$. Depending on the sign combinations of these parameters the materials can be classified as shown above.

Figure 6.1 illustrates the properties of the materials in ε – μ domain, in which the first segment (μ > 0 and ε > 0) represents the double positive or right-handed materials supporting the wave propagation in a forward direction. The second quadrant (μ > 0 and ε < 0) indicates the electric plasma and the fourth quadrant (μ < 0 and ε > 0) represents magnetic plasma supporting evanescent waves [3]. The third quadrant (μ < 0 and ε < 0) signifies the left-handed materials that support wave propagation in a forward direction. Here the electric field E, magnetic field H and the wave vector k form a double negative system [4]. Thus the materials can be classified into four categories, as described below.

6.1.1 Double Positive Materials (DPS) (ε > 0 and μ > 0)

Natural materials come under this section in which both the ε and μ are said to be positive, resulting in positive refractive index. The electric field is orthogonal to the magnetic field such that directs the wave propagation to be in forward direction.

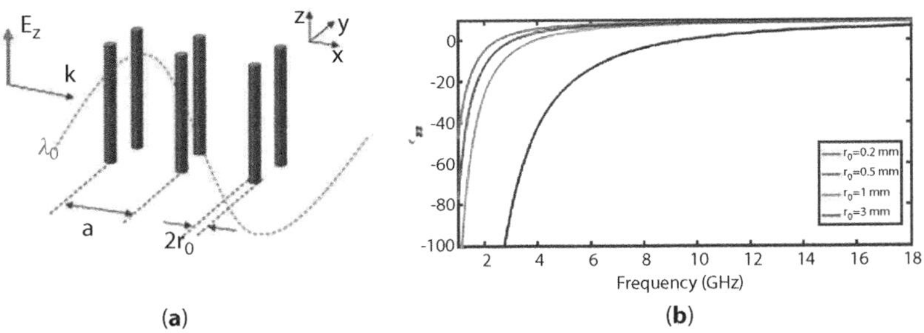

Figure 6.2 (a) Wire medium layout (b) frequency behaviour of the effective dielectric medium.

6.1.2 Epsilon Negative Materials (ENG) (ε < 0 and μ > 0)

Those materials with negative ε and positive μ are included in this. The ENG materials can be produced with a wire medium as depicted in Figure 6.2. Noble metals gold, silver exist in this domain and many eclectic plasmas exhibit this characteristic.

6.1.3 Mu-Negative Material (MNG) (ε > 0 and μ < 0)

Magnetic plasmas exhibit positive permittivity and negative permeability which can be produced by implementing repeated arrangement of split ring resonators (SRR) as depicted in Figure 6.3. This includes gyrotropic and gyromagnetic materials altered with the presence of quasi static magnetic field.

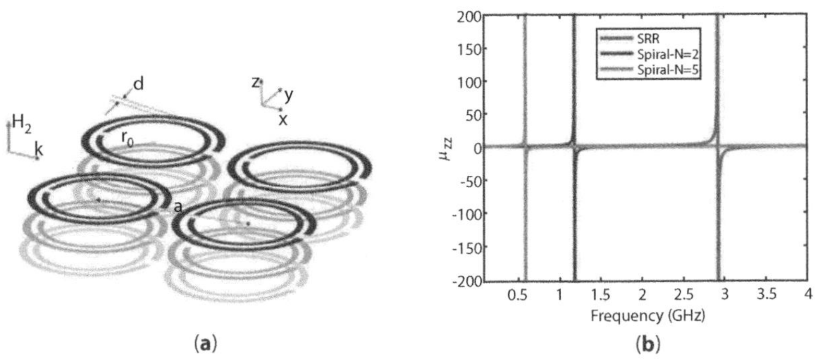

Figure 6.3 (a) SRR (b) frequency behaviour of the effective dielectric medium.

6.1.4 Double Negative Materials (DNG) ($\varepsilon < 0$ and $\mu < 0$)

Here both permeability and permittivity are said to be negative, hence it is also called negative-index metamaterials (NIM). By combining thin wires and split ring resonators, these kinds of metamaterials can be synthesised. In 1968, Dr. Veselago suggested an electromagnetic analysis of negative permittivity and permeability materials which showed a reverse radiation in NIM. NIM are also called Left-Handed Materials (LHM), which attracted growing interest after Pendry in 1996 comprehended the man-made electric plasma using wire plasma with negative permittivity [5].

Later, in 1999, the same team realized the artificial magnetic plasma with negative permeability using split ring resonator (SRR). Even though the negative refraction was achieved by Smith in 2001 by combining wire and SRRs, the applications of NIM was restricted due to its narrow bandwidth [6]. In 2002, a group of scientists along with Caloz represented LHM using a transmission line approach [7]. The first fabricated metamaterial designs composed of SRRs and rods/strips is shown in Figure 6.4.

A traditional TL consists of distributed series inductance and shunt capacitance which is modified as series capacitance plus an inductance and a shunt inductance plus a capacitance. This forms a general Composite Right-Left Handed (CRLH) that represent Right-Handed Material (RHM) and LHM. These CRLH arrangements are used to realize many microwave components and antennas despite their narrow bandwidth properties. In 2006, researchers tried to find other features like negative refractive index to bend the ElecroMagnetic (EM) waves in a controlled manner that opened a wide research area. This optical transformation helped to realize invisible cloak and metamaterials and have attracted many researchers after the experimental realization of cloaking technique.

(a) 1D design (b) 2D design

Figure 6.4 First fabricated metamaterial designs composed of SRRs and rods/strips.

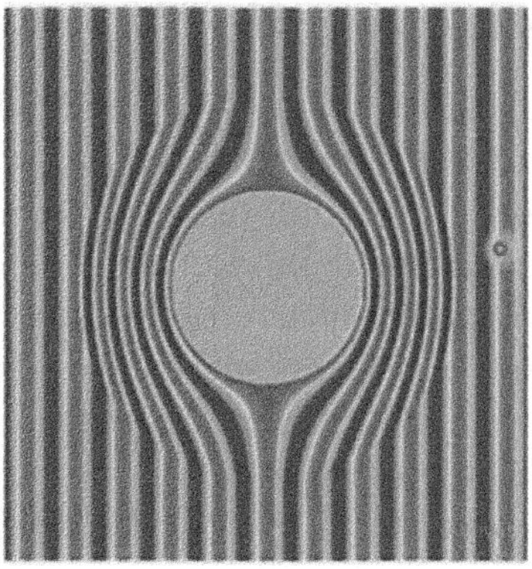

Figure 6.5 Invisible cloaking technique.

6.1.5 Applications

Because of their artificially tunable features, metamaterials find application in a wide range of electromagnetic issues. The superlens is the most promising feature of LHM which finds applications in medical and optical imaging techniques. Similarly, the CRLH structures are extensively used in antenna design and RF and microwave Circuits applications. In general, the metamaterials have gained more attention in cloaking devices in recent times. The invisible cloaking of devices is done in microwave regime [8] as shown in Figure 6.5.

Not only antenna designs, the planar metamaterials are used to sketch the microwave circuit components like filters, phase shifters and power dividers, etc. Polarizers, lens antennas can also be constructed using metamaterials to produce circular polarization and beam ending lens [9].

6.2 Characteristics Mode Analysis (CMA)

In 1968, Garbacz proposed Characteristic mode theory (CMT) which was developed later by Harrington in 1971. Characteristic Modes (CM) are used to represent the surface currents and the radiation properties that resemble the eigen vectors of a specific weighted eigen value equation comprising a comprehensive impedance matrix of the conductor. On line with the characteristic mode analysis (CMA), linear summation of characteristic mode current J_n can be used to express the total current J on a PEC (Perfect dielectric Conductor) surface.

$$J_n = \sum_n \propto_n J_n \tag{6.1}$$

Where,

J_n is the modal current for mode n which can be found by modal weighting coefficients (MWC),

$\propto_n$, is the total current in each mode.

$$J_n = \sum_n \frac{V_n^i j_n}{1 + j\lambda_n} \tag{6.2}$$

Where,

V_n, represents the modal excitation coefficient (MEC),

λ_n, is the eigen value of mode n

MEC is the coupling factor between the nth mode and excitation that concludes, whether the mode is excited because of the feed excitation or incident field.

From (1) and (2), the MWC can be written as

$$\propto_n = \frac{V_n^i}{1 + j\lambda_n} \tag{6.3}$$

$$MS = \frac{1}{1 + j\lambda_n} \tag{6.4}$$

Modal significance (MS) is the measure of resonant frequency and its significant influence to the radiation of a mode. As λ_n approaches to zero, the respective mode resonates and radiates efficiently. The value ranges from 0 to 1 and at 1 it gives better resonance and efficient radiation. From the above equations, the desired modes can be excited when the MS is high and MEC is significant. Also, these modal excitations can be altered by tuning the feeding mechanisms. Thus, the desired mode can be excited at specific frequency by feeding it properly.

In addition to these parameters, another parameter called characteristic angle (CA) also plays a major role in exciting the desired modes. It is phase angle between the modal current and its associated characteristic field, which can be expressed as:

$$CA = 180^\circ - tan^{-1}(\lambda_n) \tag{6.5}$$

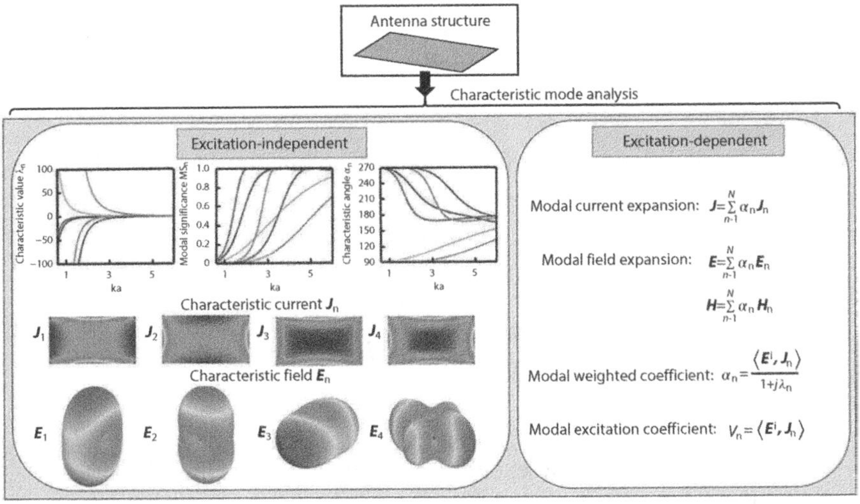

Figure 6.6 CMA steps to design a simple rectangular patch.

When the CA is 180°, the mode works as a good radiator while at 90° or 270°, it stores up energy. To obtain Circular Polarization (CP), a modal pair has to be excited concurrently with similar MS and a 90° characteristic angle difference and their modal currents should be orthogonal to each other.

Based on these formulations, it is understood that the CM depends upon the size, geometry and material of the structure, and the resonance characteristics of any conducting medium can be characterised by the three parameters $\lambda_n, MS\,and \propto_n$. The MEC V_n, is another important parameter to calculate the feeder placement in antenna design. Each parameter can be tuned in accordance with the application of the antenna. The CM results and the modal parameters of a simple rectangular patch [10] are shown in Figure 6.6. The CMA can be used to analyse different application like radiation problems, scattering problems, and electromagnetic coupling problems.

6.2.1 CMA for Impedance Bandwidth Enhancement

The impedance bandwidth, radiation pattern, polarization and gain are the radiation parameters of the antenna. CMA can be used to optimize all these characteristics and provide an enhanced performance using the

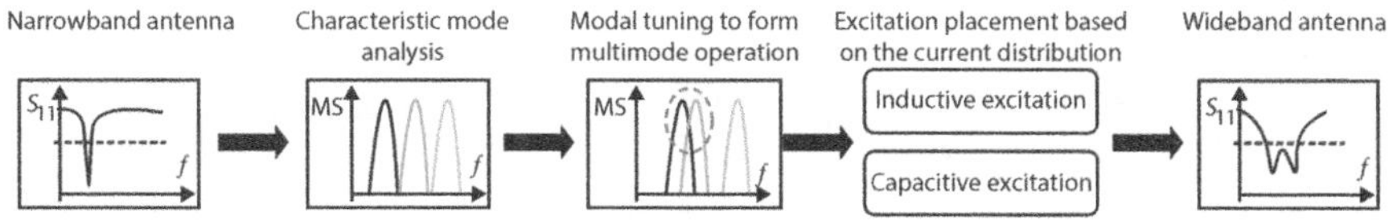

Figure 6.7 Impedance bandwidth enhancement techniques based on CM.

steps listed in Figure 6.7. Firstly, to increase the impedance bandwidth of a narrow band antenna, the modal properties are extracted by CM analysis. Then by iterative modal tuning, the multiple modes are fetched closer to form a wide frequency band. Also the location of the excitation points has to be found by calculating the modal current distributions, thereby achieving the desired bandwidth. To enhance the antenna impedance bandwidth, both excitation location identification and modal analysis is necessary [11].

Another method to improve the impedance bandwidth is to inject new modes artificially by adding parasitic elements. The parasitic patch's shape and spacing between the antenna and itself can be optimised to add a new mode, thus making the antenna operate in multimodal state. Instead of adding a parasitic patch, the slot lines can also be loaded to the antenna structure which helps in injecting new mode that improves the impedance bandwidth. Nowadays MSs containing periodic array of unit cells are used to achieve wide bandwidth. Modal analysis of these MSs expose that it resonates at quasi modes and have enhance gain bandwidth product.

6.2.2 CM-Based Circular Polarization

A circularly polarised (CP) wave is the combination of equal amplitude and 90° phase shifted two linearly polarised (LP) waves. CMA can expose the significant orthogonally LP modes which is capable of generating a CP wave. The modal significance magnitude should be equal and the characteristic angle should have 90° phase difference to achieve circular polarization. Similar to impedance bandwidth enhancement methods, the CP can also be achieved by loading metallic strips or slots or stubs to the antenna geometry or by reshaping the antenna shape in which a part of the antenna geometry is cut to introduce new modes of operation. The metasurface can also be used to tune the characteristic modes and the shape, size and position of the MS are optimised to obtain CP [12]. The steps to design circular polarised antenna using characteristic mode analysis is illustrated in Figure 6.8.

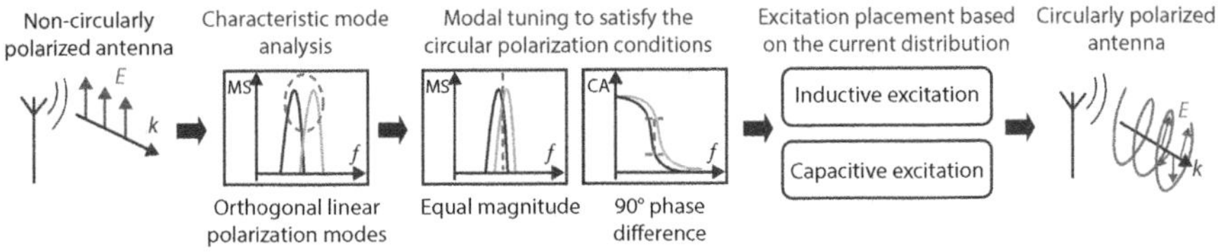

Figure 6.8 Circular polarization CM-based antenna designs.

6.2.3 CM-Based MIMO Systems

Modal analysis is much beneficial to the multiport antenna as it analyses which port excites the specific mode. An antenna structure made with multiple CM can be excited independently to generate distinct orthogonal CM which will greatly reduce the isolation between the ports. This paves the way to propose many MIMO antennas in base station millimetre wave applications. The modal analysis shows the significant modes which are chosen as the radiation modes and the feed excitation location is decided based on the modal current distributions. Thus preserving the ECC, DG of the MIMO system CP can also be implemented [13]. Figure 6.9 depicts the steps to design a CM based multimode multiport antenna.

6.2.4 CM-Based Radiation Pattern Optimization

Modal expansion of the radiation fields helps to control the radiation pattern by combining or optimising the corresponding characteristic modes. The characteristic current distribution and modal weighted coefficients are the parameters related to the radiation field. Figure 6.10 illustrates the steps for pattern optimisation and synthesis techniques. The optimisation can be done in many ways: 1) by optimising the modal current distribution, which can be done by loading or modifying the antenna geometry; 2) by optimising the feeding network and the excitation position to achieve the preferred modal coefficients, and 3) executing both steps simultaneously. In the first technique, the structure of the antenna is optimised to provide

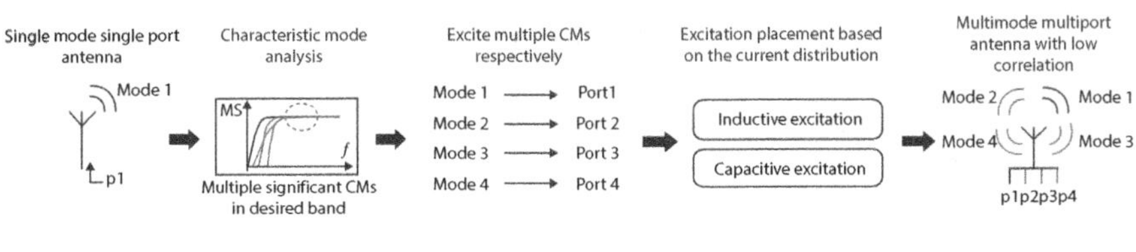

Figure 6.9 Multi-mode multi-port CM-based antenna designs.

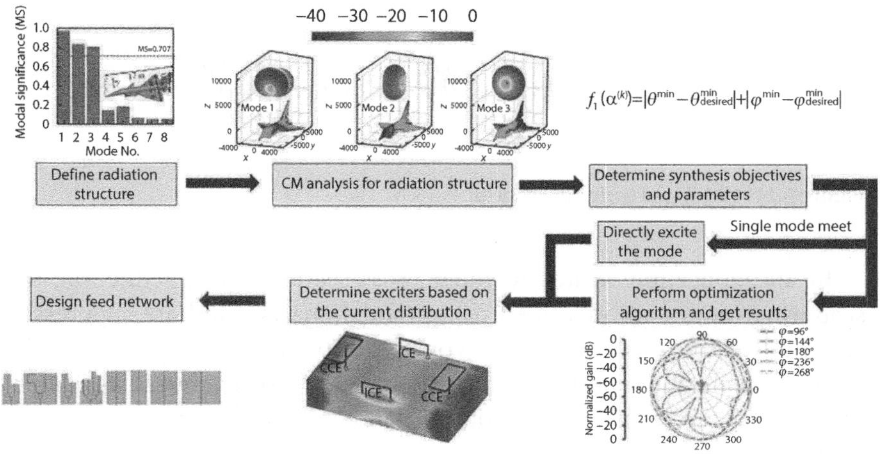

Figure 6.10 CM-based pattern optimization and synthesis techniques.

desired modal coefficients without concentrating much on the feeding network. Though this method sounds easy, the feeding network has to be optimised later to maintain the optimised modal coefficients [14].

Many pattern synthesis algorithms are available to optimize the feeding network or excitation location identification to generate the desired modal coefficients. Also, through the modal current distribution the modes can be injected or combined to create the desired radiation pattern. The main challenge posed here is to maintain the consistency of the MEC. Another method is to load the reactive lumped elements to the antenna geometry to create new characteristic modes. This reduces the focus on the excitation position a bit, but optimising the value of these elements is a bit tedious.

6.2.5 CM-Based Solution to Scattering Problems

Ideally the characteristic mode analysis was proposed initially for addressing the scattering problems. The modal decomposition computes the impact of each of the CM to the overall current distribution and radiation fields. The mode responsible for the radiation and scattering is identified individually and suppressed without affecting the overall performance as depicted in Figure 6.11. These scattering modes are to be suppressed mandatorily for certain applications microwave absorbers. Similar to impedance bandwidth, the absorption bandwidth is also enhanced by combining the multiple modes [15].

Figure 6.11 CM-based scattering control.

In an application related to radar cross section (RCS) reduction, the scattering modes are identified using modal analysis and are suppressed either by loading lumped inductors or slots into the antenna geometry. The slots are made at the hotspots of the modal currents to supress its scattering. The scattering from other sources can be cancelled by adding virtual ports that creates higher order modes.

6.2.6 CM-Based Solution to Electromagnetic Coupling Problems

From the modal analysis point of view the coupling problems can be distinguished into two groups: 1) to analyse the structure's equivalent circuit, understanding the coupling relationship between the structural parameters and optimising it to improve the isolation, and 2) designing a highly isolated array of antennas. The sequence of steps followed to analyse and control the EM coupling is illustrated in Figure 6.12. For the first type the characteristic mode parameters are analysed and the lumped element responsible for generating the specific mode is identified and the structure is optimised structural parameters either by loading or cutting or using metasurface [16].

The second approach is to create an isolated environment by exciting different orthogonal modes based on the modal current distribution and radiation field. This method is proven to provide high isolation in dual band antennas. A decoupling network is loaded at the backside of the feeding ports. These are used in most of the MIMO systems, which excites different group of characteristics modes. Isolation is also improved by slotting techniques which suppress the undesired modes and inhibits the undesired current distribution. Suppression of undesired modes can also be done by loading lumped elements, in which the position and the value of the lumped component is determined by the current distribution the desired and undesired modes. This technique also reduces the distortion in the radiation fields.

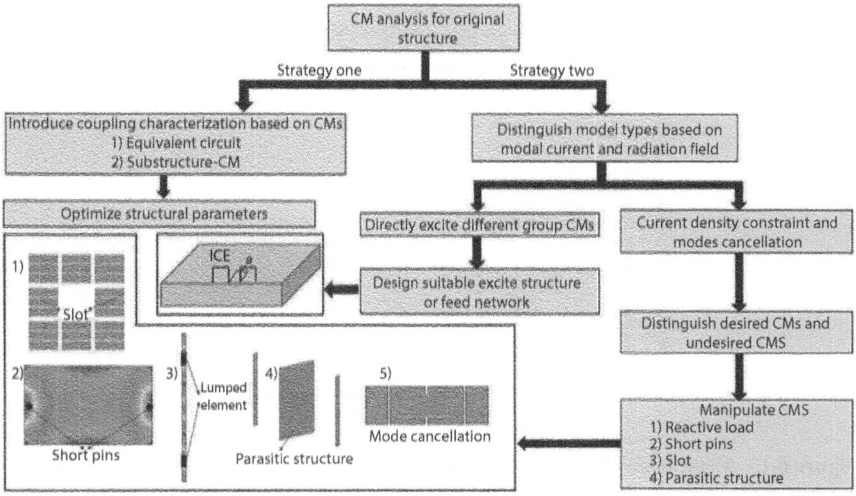

Figure 6.12 CMA to control EM coupling.

Conclusively, the recent approach is to design a radiator that excites one port whereas the current distribution in all other ports cancel each other. In this method, one single radiator is excited with multiple ports and slots or parasitic structures are introduced to optimize the characteristic modes with distinct current directions at the same resonant frequency. This opened wings to a new technique called coupled characteristic mode that helps to optimize the parasitic structures [17].

6.3 Realization and Evaluations of MS-Based Antenna Models

MSs are the 2-D planar surface with periodic arrangement of unit cells. These MSs are attached to the antenna either above or below the radiator with or without air gap to increase the gain bandwidth product of the antenna. Some of the MS-based models are discussed in this section. In [18], a planar MS-based low profile circularly polarised antenna as shown in Figure 6.13 is proposed for the entire mm- wave 5G spectrum with an average gain. The metasurface is loaded on to the top of the patch antenna without any air gap. Although the stacked patches have low gain, these radiators cover the entire spectrum from 24.2 – 29.5 GHz with decent gain value of 9-11.5 dBi. Some of the most recent literary works on the metasurface-based antenna are listed in Table 6.1 below.

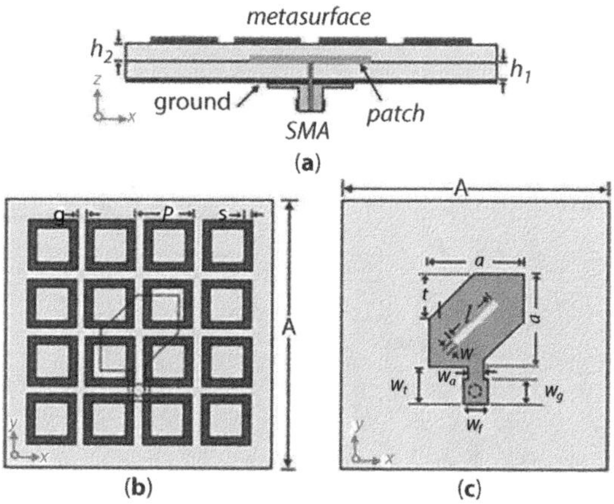

Figure 6.13 Metasurface-based antenna: (a) perspective view, (b) metasurface, and (c) patch.

Table 6.1 Literature survey on recently reported metasurface-based 5G antennas.

Ref.	Radiator and metasurface	No. of ports	Size	Operating bandwidth (GHz)	Gain (dBi)
[19]	Two substrate with square slots	8×8	$10\lambda_0 \times 10\lambda_0 \times 5\lambda_0$	5-6	3.3
[20]	Hexagonal shape patch with the square slots	1	$1.0\lambda_0 \times 1.0\lambda_0 \times 0.04\lambda_0$	25-29.6	11
[21]	MIMO square shaped patch antenna with BPF	2×2	33x33x1.778mm	6.4-8.4	8
[22]	Light filtering metasurface	-	-	Color filtering	-
[23]	Band stop filtering MS	1	240x160x0.9mm	371-500	-
[24]	MTS absorber	-	35mmx15mmx2mm	5-8	-
[25]	MTM absorber with periodic cells	-	-	8.2-12.4	-
[26]	Silicon-based MTS absorber	-	-	0.6-1.0	-

6.4 Frequency Selective Surfaces and Its Types

Frequency Selective Surfaces (FSS) is 2-D periodic array structure on a dielectric substrate which either transmits or reflects the incoming plane wave based on the characteristics of the array (Figure 6.14). This transmission or reflection befalls when the resonance frequency of the FSS equals the frequency of the incident plane wave [27]. Because of its capability to block or pass the EM wave, these are called as spatial filters. The resonance of FSS can be influenced by optimising size, periodicity and shape of the unit cell. Generally these FSS are widely used in reflector antennas, antenna radome structure and to control the Radar Cross Sections (RCS).

Conventional FSS are of narrow bandwidth and bigger in size, hence extensive research has been made to make FSS compact in size, polarization insensitive and incident angle insensitive. Conversely, to overcome the single layer FSS limitations, multilayer FSS has been proposed which is capable of providing flexibility to tune the parameters for achieving desired frequency response. For reducing the size of the FSS, recently fractal-based structures and 2.5 D structures using vias are used.

6.4.1 Operating Principle of FSS

Similar to the filtering concepts in circuit theory, the FSS also possess four different filtering characteristics like high pass and low pass, band stop and band pass. Among these, the low pass FSS allows only low frequencies to pass through by blocking the higher ones, whereas the high pass FSS is the reversal of the low pass, while the bandpass FSS allows only the designed desired band of frequencies and band stop restricts the specific set of frequencies. The functionality of these FSS depends on the shape; periodicity and size by fine tuning these parameters desired frequency of operation can be achieved.

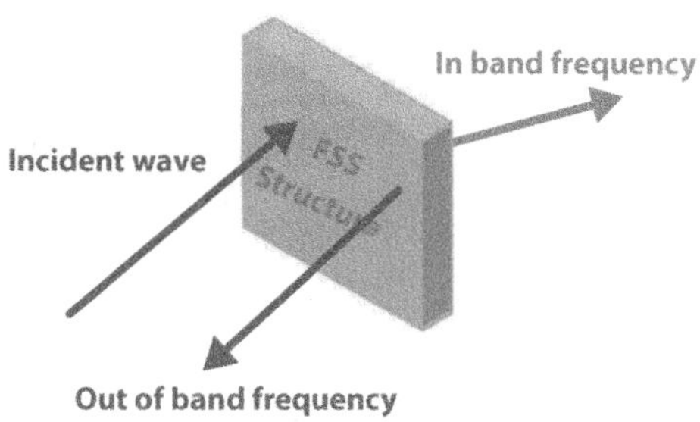

Figure 6.14 Frequency selective surfaces operating principle.

Electric currents will be stimulated in to the periodic structures when EM waves impinge on the FSS surface. The amplitude of the current induced depends on the energy coupled between the FSS and the incident wave. These currents are responsible for the scattering filed around the structure and the desired fields can be obtained by designing the array elements properly. The conventional FSS structures possess narrow bandwidth, low polarization and angular stability.

6.4.2 Equivalent Circuit of Conventional FSS

Figure 6.15 shows the equivalent circuits of a simple low pass and high pass FSS. Here, the patch forms the resistance and inductance whereas the gaps between the patch are identified as the capacitance value. When the unit cell is incident with the EM wave, the equivalent resonance circuit can be found by changing the value of these lumped components. The resonance frequency can be found by using the values of L and C,

$$f = \frac{1}{2\pi\sqrt{LC}} \tag{6.6}$$

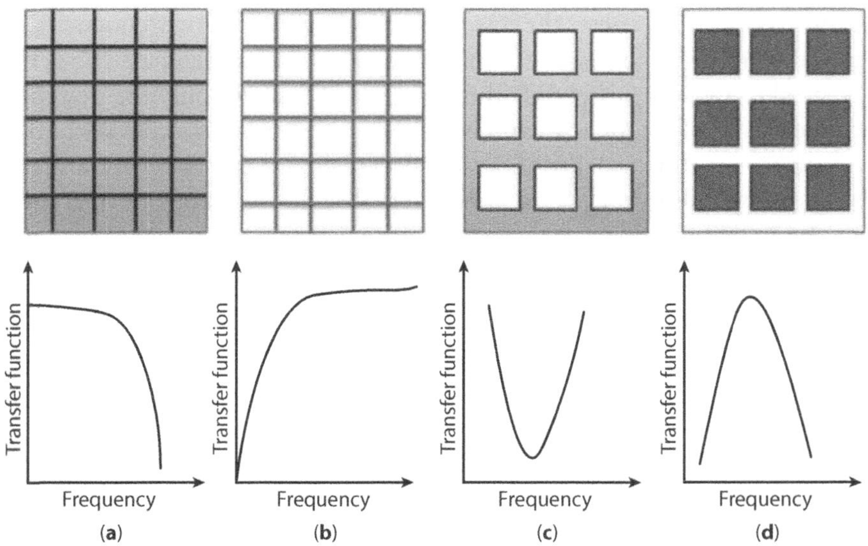

Figure 6.15 Equivalent circuits of conventional FSS.

Non-resonant elements like patch, grid and wire can be represented using a capacitive element, whereas a series combination of inductive and capacitive elements is used to represent the resonant elements like loop, cross and dipoles. Thereby, it is inferred that the number of lumped elements in the circuit decides the number of resonances [28].

6.4.3 Types of FSS

Generally, the FSS structures can be categorised into four groups as in Figure 6.16. Group 1 includes the dipole, spiral, square, cross, and Jerusalem cross, whereas the second group includes the loops like circular loop, square loop and hexagonal loops. Unique or different shapes of the patches are included in group 3 and the combination of all the above

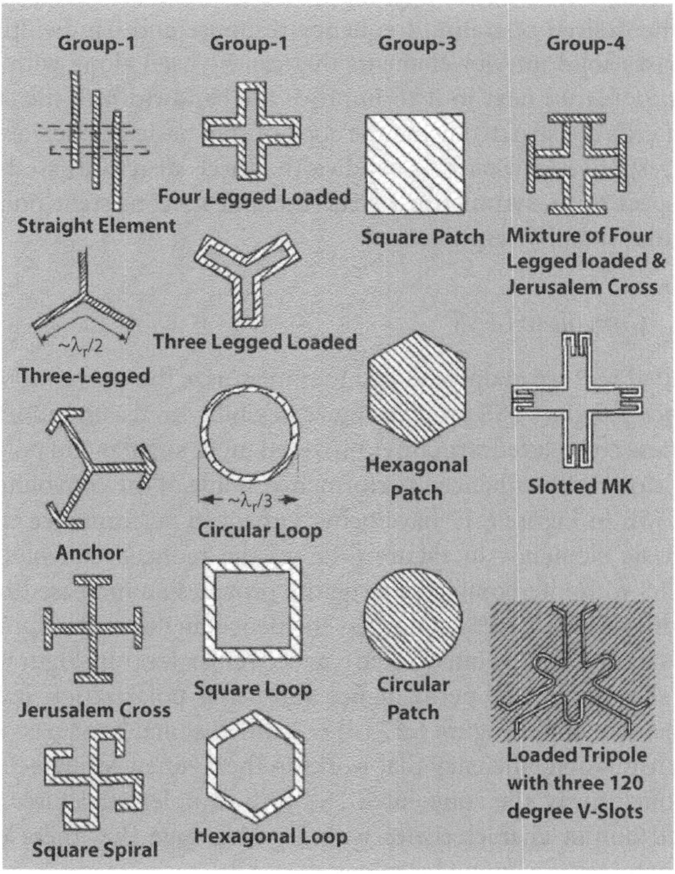

Figure 6.16 Grouping of basic geometries of FSS.

shapes comes under group 4. Among these, the loop FSS (group 2) offers higher bandwidth comparatively.

6.4.3.1 *Basic Shapes*

In light of the applications, the structure of the FSS unit cell is decided. Different groups of FSS available are shown in Figure 6.16. For wideband applications, hexagonal loops or others loops loaded with leg structures can be used. FSS resonates when the perimeter of the loop is equal to the full wavelength.

The bandwidth of the array can be varied by also changing the periodicity or the inter-element spacing in the array. If this spacing is greater than the half wavelength, then the resonance will shift downwards with varying incident angles. With proper design and inter-element spacing, the bandwidth of the FSS in group 2 and group 1 can be optimised to obtain the desired operating frequency response and bandwidth. Group 3 comprises solid interior elements that can be used along with its complementary placed next to it to improve the bandwidth of the structure. The unit cells constructed using the above-listed basic geometries exhibits limited response with narrow bandwidth. These structures are beneficial with respect to its symmetrical structure and its consistent polarization and angular stability responses.

6.4.3.2 *Convoluted FSS*

Convoluted FSS are mainly studied to miniaturize the conventional structures since compact FSS provides more flexibility to use in radome structures. These convoluted structures provided more angular and polarization stability along with enhanced performance. Some of the convoluted structures shown in Figure 6.17 have better enhanced performance compared to the basic elements. In Figure 6.17 (a) the reduced convoluted cross dipole FSS with interconnected structure provides an increased reflection bandwidth of about 63% at normal incidence angles and improved frequency stability. Convoluted square and circular loop in Figure 6.17 (b) and (c) show enhanced performance and better polarization stability up to 60° incident angle. Figure 6.17 (d) is 3-dimensional band pass FSS with good transmission efficiency that works in the frequency range 8.5 to 10.3 GHz. Conclusively, the convoluted FSS with complex structures provides enhanced output characteristics with an advantage that these distorted shapes increases the lumped element effect [29].

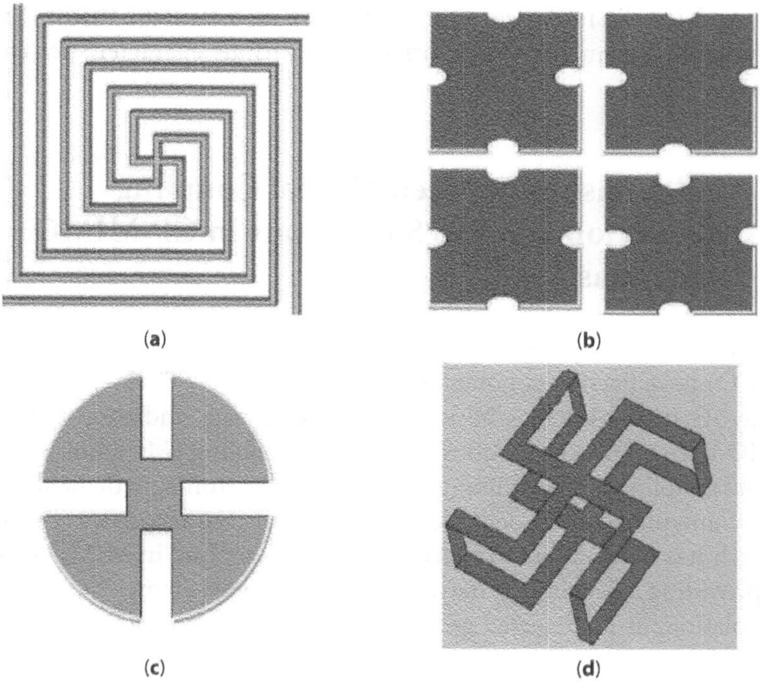

Figure 6.17 Different types of available convoluted FSS (a) meandered cross dipole, (b) square loop, (c) circular loop, and (d) 3-D miniaturized swastika.

6.4.3.3 Fractal Geometry

A basic geometric structure is used to begin the fractal design and the linear transformation operations like translation, rotation, copying and scaling are done iteratively for infinite number of times on the basic geometry to form the final arrangement. These fractal geometries give better output characteristics than the conventional structures. A fractal FSS is constructed by repeating the fractals in a periodic manner.

Figure 6.18(a) represents swastika fractal unit cell provides selectivity in frequency response and can be used in radome due to its compact size. In addition to these, it also provides polarization and angular stability. Similar to this, the structure in (b) can be used in C band radiators and (c) (d) are the Minkowski fractal structures which are more compact and made up of non-resonant patches and slots. These Minkowski structures are more compact in size and can provide a fractional bandwidth 30% more than the conventional patches. (e) represents the Sierpinski fractal patch elements made by integrating dissimilar elements which offers compact multiband FSS structures. Conclusively, the fractal structures can be made by integrating dissimilar structures and have an advantage that by tuning the individual elements size or orientation various characteristics can be achieved [30].

6.5 Relationship Between Mutual Coupling Reduction and FSS Superstrate in CP-MIMO Antennas

In millimetre wave technology, Multiple Input – Multiple Output systems (MIMO) have become a potential technique to improve the performance of the 5G networks. In addition to high data rate, radiation efficiency, MIMO have certain limitations like mutual coupling (MC) and isolation. Mutual coupling is the coupling between the electromagnetic fields of the nearby antennas which degrades the radiation characteristics. Extensive research has been done to reduce the mutual coupling in MIMO systems like providing a decoupling network, adding lumped elements to decouple the isolation, using defected ground structures, electromagnetic band gap structures, etc. These techniques occupy more space and tend to change the radiation characteristics of the system.

Metamaterials have been employed extensively recently to enhance the antenna's radiating properties, among which the FSS are used to reduce both surface wave and space wave propagation that is responsible for the mutual coupling in MIMO systems. The FSS structure allows only a band of frequencies due to which the spatial coupling is reduced between the antennas. FSS also have the disadvantage of producing insignificant reflection which can be controlled by controlling its phase responses.

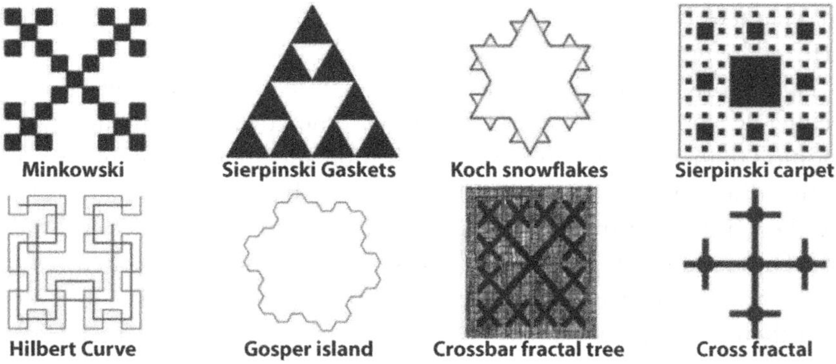

Figure 6.18 Different types of fractal-shaped FSSs.

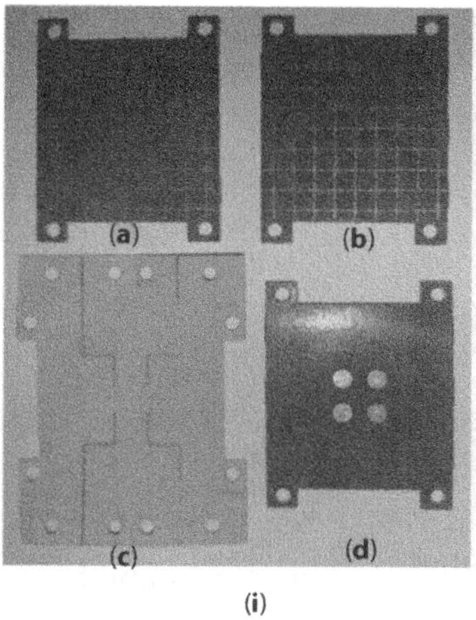

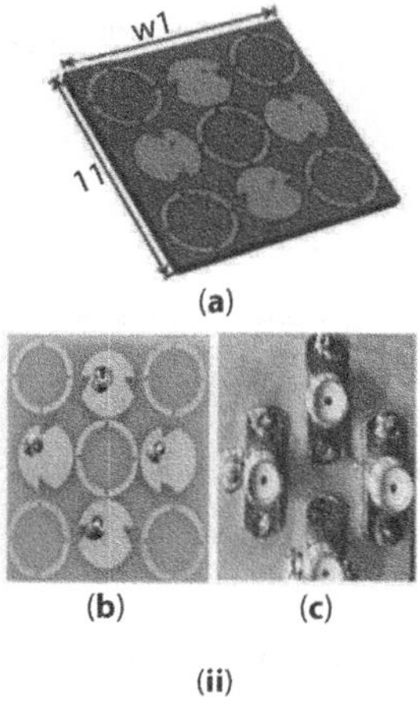

Figure 6.19 (i) MIMO antenna with FSS layers (a) and (b), (c) feed, and (d) patches. (ii) 4-port radiator with FSS (a) perspective view (b) top view (c) bottom view.

Many papers have been published by using FSS in a MIMO antenna system to lessen the effects of mutual coupling. Some are listed as follows.

In [31], a transmission type FSS is used as a superstrate as depicted in Figure 6.19 (i) to cut the spatial coupling exist in the system. The FSS used concentrated the power density which enhanced the gain and isolation factor but with a disadvantage that there exists partial reflection issues.

In [32], a band stop FSS structure was inserted on the radiator surface and above the substrate to lessen mutual coupling effects in a circular slotted MIMO. In addition to that, the gain, polarization stability and also the angular stability of the system got enhanced. A simple circular split ring band stop FSS as illustrated in Figure 6.19 (ii) helps in reducing the MC without disturbing the Envelope correlation coefficient (ECC) parameter and diversity gain (DG) parameter of the MIMO system. This paper proved that FSS is a good candidate to decrease the mutual coupling effects in a 4-port MIMO system.

All these techniques are used to reduce the MC due to surface wave propagation, while the MC occurs also due to the space wave propagation. FSS can also be used to reduce these MC due to space wave coupling. Those MIMO antennas constructed using Substrate Integrated Waveguide (SIW) technique will possess only low surface coupling due its confinement inside the cavity. In such cases, space wave coupling plays a significant role to produce mutual coupling. These can be suppressed by using 3D FSS structures as walls as shown in Figure 6.20 placed between the slot antennas [33].

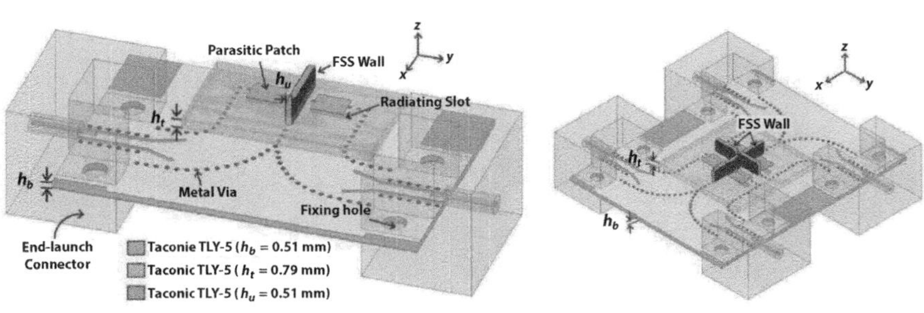

Figure 6.20 Schematic of the SO FSS wall loaded 2-element and 4-element MIMO antenna.

This second-order band stop FSS exhibits polarization stability and angular stability and reduces mutual coupling to a greater extent by preserving the efficiency and diversity of the two- and four-port MIMO system.

6.6 Conclusion

In this chapter, an extensive survey is done on the metamaterials, metasurface-based antenna, development of an antenna design using characteristic mode analysis and the functionalities of different types of FSS. In the first section, the basic mechanisms involved in the metamaterials are studied, followed by an explanation of the empirical and qualitative formulae related to characteristic modes. Then the CM-based solution for the problems related to the radiation pattern, scattering, coupling, bandwidth enhancement and circular polarization is elaborated. In the next section the realization of the metasurface-based antenna design are listed and a few are explained. In the subsequent section, the functionalities of the FSS and its operating principles are defined. Many types of FSS exist, among which some are given a brief explanation. Finally, the techniques to decrease the mutual coupling effects in MIMO system using FSS layers, metasurface and by constructing FSS walls are elaborated. This enriched review will be a better platform to establish a link between the metasurface, FSS and MIMO 5G antennas.

References

1. Sihvola, Metamaterials in electromagnetics. *Metamaterials*, 1, 1, 2–11, Mar. 2007.
2. Veselago, G., The electrodynamics of substances with simultaneously negative values of and μ. *Sov. Phys. Usp.*, 10, 4, 509, 1968.
3. Smith, D.R., Padilla, W.J., Vier, D.C., Nemat-Nasser, S.C., Schultz, S., Composite Medium with Simultaneously Negative Permeability and Permittivity. *Phys. Rev. Lett.*, 84, 18, 4184–4187, 2000.
4. Tretyakov, S., *Analytical Modeling in Applied Electromagnetics*, Artech House, 2003, google-Books-ID: MZ3tpGtadhcC.
5. Pendry, J.B., Holden, A.J., Robbins, D.J., Stewart, W., Magnetism from conductors and enhanced nonlinear phenomena. *IEEE Trans. Microw. Theory Tech.*, 47, 11, 2075–2084, 1999.
6. Tretyakov, S.A., A personal view on the origins and developments of the metamaterial concept. *J. Opt.*, 19, 1, 013002, 2017.
7. Caloz, C., Perspectives on EM metamaterials. *Mater. Today*, 12, 3, 12–20, 2009.
8. Liu, R., Ji, C., Mock, J.J., Chin, J.Y., Cui, T.J., Smith, D.R., Broadband ground-plane cloak. *Science*, 323, 366, 2009.
9. Ma, H.F., Chen, X., Yang, X.M., Xu, H.S., Cheng, Q., Cui, T.J., A broadband metamaterial cylindrical lens antenna. *Chin. Sci. Bull.*, 2009.
10. Cabedo-Fabres, M., Antonino-Daviu, E., Valero-Nogueira, A., *et al.*, The theory of characteristic modes revisited: A contribution to the design of antennas for modern applications. *IEEE Antennas Propag. Mag.*, 49, 5, 52–68, 2007.
11. Wang, C.H., Chen, Y.K., Yang, S.W., Bandwidth enhancement of a dual-polarized slot antenna using characteristic modes. *IEEE Antennas Wirel. Propag. Lett.*, 17, 6, 988–992, 2018.
12. Lin, J.F. and Zhu, L., Low-profile high-directivity circularly-polarized differential-fed patch antenna with characteristic modes analysis. *IEEE Trans. Antennas Propag.*, 69, 2, 723–733, 2021.
13. Liu, Y., Ren, A.D., Liu, H., *et al.*, Eight-port MIMO array using characteristic mode theory for 5G smartphone applications. *IEEE Access*, 7, 45679–45692, 2019.
14. Liu, N.W., Zhu, L., Liu, Z.X., *et al.*, Radiation pattern reshaping of a narrow slot antenna for bandwidth enhancement and stable pattern using characteristic modes analysis. *IEEE Trans. Antennas Propag.*, 70, 1, 726–731, 2022.
15. Elghannai, E.A. and Rojas, R.G., Interpretation of antenna scattering phenomena with the aid of characteristic mode theory, in: *Proceedings of 2018 IEEE International Symposium on Antennas and Propagation & USNC/URSI National Radio Science Meeting*, pp. 1123–1124, 2018.

16. Ghosal, S., Sinha, R., De, A., *et al.*, Characteristic mode analysis of mutual coupling. *IEEE Trans. Antennas Propag.*, 70, 2, 1008–1019, 2022.
17. Ghosal, S., Sinha, R., De, A., Further insights into coupled characteristic modes, in: *Proceedings of 2021 IEEE Indian Conference on Antennas and Propagation, Jaipur, Rajasthan, India*, pp. 820–823, 2021.
18. Hussain, N., *et al.*, A metasurface-based low-profile wideband circularly polarized patch antenna for 5G millimeter-wave systems. *IEEE Access*, 8, 22127–22135, 2020.
19. Li, S., *et al.*, Characterization of metasurface lens antenna for sub-6 GHz dual-polarization fulldimension massive MIMO and multibeam systems. *IEEE Trans. Antennas Propag.*, 68, 3, 1366–1377, 2020.
20. Hussain, N., *et al.*, Metasurface-based single-layer wideband circularly polarized MIMO antenna for 5G millimeter-wave systems. *IEEE Access*, 8, 130293–130304, 2020.
21. Yang, W., *et al.*, Novel filtering method based on metasurface antenna and its application for wideband high-gain filtering antenna with low profile. *IEEE Trans. Antennas Propag.*, 67, 3, 1535–1544, 2018.
22. Han, X., *et al.*, Inverse design of metasurface optical filters using deep neural network with high degrees of freedom. *InfoMat*, 3, 4, 432–442, 2021.
23. Deng, H., Chan, M., Zhou, S., Terahertz broadband band-stop filter based on metasurface, in: *IEEE International Conference on Electron Devices and Solid-State Circuits*, pp. 1–3, 2019.
24. Li, Z., *et al.*, A metasurface absorber based on the slow-wave effect. *AIP Adv.*, 10, 4, 045311, 2020.
25. Gogoi, D.J. and Bhattacharyya, N.S., Metasurface absorber based on water meta "molecule" for X-band microwave absorption. *J. Appl. Phys.*, 124, 7, 075106, 2018.
26. Liu, Z., *et al.*, Silicon antennas metasurface based light absorber with quantitatively adjustable operating frequency and intensity. *IEEE J. Sel. Top. Quantum Electron.*, 27, 1, 2020.
27. Munk, B.A., *Frequency Selective Surfaces: Theory and Design*, vol. 29, Wiley Online Library, Hoboken, NJ, USA, 2000.
28. Costa, F., Monorchio, A., Manara, G., An overview of equivalent circuit modeling techniques of frequency selective surfaces and metasurfaces. *Appl. Comput. Electromagn. Soc. J.*, 29, 960–976, 2014.
29. Nauman, M., Saleem, R., Rashid, A.K., Shafique, M.F., A miniaturized flexible frequency selective surface for X-band applications. *IEEE Trans. Electromagn. Compat.*, 58, 419–428, 2016.
30. Sugumaran, B. and Balasubramanian, R., Design and analysis of fractal based monopole antenna backed with modified Jerusalem Cross frequency selective surface for wireless personal area communications. *Mob. Netw. Appl.*, 25, 2092–2101, 2020.

31. Akbari, M., Abo Ghalyon, H., Farahani, M., Sebak, A.-R., Denidni, T.A., Spatially Decoupling of CP Antennas Based on FSS for 30-GHz MIMO Systems. *IEEE Access*, 5, 6527–6537, 2017, doi: 10.1109/ACCESS.2017.2693342.
32. Khan, K., Ali, L., Wu, Q., A Compact FSS-Based Four-Port MIMO Antenna for Low Mutual Coupling. *IEEE Antennas Wirel. Propag. Lett.*, 22, 12, 2836–2840, Dec. 2023, doi: 10.1109/LAWP.2023.3300837.
33. Dey, S., Keerthi, M.S., Dey, S., Broadband Millimeter Wave MIMO Antennas at 28 GHz with Low Mutual Coupling Using Frequency Selective Surface Wall, in: *2023 IEEE Microwaves, Antennas, and Propagation Conference (MAPCON), Ahmedabad, India*, pp. 1–6, 2023, doi: 10.1109/MAPCON58678.2023.10464151.

7

A Review on Electromagnetic Metamaterial Absorbers and Its Application

Surender Singh Bisht*, **Amit Kumar and Dharmendra K. Jhariya**

Department of Electronics & Communication Engineering, National Institute of Technology Delhi, Delhi, India

Abstract

Metamaterial absorbers have gained attention due to their ability to absorb incident electromagnetic radiation. They can be used for refractive index sensing, energy harvesting, electromagnetic shielding, and radar cross section reduction. These absorbers are made up of a dielectric substrate resonator layer, and metal-based ground plane. Various types of absorbers have been studied, comprising polarization-insensitive absorbers, broadband absorbers, and multiband absorbers.

The goal is to achieve near-unity absorption. Metamaterial-based absorbers utilize left-handed material properties, permittivity, and permeability to reduce the size and thickness of the absorbers. Different design approaches and configurations have been studied to increase absorptivity. These absorbers have potential applications in communication technology to reduce the adverse effects of electromagnetic radiation. The current rapid progress in wireless communication is seriously exacerbating electromagnetic interference (EMI) and contributing to EM pollution, which is destroying the climate. In addition to air, noise, and water pollution, electromagnetic radiation has been identified as the fourth major source of pollution in the public sphere. It has detrimental consequences on all living things. Moving forward, there will be a growing need to develop suitable methods and materials to overcome electromagnetic interference. Three methods exist for controlling electromagnetic interference: absorption, transmission, and reflection. Nevertheless, absorption results in the reduction of electromagnetic waves; reflection and transmission of electromagnetic waves do not weaken the EMI field. Therefore, using a suitable electromagnetic wave absorber is a workable method for addressing the problem of electromagnetic interference (EMI). To absorb the visible light spectrum, which spans frequencies from 400 THz to

**Corresponding author*: surenderbisht@nitdelhi.ac.in

Dilip Kumar Choudhary, Indrasen Singh, Manoj Kumar Singh and Amit Kumar Jain (eds.) Compact and Flexible Microwave Devices, (151–196) © 2025 Scrivener Publishing LLC

700 THz, carbon and black bodies are utilized. Materials that absorb sound waves, such as rock wool and glass fibers, are utilized to absorb frequencies between 20 Hz and 20 kHz. Similar to this, the RF and microwave regions of electromagnetic waves are absorbed by means of an electromagnetic wave absorber. Overall, research on metamaterial absorbers aims to develop materials and techniques for effective absorption of electromagnetic waves.

Keywords: Metamaterials design, electromagnetic, absorptivity, polarization dependence, energy harvesting, application, 5G/6G

7.1 Introduction

The discovery of materials having negative refraction, which V. G. Veselago initially reported in 1968, has significantly advanced the discipline of material science [1]. Pendry has since created such material after forty years [2]. Metamaterials, or materials modified beyond their inherent electromagnetic properties, are widely used in absorbers, sensors, antennas, and other devices [2–4]. For each of these uses cases, a metamaterial unit cell with subwavelength working capability was engineered to possess distinct magnetic and/or electric reactions to an incident electromagnetic wave [5–7]. This reaction in a metamaterial produces a customized medium, which increases its potential applications in antennas, sensors, cloaking devices, and other areas [8–19]. Since MTMs experience inevitable loss as a result of atomic, molecular, chemical, or structural factors, efforts have been made to optimize the structure in order to realize low loss devices [20–22]. However, it should be mentioned that absorption is necessary for applications like polymer shape, switchable absorber [23, 24], energy harvesting, heat sensing, and scattering reduction [25–27]. According to reports, in order to get MTMs of uniform absorption, magnetic and electric resonances must be tailored, which requires the use of the aforementioned intrinsic loss [28–34]. The first reported narrow bandwidth of a perfect absorber with metamaterial assigned to a resonance condition restricted the practical application of it [28]. Unit cells with several resonances are created and coupled to create MTM-based multiband absorbers [35, 36]. For close resonant frequencies, broadband absorption is achieved [37]. Broadband absorption is also achieved by MTM absorbers that are built with multilayer architectures or vertical standing nano wires [38–41].

Metamaterials comprise a broad class of artificial composite structures with features that are not obtainable in natural materials and are difficult to achieve technologically [1]. The proper selection of material parameters, in particular linear size and shape, inclusion compositions, and so on, allows for the

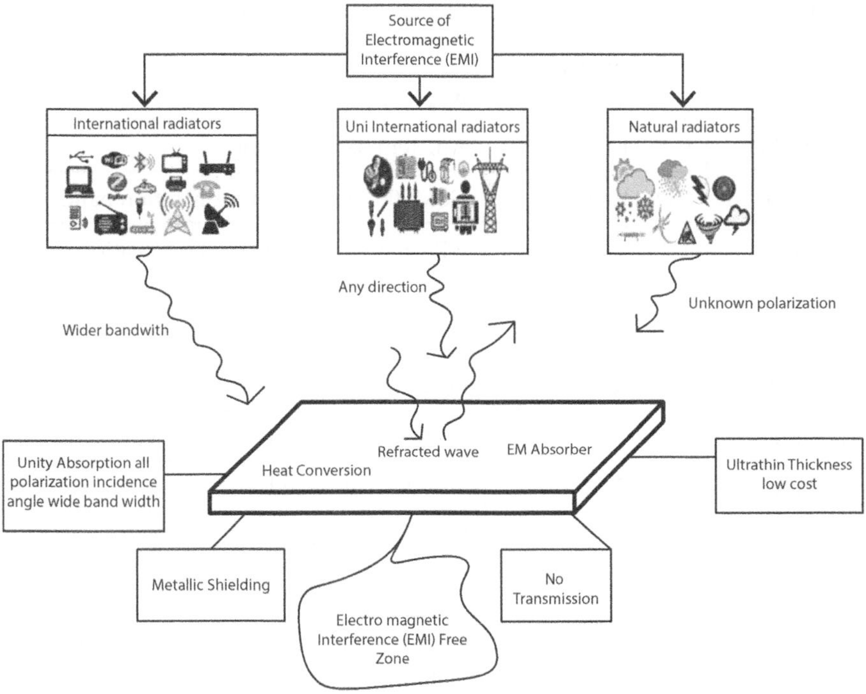

Figure 7.1 Shows the current scenario's electromagnetic absorber.

modification of permittivity and permeability and the management of material features. The current scenario's electromagnetic absorber is shown in Figure 7.1.

7.1.1 Communication Band

EM wave absorber majorly deals with the EM wave in the free space. Starting with the application point of view, absorbers have been designed to absorb the particular frequency band. Some of the most popular communication bands in space are listed in Table 7.1.

7.1.2 Classification of Metamaterial

Any type of physical substance can be categorized as shown in Table 7.2 based on its permeability and effective permittivity.

As shown in Figure 7.2, the majority of materials found in nature are classified as DPS materials with a double positive because their permeability and permittivity both have values higher than zero. Materials designated

Table 7.1 Popular communication bands and their respective applications.

Band	Frequency range (GHz)	Application
UHF Band	0.432 to 0.438	Amateur satellite band
UHF Band	0.890 to 0.960	GSM900 Mobile communication band
L Band	1.2 to 1.8	GPS, GNSS, Mobile Communication satellite band
L Band	1.67 to 1.71	Meteorological Satellite band
S Band	2.025 to 2.3	Space operation and research
S Band	1.92 to 2.17	3G Spectrum band
S Band	2.3 to 2.4	4G Spectrum band
S Band	2.4 to 2.483	Wi-Fi and ISM band
C Band	3.3 to 3.8	5G Spectrum band
C Band	3.4 to 6.4	The frequency range utilized for Fixed Satellite Service (FSS) and Broadcast Satellite Service (BSS)
X Band	8 to 9	Environmental and military communication satellite
Ku Band	10.7 to 12.2	FSS and BSS downlink, Domestic TV Program
Ku Band	14.5 to 18.1	FSS and BSS uplink
Ka Band	23 to 28	5G Spectrum, broadcast, environmental and space operations satellites
Ka Band	7 to 20	6G Spectrum support various application, such as augmented reality (AR), advanced IoT application and a Virtual reality (VR)

Table 7.2 Physical material categorized.

Metamaterial			
Double Positive (DPS)	**Epsilon Negative (ENG)**	**Double Negative (DNG)**	**Mu Negative (MNG)**
ε > 0, μ > 0 Double positive (DPS) materials, or conventional materials, are those where the permittivity and permeability polarities are positive at the same time.	ε< 0, μ > 0 Materials are classified as epsilon-negative (ENG) materials if they have positive permeability (ε > 0) and negative permittivity (ε < 0).	ε< 0, μ < 0 Double-negative (DNG) materials, also referred to as MTMs generally, are specifically specified when both of these characteristics are adjusted to be negative.	ε > 0, μ < 0 Mu-negative (MNG) materials are those in which the permittivity is positive and the permeability is negligible (ε > 0, μ < 0)

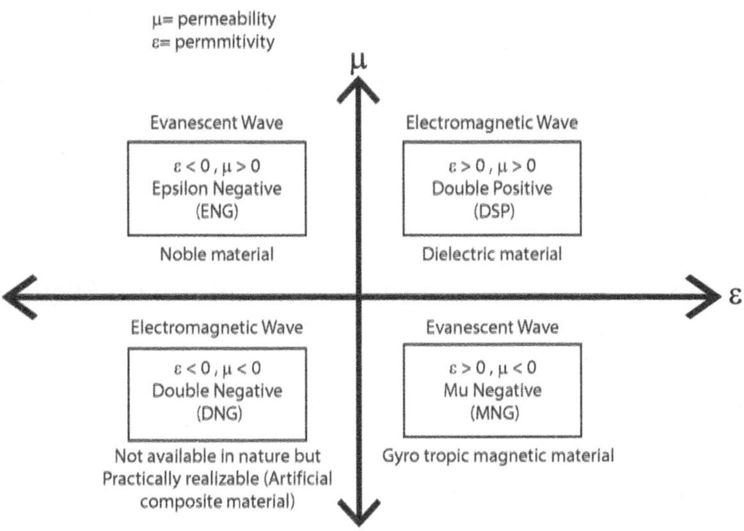

Figure 7.2 Classification of material based on permittivity(ε) and permeability(μ).

as SNG (single negative) only have negative permittivity (ε) or permeability(μ), and they are further classified into two classes, ENG (ε-negative) and MNG (μ-negative), based on negative effective parameters. Plasma is the most well-known natural material to be an ENG-material. Certain gyro tropic magnetic materials might be referred to as MNG-materials since they exhibit negative permeability within a specific frequency range. Materials having concurrently negative ε and μ allow for modifications to radiation characteristics in a certain frequency range, such as the doppler shift being inverted, Cerenkov radiation, and the change in the sign of group velocity. The modification of Negative refraction, or Snell's rule, is the most important and most carefully thought-out impact. In various works, materials exhibiting the aforementioned characteristics are referred to as left-handed materials (LHM), backward-wave media (BW) or double negative materials (DNG). Nowadays, materials for the microwave domain are represented by a mix of split ring resonators and thin metal grid mesh [2]. The first material is synthetic ENG material, and the second is MNG material. By arranging these unit cells periodically, the composite material produced has concurrently negative ε and μ. It was shown that this medium's boundary exhibits anomalous refraction, which is caused by negative refraction [2, 3]. Additionally, according to [4], there are two main classes into which all metamaterials can be classified: DNG and SNG structures are included in the first class, and EBG structures (photonic crystals) are included in the second class. Thanks to methods for expressing such materials mathematically, classification was achieved. Since the inclusions and inter inclusion distances in DNG and SNG-structures are significantly less than wavelengths, homogenization and successful media concepts can be used to characterize these types of media. The EBG metamaterials are characterized by Bragg reflection and other periodic media principles and involve distances of half a wavelength or more.

7.2 Types of Electromagnetic Metamaterial Wave Absorbers

Electromagnetic wave absorbers fall into two main categories:

7.2.1 Resonant Absorbers

Resonant absorbers depend upon frequency because these materials are intended to resonate at a specific wavelength as shown in Figure 7.3.

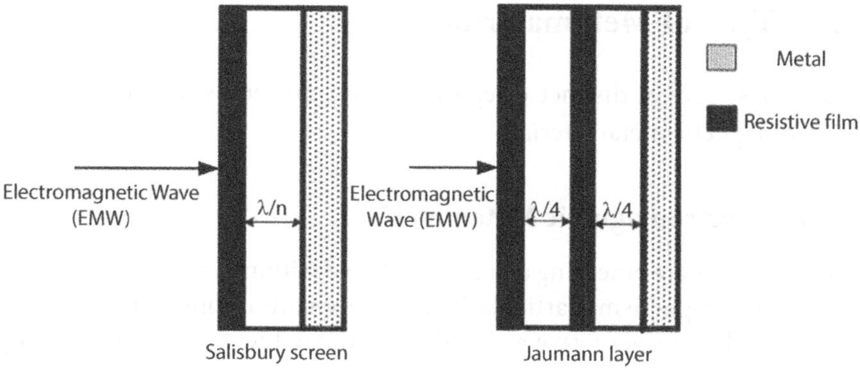

Figure 7.3 Common designs for impedance matching resonant absorbers. Adapted from [25].

In conclusion, the effectiveness of these absorbers depends on the material's characteristics interacting resonantly at a particular frequency at the incident radiations. Salisbury screens, Jaumann absorbers, crossed grating absorbers, and so forth are examples of resonant absorbers.

7.2.2 Broadband Absorbers

The broadband absorber is not dependent on a specific frequency; broadband absorbers are able to function efficiently throughout a wide region of the electromagnetic spectrum. In general, these absorbers involve the utilization of materials that possess properties that are not reliant on frequency and, as a result, have the capability to absorb radiations throughout a broad spectrum.

The electromagnetic spectrum is often composed of a variety of frequency bands, in addition to the electronic gadgets and phenomena that operate inside those ranges of frequencies. These days, a significant amount of attention is being paid by researchers to the optimization of microwave absorbers. This is due to the fact that the majority of mobile devices for communication and the introduction of 6G and 5G technology are inflicting significant damage in the form of harmful microwaves in that region, which normally extends from 1 GHz to 100 GHz. Microwave-absorbing materials (MAMs) are materials that absorb microwave radiation are sometimes referred to as electromagnetic (EM) wave absorbers or protectors or EMI shielders. This is because microwaves constitute a subset of the electromagnetic spectrum as a whole.

7.3 Type of Metamaterial

There exist several distinct categories of metamaterials, one of which is electromagnetic metamaterials.

7.3.1 Electromagnetic Metamaterial

Metamaterials are emerging as a novel subfield within the realms of physics and electromagnetism, particularly in the domains of optics and photonics. Optical and microwave applications employ these materials in many capacities, including novel modulators, lenses, beam steerers, microwave couplers, antenna radomes and band-pass filters. Metamaterials are composed of many constructions. Metamaterials exert an influence on electromagnetic waves through the presence of structural characteristics that have smaller size than the wavelength of the electromagnetic radiation with which they interact.

7.3.2 Refractive Index with a Negative Value

The ability to fabricate a structure with a refractive index is a negative for the most promising aspect of metamaterials, as this characteristic is not

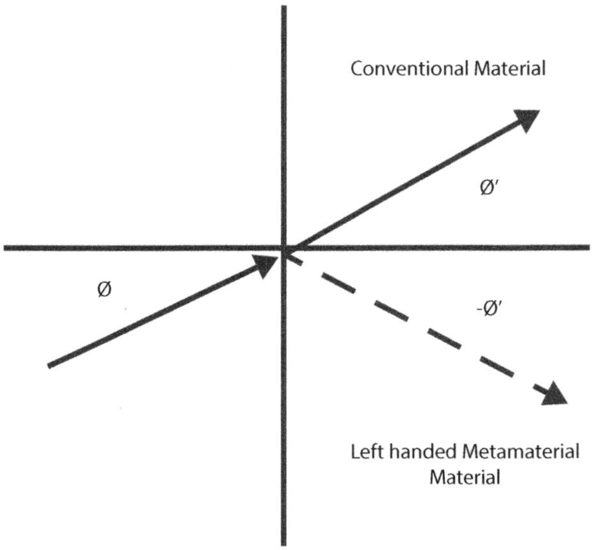

Figure 7.4 Comparison of refraction in a left-handed metamaterial with an ordinary material.

present in all naturally occurring substances. Permittivity ε and permeability μ are both positive for the majority of optics-related materials, including glass and water.

However, at visible wavelengths, numerous metals (including gold and silver) have a negative ε. Opacity towards electromagnetic radiation is exhibited by materials with either ε or μ negative, but not both. The values permittivity ε and permeability μ give a detailed explanation of the optical characteristics of a clear material, but in practice, value n is chosen for the refractive index. Figure 7.4 indicates the refraction in left-handed metamaterial (LHM) and normal material.

All transparent materials that are not metamaterials are known to have positive ε and μ. The standard practice is to make use of the positive square root of n. Even so, specific constructed metamaterials possess $\mu < 0$ and $\varepsilon < 0$. The reason n is a real number is that the product εμ is positive. The negative square root of n must be computed in these cases. The ability of such materials to transmit light was demonstrated by physicist Victor Veselago.

7.3.3 Various Categories of Electromagnetic Metamaterials

The refractive index that is negative in double negative metamaterials (DNG) is attributed to both of their negative values of both permittivity (ε) and permeability (μ). DNGs are commonly known as negative index metamaterials (NIM). Other terms used to refer to DNGs include "left-handed media", "the media having a negative refractive index," as well as "backward-wave media."

7.3.3.1 Metamaterials with a Single Negative Charge

In the context of single negative (SNG) metamaterials, it is uncommon for both permittivity and permeability to be negative. The following section will address the topics of MNG metamaterials and ENG metamaterials. Exciting research has been carried out by merging two layers of SNG into a single metamaterial. All of these entities effectively generate an alternative form of DNG metamaterial. Wave reflection experiments were conducted by joining two slabs of MNG and ENG material together. As a consequence, the material displayed characteristics like resonances, abnormal tunneling, transparency, and complete absence of reflection. Similar to Double negative (DNG) metamaterials, SNG possess inherent dispersive properties, resulting in variations in their permeability (μ), refraction index (n), and permittivity (ε) as a function of frequency.

7.3.3.2 Metamaterials with Electromagnetic Bandgaps

The propagation of light is regulated by metamaterials with varying electromagnetic bandgaps. The achievement of this objective is made possible either through the utilization of a category of metamaterial called photonic crystal (PC) or an alternate category referred to as left-handed materials (LHM). The two entities belong to a distinct category of purposefully designed structures, and they both possess the ability to regulate and modify the transmission of electromagnetic waves, specifically light.

7.3.3.3 Medium with Double Positivity

Natural dielectrics are examples of double positive mediums (DPS) that can be found in nature. Both permittivity and magnetic permeability exhibit positive values, and the propagation of waves occurs vertically.

7.3.3.4 Metamaterials with Bi-Isotropic and Bi-Isotropic Properties

Metamaterials are materials that usually fall into two categories as either double or single negative, or double positive, on the basis of the belief that they exhibit separate electric and magnetic responses, which are determined by the permeability (μ) and permittivity(ε) parameters. In numerous examples of electromagnetic (EM) metamaterials, the presence of an electric field results in the occurrence of magnetic polarization, which then generates an electrical polarization. This phenomenon is commonly referred to as magnetoelectric coupling. These types of media are sometimes referred to as bi-isotropic. Media that demonstrate magnetoelectric interaction and possess anisotropic properties are referred to as bi-anisotropic.

7.3.3.5 Chiral Metamaterials

The term "chiral metamaterial" is used to describe a metamaterial that is composed of chiral elements.

7.3.4 Split-Ring Resonators

A double negative metamaterial (DNG), sometimes referred to as a negative index metamaterial (NIM), is composed in part of split-ring resonators (SRRs). Furthermore, they are constituent elements of other metamaterial kinds, such as a Single Negative Metamaterial (SNG).

Split-ring resonators (SRRs) are also employed in the research of acoustic metamaterials, Terahertz ranges metamaterials, and metamaterial antennas. SRRs are structures consisting of two concentric circular rings that have splits at opposing ends. The rings consist of nonmagnetic metals, such as copper, and exhibit a small spacing between them.

7.3.5 Terahertz Metamaterial

Terahertz metamaterials are metamaterials that engage in interactions at frequencies in the terahertz range. In the context of research and applications associated with metamaterials and another material, the terahertz range is commonly specified as a range of frequency spanning 0.1 THz to 10 THz. The wavelengths within the range of 3mm (Extremely High Frequency band) to 0.03mm (long-wavelength edge of far-infrared light) are connected to this phenomenon.

7.3.6 Photonic Metamaterials

A photonic metamaterial refers to a synthetically produced, sub-wavelength, periodic arrangement that is specifically engineered to interact with optical frequencies. From photonic band gap structures, the photonic metamaterial is differentiated by its sub-wavelength period.

7.3.7 Nonlinear Metamaterials

Metamaterials can also be manufactured that include nonlinear media, such as materials with properties that vary in response to the power of the incident wave. Non-linear media have a crucial role in the field of nonlinear optics.

7.3.8 Metamaterials Absorber

In order to achieve a high level of electromagnetic absorption, a metamaterial absorber is capable of manipulating the loss components associated with the complex and efficient features namely magnetic permeability and, electric permittivity of metamaterials.

7.3.9 Frequency Selective Surfaces (FSS) Metamaterials

Metamaterials based on FSS are now available as an adequate replacement for fixed frequency metamaterials.

7.4 The Metamaterial (MTM) Absorbers Theory

The primary operating principles of MTM absorbers are Impedance Matching and Interference Theories.

7.4.1 Theory of Impedance Matching

This theory states that a metamaterial's perfect absorption can be achieved by manipulating its permeability and effective permittivity values through the manipulation of its electric and magnetic resonances in order to get an impedance match with empty space [41, 42]. The subsequent principle potentially contributes to the electromagnetic (EM) absorption phenomenon of impedance matching. This phenomenon is widely recognized; it arises when electromagnetic wave propagates across two mediums, resulting in the reflection of some EM energy and the transmission of the remaining energy. Figure 7.3 illustrates that the minimization of reflection occurs whenever the characteristics impedance of the reflected medium aligns with that of the incident medium. The job of impedance matching poses a significant challenge in achieving optimal performance in absorber design. Typically, the air is initial medium, which has a characteristic impedance of around 377Ω. Consequently, impedance of the absorbers should be very close to this value at the target frequency to achieve absorption close to unity [46–49]. Additionally, it has been claimed that impedance matching in MTM absorbers is impossible without simultaneous electric and magnetic resonances. This suggests that MTM of a single resonance, either electric or magnetic, cannot provide a perfect absorber [43].

7.4.2 Electrical and Magnetic Resonance

Perfect absorbers utilize electric and magnetic resonances for their absorption mechanism. Closed loop-like structures can be utilized to generate magnetic resonances, while gaps in the structures can be employed to achieve electrical resonances. The electric and magnetic characteristics can be adjusted through the use of appropriate structural design. The most commonly used form of resonator is a split-ring resonator (SRR) that employs magnetic and electrical resonances to achieve absorption properties. It is extensively accepted and can be seen in Figure 7.5. The initial metamaterial absorber developed by Landy *et al.* is founded upon the identical idea. Concentric solid-repellent resonators (SRRs) are commonly

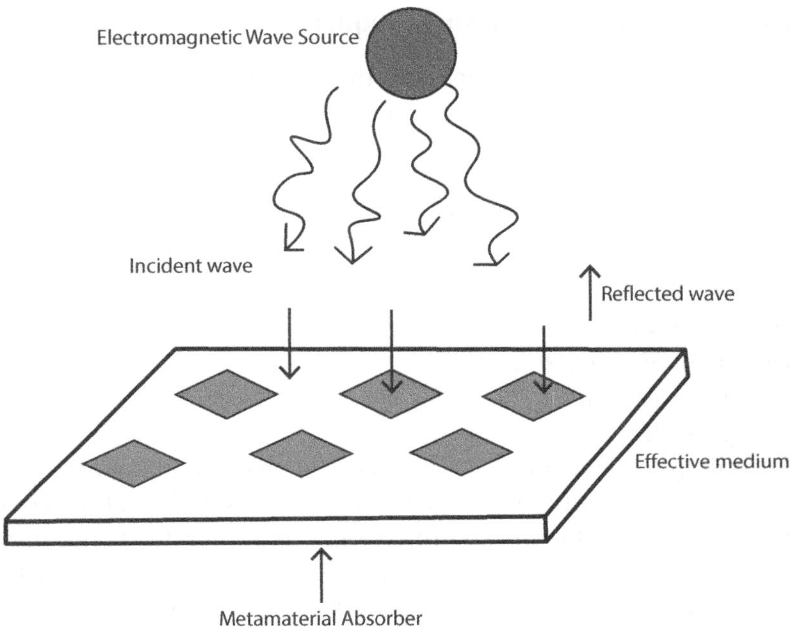

Figure 7.5 Impedance matching in metamaterial absorber.

employed in order to attain multiband absorptions properties [40–45]. The mutual dependency of these absorber's generates supplementary absorptions bands, while closely spaced concentric solid-repellent resonators (SRRs) provide wide absorption properties.

7.4.3 Theory of Interference

Interference theory is based on the fact that there is a destructive interference between many reflections in a given dielectric substrate. On either side of a substrate, an MTM absorber was built using high conducting metallic planes and metallic patterns. The layer of metallic patterns can change the transmission and reflection coefficients and functions as a partial reflector. A phase shift (180°) delay between the incident wave and reflecting wave of the electromagnetic waves is produced by the conducting plane acting as a perfect reflector [44, 45]. Absorption is the result of this combination, depending on each particular parameter.

7.4.4 A Reduction in Plasma Frequency

The frequency at which the density of the electron gas oscillates is known as the material's plasma frequency, and it is determined by:

$$\omega_{p=}\sqrt{\frac{N_{e^2}}{m_{\varepsilon_0}}}\omega_p \tag{7.1}$$

Where, Plasma frequency = ω_p
Density of Free electron = N
effective mass = m
Charge of electron = e

According to Equation (7.1), it is evident that the plasma frequency, denoted as ω_p, is entirely contingent upon the density (N) of the free electron carriers within the metals. The plasma frequency (ω_p) in semiconductors is capable of being altered by introducing doping into the medium. By decreasing the plasma frequency, which is determined by the operating frequency of the metamaterial absorber, it is possible to create materials with negative permittivity. The primary objective behind the decrease in plasma frequency is to manufacture MM absorbers capable of functioning across several frequency ranges. Thus, it is crucial to adjust the frequency in accordance with the desired frequency range [50–52].

7.4.5 Working of Electromagnetic Absorbers

A significant amount of electromagnetic wave pollution is being produced due to the quick advancement of technology in electromagnetic radiation creating devices such as medical equipment, laptop, computer, radar systems, and microwave ovens, amongst other technological advancements. This pollution is becoming a hazard to the human race. In addition to being dangerous for the electronic devices themselves, it also has negative impacts on other electrical devices. In the modern world, there is a significant demand for electromagnetic interference (EMI) shielding devices. The phenomenon of shielding is primarily brought about by two mechanisms: The process by which some particles absorb electromagnetic radiations (EMR) or by EMR's reflection pointing in a particular direction. On the flip side, the first option is often favored because it contributes to the appropriate attenuation of EMR. Through the processes of absorption, transmission, and reflection, the manner in which electromagnetic wave or microwave absorber's function is depicted in Figure 7.6.

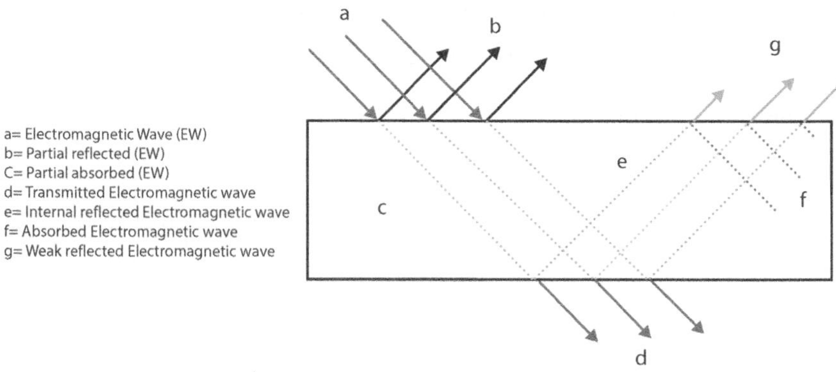

Figure 7.6 Working of electromagnetic metamaterial absorber.

It is necessary for a material to have either no transmission or very little reflection in order for it to be considered an effective absorber. A material must possess permanent magnetic, strongly dielectric properties, qualities such as high resistivity, high permeability, low coercivity and considerable magneto-crystalline anisotropy and a high Curie temperature and high saturation magnetization and low coercivity, among other characteristics, in order to achieve a lower proportion of transmission and reflection. In the context of electromagnetic interference (EMI) suppression applications, the desirable characteristics consist of attributes for thermal stability, high dielectric losses, and high magnetic losses. Even though a significant amount of investigation has already been conducted in this area, the fulfillment of optimal requirements for electromagnetics wave absorbers, which include a tiny matching thickness, a wide absorption bandwidth and very low reflection loss and perfect impedance matching is still a difficult challenge to accomplish.

7.5 Different Approaches for Analysis of Microwave Absorption

7.5.1 Methodology for Open Circuit

With this method, an electromagnetic wave that strikes a sample can be transmitted, absorbed, or reflected. The technique is known as open-circuit since no device is obstructing the substance. Thus, incident power = Transmitted power + Reflected power + Absorbed power.

Using experimentally determined S-parameters from VNA, the absorption percentage is computed according to the following relation:

$$\begin{aligned}\text{Absorption (A) in percentage (\%)} &= 100 - \text{Reflected power (R)} \\ &\quad - \text{Transmitted power (T)} \\ &= 100 - \left[100\left(10^{\frac{-RL}{10}}\right)\right] - \left[100\left(10^{\frac{-TL}{10}}\right)\right]\end{aligned} \tag{7.2}$$

Where, RL = 20 $log_{10} S_{11}$ and TL = 20 $log_{10} S_{21}$ and S_{11} and S_{21} are S- parameter

$$S_{11} = \text{reflection coefficient}$$

$$S_{21} = \text{Transmission coefficient}$$

7.5.2 Methodology for Short Circuits

In this technique, using complex electromagnetic parameters generated through experimentation, the values of reflection loss are simulated throughout the sample's different thicknesses. This technique is also known as the "back-metal plate technique" since it is supposed that a metal plate is placed on the rear side of the material. The metal plate blocks the transmission of electromagnetic waves, so when they strike the sample, they are either absorbed or reflected.

As a result, incident power is equal to the addition of solely reflected power and absorbed power. Incident power = Reflected power + Absorbed power.

Calculating the absorption in % is done as follows:

$$\begin{aligned}\text{Absorption (A) in percentage (\%)} &= 100 - \text{Reflected power (R)} \\ &= 100 - \left[100\left(10^{\frac{-RL}{10}}\right)\right]\end{aligned} \tag{7.3}$$

In this method, absorption maxima and reflection loss minima simply match, therefore these terms have interchangeable usage.

7.5.3 Impedance Matching

The requirements of impedance matching must be met for perfect absorption. The following relation is used to compute reflection loss:

$$\text{Reflection Loss (RL)} = 20\log_{10}\left[\frac{Z_n - 1}{Z_n + 1}\right], \text{ where } Z_n \text{ is normal wave impedance}$$

$$\text{Now, } Z_n = \frac{Z_i}{Z_o} = \sqrt{\frac{\mu_r}{\varepsilon_r}}\tan\left(\frac{2\pi ft\sqrt{\mu_r\varepsilon_r}}{c}\right), \tag{7.4}$$

where Z_i is input impedance, Z_o is the characteristic impedance (377 Ω). μ_r is complex permeability, ε_r is complex permittivity, f is frequency of operation, t is the thickness of sample and c is speed of light in vacuum.

The condition for the Perfect absorption is that there should be no reflection, i.e., $Z_n \rightarrow 1$. It signifies that the input impedance of the wave (Z_i) must be identical to the characteristic impedance (Z_o). Z_o is equivalent to a resistance of 377 Ω without any imaginary component. Consequently, the real component of Z_i should be exactly 377 Ω, while the imaginary component should be nearly zero. The Z_n values are computed and matched with the RL spectra. If the RL dips correlate to Z_n values that are almost equal to unity, it can be claimed that the criterion of impedance matching has been satisfied.

7.6 Narrowband Metamaterial Absorbers

The initial development of the Metamaterial (MTM) absorber may be traced back to 2006, when a design employing split-ring resonators (SRR) with the support of a resistive sheet was developed [47]. The electromagnetic wave/magnetic field in this structure is either perpendicular or parallel to the split-ring resonators (SRR) array/split-ring resonators SRR plane. A resistive sheet is used to deposit an SRR array in order to achieve impedance matching with the surrounding free space. Both transmission as well

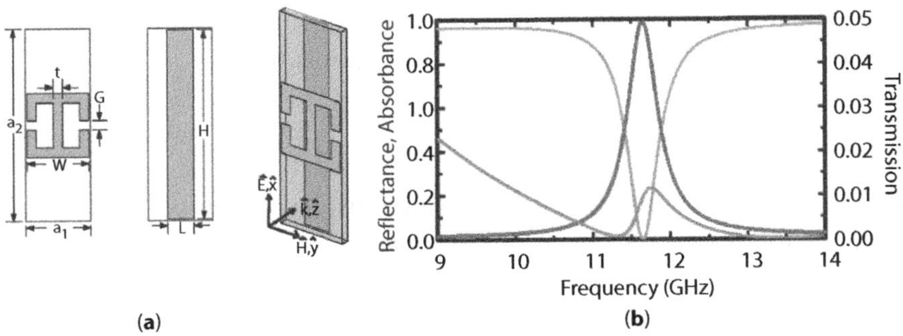

Figure 7.7 The image displays a planar MTM absorber, with (a) representing the unit cell and (b) providing a plot of absorbance, reflectance, and transmission values as a function of microwave frequency. Reproduced from [2] with permission.

as reflection coefficients are measured to be below -20dB at a frequency of 2GHz., indicating complete absorption. This configuration is superior to a flat structure with a limited absorption bandwidth

In 2008, a novel planar MTM absorber was introduced, featuring a flame retardant (FR-4) substrate positioned between electric ring resonators (ERR) and cut wires [27]. This study presents the initial planar metamaterial absorber featuring a sub wavelength structure. The predicted absorption of the absorber is around 96% at a frequency of 11.65 GHz, whereas the experimental result is 88% at a frequency of 11.5 GHz. The absorption frequency and intensity are contingent upon the resonator's geometry and the thickness of the substrate. Numerous MTM absorbers that have different spectral ranges have been implemented based on the aforementioned designs shown in Figure 7.7 [2, 28–38].

7.6.1 Broadband Metamaterial Absorbers

The enhancement of bandwidth in metamaterial absorbers can be achieved by employing multiple methodologies. The design incorporates several advanced techniques, including (a) structures with multiple layers [37, 38], (b) numerous unit cells with resonant properties [49, 50], (c) lumped components [52], and (d) dielectrics having significant amounts of loss [52, 53].

A proposal was made for a broadband metamaterials absorber that consists of in a manner stacked resonant patches of varying diameters. As illustrated in Figure 7.8, the device comprises an metamaterial absorber with twenty metal patch layers, each having a thickness of the net that is smaller than the wavelength at which it operates. The entire width absorption at half maximum is claimed to be approximately 86%. Ultra-broad

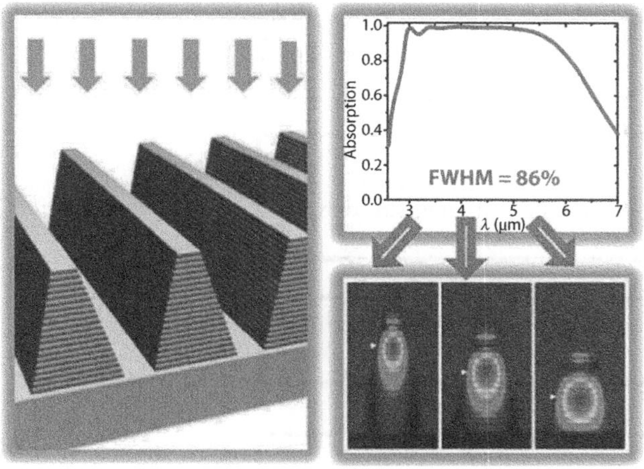

Figure 7.8 Displays an image showing a saw-toothed MTM absorber, accompanied by its corresponding absorption spectrum. Courtesy [39].

bandwidth is achieved by absorbing higher frequency electromagnetic waves at upper portion of patches and blocking lower frequency electromagnetic (EM) waves at lower portion of patches [36].

7.7 Electromagnetic Metamaterial Design Consideration

The methodology of electromagnetic metamaterial design is shown in Figure 7.9.

7.7.1 Design Criteria and Their Limitations

A further way to modify the absorptivity is to alter the various planned parameters. Using the adjusted parameters, the highest level of absorption may also be achieved by adjusting the substrate thickness (t), microstrip line width, and unit cell periodicity (p) [27]. The formula for substrate thickness and unit cell periodicity expressed in terms wavelength (Λ_0), can be described as follows:

$$\text{thickness}(\text{t})\text{of substrate} < \Lambda_0/20.$$

$$\text{Unit cell}(\text{p})\text{periodicity} < \Lambda_0/4 (8).$$

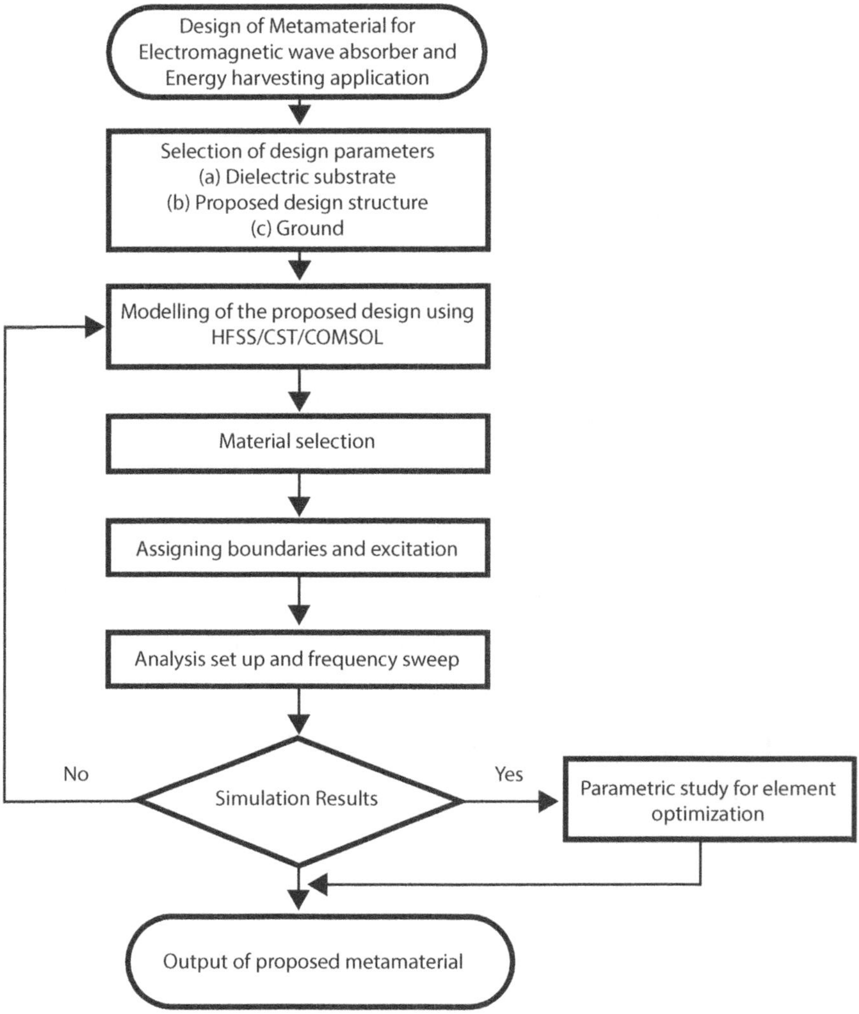

Figure 7.9 Flow chart showing metamaterial absorber simulation step.

7.7.2 Dielectric Characteristics of the Substrate

To achieve maximum absorption, the effect of the refractive index of the dielectric material is adjusted while maintaining the same values for other design parameters. Changes in the refractive index of the dielectric's materials cause a significant variation in the resonance frequency. Nearly optimal absorption is achieved with a refractive index of 2.5. Materials with a refractive index greater than 5, i.e., $n > 5$, are not recommended for achieving perfect absorption.

7.7.3 Polarization Angle and Oblique Angle

In electromagnetic waves, the polarization angle refers to the orientation of the electric field vector that either strikes or enters an item, while the oblique angle refers to an angle that is not perpendicular or parallel to a certain reference line or surface.

A properly polarized Metamaterial Absorber (MA) is one whose absorption remains constant over a range of polarization angles. As a result of oblique incidence, the following is the reflection coefficient in TM and TE [28]:

$$\Gamma_{\text{TM}}(\omega) = \frac{Z(\omega)Cos\theta_{t\_} - Z_0 Cos\theta_{i\_}}{Z(\omega)Cos\theta_{t\_} + Z_0 Cos\theta_{i\_}} \tag{7.5}$$

$$\Gamma_{\text{TE}}(\omega) = \frac{Z(\omega)Cos\theta_{i\_} - Z_0 Cos\theta_{t\_}}{Z(\omega)Cos\theta_{i\_} + Z_0 Cos\theta_{t\_}} \tag{7.6}$$

Where Z(ω), θ_t and θ_t represent the wave impedance, transmission angle and incidence angle, respectively. These two angles may have an impact on the reflection coefficient, which in turn may have an impact on the absorption in the TM or TE mode. Designed when building a wideband and multiband metamaterial absorber, it is essential to consider a few key features.

7.7.4 Frequency of Resonance

The resonant frequency refers to the specific frequency at which the MA system is functioning. In the event of a multiband system, there will exist many working frequencies. Conversely, in the case of a wideband system, the absorber will operate within a range of frequencies. The intended resonance frequencies are contingent upon the structural design as well as the dimensions of the substrate, including its length and width.

7.7.5 Substrate Dimensions

The substrate functions as the intermediary layer in the design and is a crucial parameter in terms of both material composition and thickness. The substrates that are commercially available include FR4 and Rogers. The variation in thickness is contingent upon the resonance frequency.

7.7.6 Design of Patches

The design of patches is a crucial parameter in metamaterial absorbers, with various reported absorbers exhibiting distinct and innovative designs. The absorbers work at varying frequencies depending on the designs.

7.8 Applications of Electromagnetic Metamaterial Absorbers Are Classified on Frequency Range

Metamaterial absorbers are classified on the basis of frequency range from microwave to optical as shown in Figure 7.10.

7.8.1 Microwave Absorber

The 300 MHz to 30 GHz frequency band comprises where the microwave MMA works. Electromagnetic shielding (EMS) is useful in military surveillance and other radar applications, and most microwave frequency MMAs have been developed for X-band applications. To build metamaterial absorbers (MAs) that have multiband absorption, this can be achieved by connecting multiple unit cells employing fractal structures or a coplanar configuration. This is possible by using.

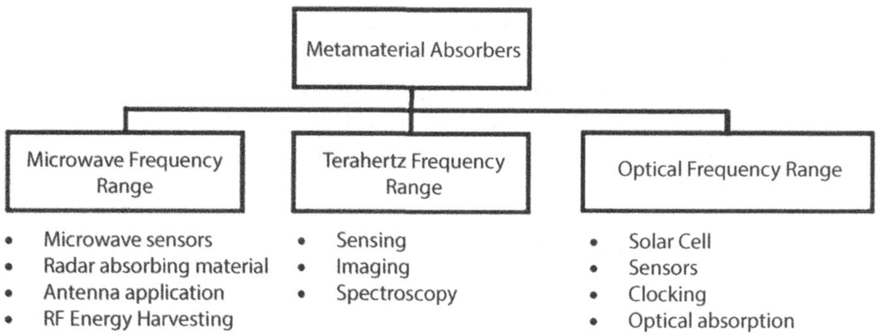

Figure 7.10 Application metamaterial absorber with respect to different frequencies.

7.8.2 Terahertz Wave Absorber

The terahertz MMA operates throughout the frequency range of 300 GHz to 10 THz. Terahertz technology has recently become prominent as a broad sector for the discovery of technologies that will be used in the next generation. In addition, THz absorbers have been investigated because of the potential applications they have in a variety of fields, including astronomy, medical sensing, military, security, industrial operations, and wireless communication, among others. Researchers are interested in terahertz MMA because of its ability to permeate materials like cloth, paper, and plastics, as well as its potential applications in imaging. They have the ability to operate within a spectrum that spans terahertz (THz) to visible frequencies, and their geometrical dimensions are modifiable. One potential feature of the structure's building design that helps researchers bridge the THz gap is its flexibility. The use of sensing in the biomedical field has drawn scientists interested in terahertz multiplexing.

7.8.3 Millimeter Wave Absorber

The millimeter wave MMAs, which operate within the frequency range of thirty gigahertz to three hundred gigahertz, i.e., 30 GHz to 300 GHz, are characterized by their small size, great performance, and ability to demonstrate unique functions.

Although water and water vapor greatly absorb these millimeter waves, dielectric materials like polymers and textiles allow them to pass through easily. An important use for a material possessing millimeter wave qualities is in the encoding of invisible to the untrained human eye marks, signs, and barcodes on items like railroad cars and cargo containers. Their high bandwidth and restricted range are the cause of this. The main disadvantage of millimeter wave absorbers is their low light transmittance, which makes it impossible for them to be utilized as transparent shielding windows in some circumstances and limits their versatility in conformal applications. The wave in millimeters nearly one millimeter is the wavelength at which MMA was intended to operate. The use of millimeter wave MMA in wireless communications, radar, and imaging has drawn the attention of scientists and researchers in recent times. When it comes to improving the overall efficiency of the systems and providing necessary electromagnetic protection, millimeter wave absorbers are extensively used for the purpose of disperse jamming signals. A novel method for implementing millimeter wave absorber that may separately alter electric and magnetic responses is offered by conformal absorbers.

7.9 Applications and Research Area of Electromagnetic Metamaterial Absorber

There are specialized materials called microwave absorbers that can attenuate or even completely absorb the power of microwaves. A wide range of issues, including internal cavity resonance, antenna pattern shaping, and high-frequency interference are resolved by MAs [37]. The finding of enhanced applications in the range of optical to microwave frequencies has been made possible by intense study of Metamaterial Absorber. Electromagnetic wave (EMW) absorbers are utilized in many applications across distinct frequency bands of the electromagnetic spectrum. A few examples are shown in Figure 7.11.

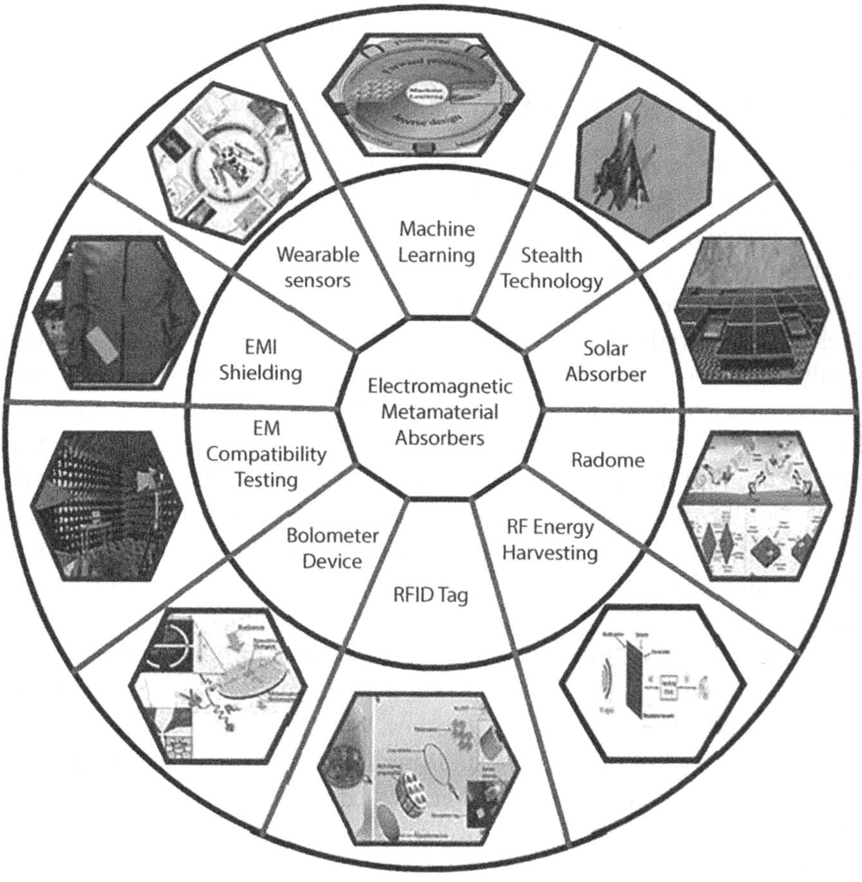

Figure 7.11 Application of electromagnetic metamaterial absorber.

7.9.1 Machine Learning

Machine learning-assisted metamaterials in biomedical applications are used for sensing with high accuracy to learn about the behavior of absorbers and to make predictions about the absorption values for intermediate frequencies. An Extreme Randomized Tree (ERT) regression model that is helped by machine learning is employed. The MMA sensor that is being suggested, which has been designed using an ERT model, has the potential to be utilized in biological applications for the detection of glucose and malaria [54]. Framework predicts and design metamaterial absorber accurately and efficiently. It achieved high fitting coefficient for absorption and reflection spectra predication. On demand design framework suitable for different structures and material. Future work includes applying the framework to more complex material [55–58].

7.9.2 Stealth Technology

Broadband metamaterial absorbers have demonstrated the highest absorption levels at X-band, indicating potential for stealth applications against X-band radars [59, 60]. The RCS, an ideal metamaterial absorber, is wrapped around a metal cylinder, which was reduced 232 cm 2 to 0.60 cm 2 at frequency 0.87 THz, demonstrating the effectiveness of flexible metamaterial film in reducing the radar cross section of metallic object [61]. An absorber of broadband infrared stealth metamaterial with a metal-dielectric-metal structures featuring multilayers is proposed. This arrangement achieves selective heat radiation in the infrared band by using high-temperature-resistant materials rather than precious metals with low melting points. The structure's five-layer structure matches atmospheric absorption spectra and maintains radiation reduction rates over 80% [62, 63].

7.9.3 Solar Absorber

This is a metamaterial absorber design that achieves perfect absorption in microwave, infrared, and visible frequencies for solar cell applications, regardless of polarization angle [64, 65]. Metamaterial absorbers achieve 99.99% absorption at 403.5 THz, with a structure that is polarization and angle of incident insensitive for solar cell efficiency [66]. A wideband perfect absorber featuring three concentric circular ring resonators for solar cells, demonstrating over 99% absorption in the visible spectrum and evaluating its thermal performance [67]. A dual-band perfect metamaterial absorber with 99.9% absorption, suitable for solar cell applications, and a wide-frequency tunable ideal absorber with perfect absorption, offering potential applications in filters and solar cells [68]. Titanium Carbide pyramid-shaped absorber with 88% efficiency for solar spectrum (400-2000nm) suitable for solar cell applications, using MIM configuration and magnetic resonance for high absorptance [69]. A dual-band metamaterial absorber with circular shapes and rectangular gaps was developed to improve solar cell efficiency, achieved absorption rate of 99.32% at 68.35THz and 99.98% at 80.2 THz [70]. A broad angle of incidence, polarization insensitive absorption, and broadband metamaterial solar spectrum absorber is presented in the study. The three-layer absorber uses the dielectric of a single silicon dioxide (SiO_2) layer sandwiched between the tungsten metal and the meta surface. It attains near-unity absorption at the 572.23 nm wavelength and 99% average absorption between 400 and 750 nm. Solar cells, thermo-photovoltaics, and energy harvesting devices can all use this type of design [71].

7.9.4 Radome

EM performance of Frequency Selective Surface (FSS) structures for dual/multiband metamaterials for microwave and millimeter-wave (MMW) radome applications using the TLTM method. The proposed four-layer structure shows superior transmission efficiency over 45.8-53.1 GHz and 93.0-97.1 GHz, making it suitable for designing normal incidence and streamlined nosecone radomes [72]. Metamaterial-based FSS structure using the TLTM method. The structure demonstrated superior performance compared to conventional monolithic radomes, with over 95% power transmission over a wide frequency range and low reflection, making it suitable for normal incidence and streamlined broadband airborne radome design [73]. High dielectric permittivity substrates can improve angular stabilization for transverse electric polarization and metal vias for transverse magnetic polarization, but high temperature and pressure pose challenges to practical application of invisible radomes [74]. Microstrip patch antenna design both with and without a metamaterial radome composed of many layers of liquid split ring resonator. The design improves gain by 11% and S_{11} by 27%. This liquid metamaterial radome is suitable for electronic warfare radar antennas, aiding in sensitive target detection [75]. Advantages, including polarization independence, highly targeted electromagnetic properties, and a propensity to spontaneously unite with the magnetic field, were demonstrated by the constructed swastika-shaped MTM-FSS cell. In contrast to a half-wave monolithic radome that has been optimized, the proposed hemispherical radome wall demonstrated better electromagnetic performance. The MTM radome is multilayered, with an Arlon inner layer and quartz laminate outer layer. Although the development cost is higher than monolithic radome, the EM performance is better than monolithic radome for modern airborne radar systems [76]. Multifunctional sandwiched composite with pyramid-shaped metamaterial dispersion engineering and radome integration into a metamaterial antenna array. The metamaterial (MA) provides mechanical strength and functions as a high pass and low absorption filter. The metamaterial MA serves as an antenna radiator, providing high band efficiency radiation performance and features of out-of-band RCS reduction. The radome Integrated sandwiched antenna provides improved mechanical strength, reduced RCS characteristics, and good radiation performance [77]. A phase- and amplitude-adjustable metasurface radome enables low radar cross section (RCS), wideband higher gain, and lower side lobe level (SLL) antenna performance at 9.8 GHz, validated through simulations and measurements [78]. Researchers developed and created a bilayer metasurface that is optically transparent, light weight, and possesses extreme asymmetry in both microwave absorption and reflection. This invisible metasurface has the ability to increase the gain of a multifunctional antenna modulus while simultaneously decreasing its RCS, all without compromising the antenna's optical or optoelectronic operational performance. The transparent radome has the ability to reduce the relative cross section of a microstrip patch antenna by above 10 dB in the frequency band between 9 GHz and 7.5 GHz, and it can boost the broadside gain of the antenna by 6.1 dBi at 8.1 GHz [79]. To increase the range of detection of commercial millimeter wave radar sensors by fastening the wire structure MTM radome for the 3T4R series-fed patch antenna arrays and a composite MTM radome to the 60 GHz AiP radar sensor. The MTM radome's cross-type star structure to overcome beam offsets and improve overall radar detection range by the proposed structure of square periodic. Additional Cheaper FR4 substrates can be used to build metamaterial radomes [80]. For Ka-band satellite communication, design a low-power RCS using (AFSR) radome with great performance. To be able to function, the antennas, which are frequency-selective surfaces composed of a band-pass bottom layer and a metamaterial absorber top layer, work at frequencies of 19 and 29 GHz. Simulations and measurements show minimal gain degradations and 10dB bandwidth of radar cross section reduction [81].

7.9.5 Radio Frequency Energy Harvesting

Electromagnetic wave absorbers are utilized in solar cells to enhance the collection of solar energy by virtue of their exceptional absorptive properties. The cells have been designed so that they possess a surface impedance that is matched to free space, leading to complete absorption and, therefore, maximum energy harvesting. The field of vibrational energy collection is expanding rapidly due to the growth of networks of wireless sensors. A substitute method to battery power is required, which involves the utilization of a micro-engineering device to extract mechanical stimulation from the vibrations of the surrounding environment [82, 83]. A new multiple bands and multilayers metamaterial absorber-based harvester, which has been created, tested experimentally and designed demonstrated. A multiband structure, with three layers resonator, possesses larger absorption bandwidths and higher degrees of absorption in the microwave frequency range like satellite communication WiMAX and, GSM, bands. The structure's absorption level and response to frequency are largely unaffected by incident angles, making it a promising candidate for wireless communication bands in energy harvesting instruments [84]. Design RF energy harvesting retractable antenna employing Schottky diodes and the metamaterial perfect absorber. The Fabry-Perot cavity resonance enhances energy capture and rectification efficiency, resulting in a factor of 16 improvement in radio frequency (RF) to direct current (DC) conversion [85]. A triple band is present in the ultrathin dual-layer foldable metamaterial absorber for use in applications involving radio frequency energy harvesting. Absorber consists of six concentric annular units with metallic resonators made of copper foil self-adhesive tape. The absorber is compact, thin, and exhibits triple absorption peaks at different frequencies. The absorber's RF performance is numerically computed, showing improved absorption values for different polarization and incidence angle variations [86]. A metamaterial absorber achieved ultra-wideband absorption over 90% from 4.8THz to 15.65 THz, with relative bandwidth up to 100%. Surface currents, resonances, and current distributions enhance absorption [87]. PCB-fabricated triple-band absorber with a single-layered metallic patch meets angular stability criteria for normal and oblique incidences, making it suitable for real-time applications [88]. Metamaterial (MTM) perfect absorbers offer an option that shows promise for gathering electromagnetic energy from the surrounding environment in areas with low levels of power density. These adjustable, extremely effective, and compact in size rectennas improve RF-DC conversion efficiency, eliminate reflection, and overcome high resistance. Their ultra-small thickness allows for portable, low-profile wireless power transferring (WPT) devices [89]. Compact, thin microwave energy harvesting absorber with high absorptivity rates, suitable for use in unmanned aerial vehicle devices with microwave energy harvesting systems [90]. The polarization-insensitive triple band perfect meta surface absorber for radio frequency energy harvesting, which has a high harvesting efficiency of 84% and 94.4% at 5.97 and 3.07 GHz, respectively, has been addressed, in line with simulation results [91].

7.9.6 Wireless Communications

Electromagnetic wave (EMW) absorbers have become essential for absorbing the harmful radiation released by electronic consumer devices like cell phones, satellite communications, 4G/5G/6G communications, RFID systems, Wi-Fi devices, wearable devices, and other technologies. This absorption enhances the safe utilization of these gadgets for humanity. Wearable Metamaterials Absorber (WMMA), a promising material of interest for indoor radar clear applications, consists of a backing ground plate, square ring resonators, along with a textile substrate with 18.9% absorptivity [92]. A flexible broadband microwave absorber (MA) is made from metallized fabric, scuba knitting fabric and resistive film patterns with absorption bands of 8.9GHz to 15.2 GHz and 11.2GHz to 24.1GHz, respectively. The metamaterials absorber (MA) is a suitable application in flexible microwave products, such as electromagnetic (EM) shielding and microwave stealth fabric [93, 94]. MMA in UHF-band, with excellent absorption properties MMA in the UHF band, which operates throughout the global UHF-RFID operating band (860–960 MHz), has good absorption qualities. The RFID experiment demonstrates its feasibility, and further investigation is going on about how miniaturization of thickness and wide-angle absorption could enhance system reliability [95]. The Minkowski fractal shape is employed in the creation of a lightweight metamaterial panel for multipath mitigation in UHF-RFID systems, offering excellent angular stability and high miniaturization capabilities [96]. Develop a thin, multi-resonance absorber using metamaterials on a grounded dielectric substrate to suppress electromagnetic interference in RF-ID systems, achieving two absorption peaks at different wavelengths at 2.45 GHz and 0.88 GHz, and maintaining high absorption levels up to 30° [97]. The design methodology focuses on external coupling rather than internal losses, resulting in an ultra-thin and compact structure. The MPA has a 175.6% higher gain and a low-profile design, making it is a bright prospect for future portable or stationary RFID applications [98]. The square loop FSS design allows control of reflection coefficient, allowing easy setting of 3.5 GHz and 5.8 GHz resonance frequencies [99]. A bilayer poly di methyl siloxane (PDMS) composite microwave absorbers, enhancing RFID systems on conductive surfaces with high reflection loss and shielding, enhancing tag detection and reducing interference [100]. Metamaterial absorber (MMA) for microwave signal absorption from Wi-Fi frequencies, offering 99.2% and 99.9% maximum absorption, flexibility for frequency tuning, and excellent angular stability [101].

7.9.7 Bolometer Devices

Demonstrated metamaterial metal-based bolometer elements, enabling the development of arrays of metal-based, integrated broadband metamaterial bolometer spectrometers, allowing simultaneous light polarization analysis without external components [102]. A researcher developed a monolithic resonant THz detector, using a micro-bolometer sensor and metamaterial absorber (MA), which offers real-time THz imaging capabilities and is compact, low-cost, and easily extending to focal plane array image formats [103]. A metamaterial absorber-based microbolometer with 185 nm thickness allows for adjustable wavelength and thermal distribution. The absorption wavelength can be adjusted from 2.4 nm to 10.2 nm, with a peak absorption of 90%. This technology offers potential for thermal imaging in mid-infrared and far-infrared regimes [104]. A microbolometer using a broadband metamaterial absorber (MMA) is improved in functionality, enhancing its temperature sensors. The metamaterial absorbers are included in the device using square shape resonators on the silicon nitride layer. Comparatively, MMA improves IR responsivity by 60% without sacrificing response time, which is minimized since the thermal mass is small [105]. A bolometer device in the THz range, which is also highly sensitive and compact in size, was developed and tested. It uses a carbon black (CB) - poly di methyl siloxane layer with TCR ranging from $3.11\%/K$ to $1.88\%/K$ and a metamaterial absorber to detect irradiated THz waves. The maximum change in resistance was 1.02%, higher than background thermal noise [106]. Two MAs with nanostrip antennas were designed using MIM structure. The TM polarized light absorption averages are 0.8300 and 0.7969 in 5.3 μm – 6.6 μm spectral bands, respectively. For spectral and polarization selective detection, the metamaterials absorbers are integrated with VOx microbolometers [107].

7.9.8 EM Compatibility Devices and EMI Shielding

An electromagnetic wave absorber is commonly employed in the industry of consumer electronics to reduce electromagnetic interference (EMI), improve electromagnetic compatibility of devices, and advance technologies related to EMI shielding in both consumer and industrial electronics. The modeling and analysis of ferrite-based absorbers for applications in the low-frequency range, in the broadband microwave frequency range, pyramidal absorbers were used, and the combination of the ferrite tile and pyramidal dielectric absorbers. For the practical point of view, aspects of designing hybrid absorbers, including carbon loading and matching layer influence, and the use of metamaterial structures or graphene material for millimeter-wave spectrum extension [108]. Screen-printing technology has been used to design and fabricate a compact, ultrathin, and flexible meta surface for band stop electromagnetic interference shielding. The prototype, a 1.8 GHz shield, has been validated, offering a flexible, lightweight shield for protecting critical electronics instruments [109]. For electromagnetic shielding applications, use reconfigurable frequency-selective surfaces (RFSS). The RFSS features square loops shorted separated by uniform distance, offering wideband frequency tuning with a 1:2,3,4 ratio. It covers 3.5, 5, and 5.8 GHz, shielding, ISM/WiMAX, and WiMAX WLAN bands. The initial model is fabricated and validated with measurements [110]. The study explores the use of metamaterial-based absorbers to reduce electromagnetic emissions from high-speed system enclosures, demonstrating significant reductions in measured emission patterns [111]. Metamaterial absorbers are custom-designed to reduce radiated emissions from system shield boxes, using cavity analysis to evaluate efficacy. Complex permittivity and permeability design expedites emission reduction in high-speed differential signaling systems [112]. In investigations of the application of a metamaterial absorber in 7T and 9.4T MRI systems as an RF shield, results showed improved transmitted efficiency and local-specific absorption rate (SAR) distribution, with a 22% reduction in peak specific absorption rate (SAR) value. This approach could lead to new applications in MRI [113]. Proposes a deca-band dual-sided FSS absorber suitable for applications in the X- to K-band, reducing transmission minimum by 5.5%. The unit cell is polarization insensitive, stable up to 60°, and has potential for versatile applications [114]. Metamaterials Absorber with double elliptical resonator based electromagnetic interference shielding application for TE mode, achieved quadruple absorption, polarization, and incident angle insensitivity up to 60°. Metamaterial Absorber achieved above 98% absorption and measured SE above 80 db. The equivalent circuit model was verified using an ADS simulator, for future EMI shielding applications [115]. Proposes a wideband mirror symmetric metamaterial for electromagnetic interference shielding applications. The structure consists of an alphabet U-shaped metal connected split ring and four similar quarter-circles on a low-loss compact dielectric substrate. The metamaterial enhances the range of frequencies that are blocked or attenuated by a shield from 4.33GHz to1.6GHz, with a 170.63% improvement in SE. Further, the structure displays wideband near-zero and ENG properties. A novel metamaterial in the C / X band is being designed for wideband EMI shielding applications [116].

7.9.9 Biomedical Sensors

Electromagnetic wave absorbers are utilized in a range of sensors, including healthcare sensors, multi-frequency sensors, and temperature sensors. These sensors are employed in numerous application fields like glucose level assessments, cancer detection, and the diagnostics of blood disease. A novel device uses terahertz electromagnetic waves to detect colon cancer using surface plasmon polaritons. This method detects water concentrations in health and cancerous colon tissue, indicating cancerous tissue. The device is believed to be less invasive, faster, and cheaper, potentially reducing colon cancer death rates [117]. Researchers present a metamaterial biosensor based on gold layers arranged in a hexagonal pattern on a substrate made of polyamide for early cancer detection. Strong linear performance, high field confinement, high absorption, and quality factor are attained for cancer detection in early stage by basal cell, which refers to a type of cell found in the basal layer of the skin. Breast cell refers to a cell that is part of the breast tissue, and brevican cell detection, having a typical sensitivity of 1650 GHz/RIU with an average sensitivity of 1649.8 GHz/RIU [118]. Terahertz metamaterial absorber for cancer detection, featuring combined circular ring resonators over a gallium arsenide substrate. With a high Q factor of 91.99 and sensitivity of 1450 GHz/RIU, the sensor's resonance mechanism is studied, making it appropriate for applications in biomedical sensing [119]. The sensitivity of a metamaterial-based near-infrared biosensor has been enhanced for detecting cancer cells, malaria infection, bacillus bacteria, and urine concentration, with an Au layer and graphene layer providing near-unity absorption [120]. An innovative metamaterial absorber intended to identify cancer cells in the terahertz range. This absorber has a high level of sensitivity towards even little fluctuations in the refractive index. It achieves a remarkable sensitivity of 1.491 THz/RIU across a wide range of refractive indices, from 1.34 to 1.40. The design's efficacy, determined by a Q-factor, is very high [121]. A dual-band terahertz MTM is made of aluminum, simplifying production and reducing costs. The TMA operates in dual frequency bands at 1.803 THz and 1.887 THz, with strong absorption of 97.27% and 98.04%, respectively.

The characteristics of detection are examined in biomedical applications, with corresponding sensitivities of 0.780 THz/RIU and 0.892 THz/RIU. Given that a wide variety of samples, including malignant cells, basal/breast/cervical cells, and human blood, are present in this range of RI, for practical uses, the THz (MTM) sensor could be a useful bio-sensor for identifying biological specimens for real-world applications [122].

7.9.10 Aeronautics and Defense

Electromagnetic wave absorbers are extensively utilized in stealth technologies particularly for hiding engines and radar absorbing materials. These devices are employed to mitigate the strength of the reflected signals emitted by the aircraft coverings, hence impeding the enemy's ability to readily detect defensive aircraft. The absorbers are comprised of very small layers of absorbent paints, which are applied to the aircraft's surface. Metamaterial absorber three - D specimen using a resistive films patch grid that stands up for ultra-wideband absorptions. The absorber achieves over 90% absorption from 3.9 to 26.2 GHz, with a lightweight areal density of 0.062 g/cm2. Design is similar to conventional honeycomb absorbers but offers wider absorption bands and more tunable performance [123]. A radar absorber system design method for multiple-band frequency applications, analyzing FSS parameters on TiO2/Al2O3 coating properties. A genetic algorithm approach is proposed for better absorption [124]. The research provides the measurement, insight, also design with small, absorbent substance for use in space applications. To tackle the issue of scan and mismatch phenomena, the initial surface was divided into two sectors, each optimized for a smaller angular range. The absorber achieved a reflection coefficient below -11.49 dB and absorption above 0.955 over the 13.99% frequency band. The multi-sector absorber approach absorber could be extended to more sectors for improved performance [125]. A radar absorber fabricated using a patch made of metallic coated use graphene material. The design yields good absorption (99.93%) in ultrawideband (1-60 GHz) and allows electric potential tuning by changing the graphene layer's fermi energy. Design's significant absorption in ultrawideband indicates potential applications in RF stealth technology, despite constraints on fabrication facility [126]. A design for a wideband metamaterial absorber for military and defense applications, optimized for 14.79 GHz and 13.1 GHz frequencies range in Ku band zone, utilizes low-cost materials and is suitable for indoor radars and airborne surveillance [127]. Integrated frequency selective surface (IFS) absorber is manufactured, modeled, and engineered to have good stealth qualities. The absorber is made up of a closed centroid honeycomb structure that is split, encased in four L-shaped sections, and ringed by four circular hexagonal rings. For glass fabric, the simulated pattern was tuned to minimize reflections. Custom Glass cloth imprinted with a resistive ink based on carbon was used to build the absorber. The simulated and experimental RC performances were found to be in good agreement, spanning Ku and X bands with 75.99% fractional bandwidth [128].

7.9.11 Imaging

Absorbers are necessary in imaging applications, including phase imaging, medical imaging, and thermal imaging, due to the utilization of various electromagnetic waves for imaging purposes. They are used to reduce the interference between closely positioned antennas, and to mitigate cavity resonance's detrimental impact in enclosed microwave integrated circuits (MMIC). For the purpose of stopping leaks from the microwave oven into the surrounding area, protective shields are utilized in these appliances. Regarding terahertz imaging that is multispectral and has polarization resolution, a multispectral 24 x 24 bolometric matrix structure has been developed. The construction has polarization selective absorption in an ultra-thin metamaterial absorber and terahertz to infrared conversion. Additionally, an excellent IR emissive layer is a component of its structure [129]. The study showcases the integration of broadband THz metamaterial and single band absorbers in a 180 nm CMOS process, forming THz detectors with NEPs of at least 108 pW/Hz and 10.4 n W/Hz, suitable for THz imaging systems [130]. A metal-insulator-metal metamaterial absorber that is compatible with CMOS geometry has been described, achieving 93% absorption for 10 bands in the MWIR spectrum. The absorption characteristics are invariant as much as 25° angles, making them appropriate for imaging systems. These absorbers can be made into inexpensive focal plane arrays by integrating them with detectors, with applications in gas detection, biological material identification, monitoring of pollutants and chemical sensing. Hybridizing MTM absorber and plasmonic metasurface technologies can create a synthetic multispectral substance that absorbs MWIR and visible light filters [131]. Metamaterial-based technology is used in a novel radar system for applications with higher sensing capacity imaging CRAs coated on the reflector antenna surface. Sensing capacity increases and creates spectral patterns and uncorrelated spatial in the near-field. An ADMM-based norm-1 regularized iterative technique is used to assess the system's performance. Standoff detection of security threats is made possible by the system's easy reconfiguration to work in the far field. There are intriguing new avenues for research when using other metamaterial absorbers combinations or all dielectric materials [132]. A genetic algorithm-based program has been developed to design metamaterial absorbers metal-based metal-insulator antennas using nanostrips for broadband, polarization-selective higher absorption in the mid-range IR. The top antenna pattern is iteratively optimized by the computer until the intended design target is attained. With a normal incidence polarization extinction ratio of 30 and an average absorption coefficient of 72.8% in the MWIR band, MIM absorbers with two-polarization selectivity and broadband high absorption were discovered. Additionally, the lightweight multiband infrared polarimetric imagers can be enabled by the program, and develop optimum solutions for various spectral bands [133]. Metamaterial absorber-based microwave imaging detector are designed for industrial electronics, medical (ISM) band, and scientific applications. The structure achieves excellent 2.51 GHz and 2.39 GHz absorption in simulation and empirical measurements. Schottky diodes are used for energy-harvesting applications, resulting in 84.2% dc conversion efficiency. The detector generates accurate images with minimal distortions, making it an innovative solution for wireless appliances [134]. Metamaterials are promising artificial electromagnetic materials that enable the creation of innovative imaging components and serve as a platform to verify exotic imaging concepts. The metamaterials design paradigm provides versatility, insight, and utility to many components in imaging systems, including lenses, spatial light modulators, objects, holograms, polarizers, sources, and detectors. These special qualities will be tapped by future imaging systems to advance the state of the art. While much research has been on individual imaging components or proof-of-concept imaging modalities, metamaterial-based imaging systems still have space to grow. For instance, traditional focal plane array-based imaging systems and the scarcity of low-cost, high-performance pixels make imaging at longer wavelengths challenging. Future research in metamaterials based tunable imaging components and systems might make long-wavelength metamaterial imaging more feasible, which would have an influence on infrared thermography, non-invasive cancer screening, and other medical imaging applications [135]. Four ultra-wideband metamaterial THz absorbers have been introduced for use in devices like bolometer detectors. The structures have high absorption rates of over 90%, 80%,70%, and 50%, having the bandwidths for relative absorption of 0.72,0.93, 1.29, and 1.43, respectively. Nickel and SU8 negative photoresist were used as the ground and metamaterial layers, with a 3μm minimal size for feature. The structure's broadband absorption allows for applications in bolometric imaging, scattering reduction, and thermal sensing [136]. A THz perfect metamaterial absorber (PMA) developed on a 3.5 dielectric constant polyimide substrate. With an absorptivity of above 98%, the PMA has five unique absorption peaks and four connected arms with asymmetric convolution. It delivers up to 60° of angular stability and polarization-independent operation. The PMA has a sensitivity of 16.99 GHz/PU on average and 88.4 GHz/PU at 2.90 THz at its peak [137]. A sandwich construction composed of compact and asymmetric metamaterial for THz imaging demonstrates distinct NIM behavior. Miniaturization principles are used, and various design variables are perturbed to identify the optimal metamaterial configuration. The study shows innovative performance by changing the s_{21} response at higher frequencies and revealing novel absorbance as a consequence of switching to sandwich architectures for the unit cell design [138].

7.9.12 Microwave Components

Electromagnetic wave (EMW) absorbers are utilized in a variety of microwave components, including filters, emitters, amplifiers, and switches, to ensure optimal performance. These components can effectively manage exceptionally high peak power levels with the assistance of absorbers.

7.10 Advancements in Metamaterials in Recent Times

2002: Lucent Technology developed the first resonant antenna.
2003: Making use of photonic crystal in metamaterials and techniques for producing electromagnetic metamaterials.
2005: Metamaterials were described as a grouping of man-made building blocks that are meant to have special electromagnetic properties.
2010: Metamaterials have been employed as artificial media structures. Metamaterials emerged as artificially engineered media that offer the ability to manipulate electromagnetic characteristics as desired.
2017: A commercially available program facilitating the utilization of metamaterial-based satellite antennas was introduced.
2023: Hepta-band THz metamaterial absorber for biomedical application with high sensitivity.

Potential application in biomedical field like bacterial infection and malaria.

7.11 Conclusion and Prospects for the Future

This article provides a comprehensive analysis of the historical progression of metamaterial-based absorbers across different frequency ranges, spanning microwave to optical. Metamaterials exhibit great potential in the development of absorbers and the investigation of many unconventional electromagnetic phenomena. The proposed metamaterial absorbers with uncomplicated designs can achieve optimal absorption at either lower or higher frequencies. These designs have the potential to be modified in order to showcase supplementary components that are relevant to the real applications that are intended.

The size of the unit cell poses the greatest challenge for MMAs operating at gigahertz (GHz) and low frequency ranges. Alternatively, microwave frequency flexible metamaterial absorber (MMAs) can be achieved through straightforward manufacture. Nevertheless, the ability to function in various situations and the intricate process of manufacturing continue to pose challenges for absorbers functioning at higher frequencies. The MMAs that have been optimized in the terahertz (THz) regime exhibit promising prospects for utilization in the domains of imaging and spectroscopy. Furthermore, the utilization later on of metamaterials (MMAs) in optical frequency applications necessitates a greater level of manufacturing tolerance. MMAs operating in the THz to GHz frequencies, such as absorbers in the visible range, necessitate less complex designs, more convenient manufacturing processes, and reduced production expenses.The primary objective behind the progress of metamaterials is to enhance research and development endeavors in the fields of defense, aerospace, and telecommunication. The employment of metamaterial absorbers has experienced significant growth in recent years due to their effective application in radar systems, warships, and specialized cellphones. Currently, international market producers include NKT Photonics AS, Fractal Antenna Systems Inc., Kymeta Corporation (US), JEM Engineering LLC (US), Multi wave (Switzerland), Metamaterial Technologies Inc. (Canada). Midiwise (UK) is the main player in the metamaterial market, specializing in the use of metamaterials for antenna and radar applications. The tremendous rise of metamaterials and their corresponding market can be attributed to several prominent operational companies. In recent times, numerous advanced nations have augmented their national defense spending, which may result in a rise in the utilization of (MTM) metamaterial absorbers for defense purposes. Considering the satellite communication growth, it will be necessary to deploy additional satellites in the future to guarantee seamless and secure connectivity worldwide. In essence, this would also result in a higher deployment of metamaterials. This review has undertaken a deliberate endeavor to encompass relevant scholarly works pertaining to the optical frequency to microwave frequency range, metamaterial absorbers encompassing their previous history progression, and additionally their numerous uses across many sectors.

References

1. Veselago, V.G., Electrodynamics of materials with negative index of refraction, in: *Electromagnetic Materials*, pp. 115–122, World Scientific, 2003.
2. Landy, N.I., *et al.*, Perfect metamaterial absorber. *Phys. Rev. Lett.*, **100**, 20, 207402, 2008.
3. Smith, D.R., *et al.*, Composite medium with simultaneously negative permeability and permittivity. **84**, 18, 4184, 2000.
4. Smith, D.R. and Kroll, N., Negative refractive index in left-handed materials. *PRL*, **85**, 14, 2933, 2000.
5. Zhang, X. and Liu, Z., Superlenses to overcome the diffraction limit. *NM*, **7**, 6, 435–441, 2008.
6. Zhu, W., *et al.*, Polarization conversion in U-shaped chiral metamaterial with four-fold symmetry breaking. **115**, 14, 2014.
7. Zhu, W., *et al.*, Hiding in the corner. **19**, 21, 20827–20832, 2011.
8. Yang, J.J., *et al.*, Metamaterial sensors. **2013**, 2013.
9. Raghavan, S. and Rajeshkumar, V., An overview of metamaterials in biomedical applications. *PER*, **25**, 369, 2013.
10. Wang, B., *et al.*, Chiral metamaterials: simulations and experiments. **11**, 11, 114003, 2009.
11. Zhu, W., *et al.*, Wideband giant optical activity and negligible circular dichroism of near-infrared chiral metamaterial based on a complementary twisted configuration. **15**, 12, 125101, 2013.
12. Kang, M., Wang, H.-T., Zhu, W., Wavefront manipulation with a dipolar metasurface under coherent control. *JAP*, **122**, 1, 2017.
13. Cui, T.J., *et al.*, Coding metamaterials, digital metamaterials and programmable metamaterials. **3**, 10, e218–e218, 2014.
14. Liu, Y., *et al.*, Transformational plasmon optics. **10**, 6, 1991–1997, 2010.
15. Zhu, W., Rukhlenko, I.D., Premaratne, M., Linear transformation optics for plasmonics. *JOSAB*, **29**, 10, 2659–2664, 2012.
16. Zhu, W., Rukhlenko, I.D., Premaratne, M., Maneuvering propagation of surface plasmon polaritons using complementary medium inserts. *IPJ*, **4**, 3, 741–747, 2012.
17. Hong, W., *et al.*, Multibeam antenna technologies for 5G wireless communications. **65**, 12, 6231–6249, 2017.

18. Si, L.-M., *et al.*, A compact, planar, and CPW-fed metamaterial-inspired dual-band antenna. **12**, 305–308, 2013.
19. Lin, F.H. and Chen, Z.N., Low-profile wideband metasurface antennas using characteristic mode analysis. *ITAP*, **65**, 4, 1706–1713, 2017.
20. Cao, W., *et al.*, Low-loss ultra-high-Q dark mode plasmonic Fano metamaterials. **37**, 16, 3366–3368, 2012.
21. Al-Adhami, A. and Ercelebi, E., A flexible metamaterial based printed antenna for wearable biomedical applications. *S*, **21**, 23, 7960, 2021.
22. Zhu, W. and Zhao, X., Adjusting the resonant frequency and loss of dendritic left-handed metamaterials with fractal dimension. *JAP*, **106**, 9, 2009.
23. Yi, J., *et al.*, Frequency-tunable and magnitude-tunable microwave metasurface absorbers enabled by shape memory polymers. **70**, 8, 6804–6812, 2022.
24. Li, X., *et al.*, Frequency-tunable and absorption/transmission-switchable microwave absorber based on a chitin-nanofiber-derived elastic carbon aerogel. **469**, 144010, 2023.
25. Wang, H., *et al.*, Highly efficient selective metamaterial absorber for high-temperature solar thermal energy harvesting. **137**, 235–242, 2015.
26. Culhaoglu, A.E., *et al.*, Mono-and bistatic scattering reduction by a metamaterial low reflection coating. **61**, 1, 462–466, 2012.
27. Guddala, S., Kumar, R., Ramakrishna, S.A., Thermally induced nonlinear optical absorption in metamaterial perfect absorbers. *APL*, **106**, 11, 2015.
28. Faktorová, D., Metamaterials applications in radiocommunication and biomedical engineering, in: *Proceedings of the 4th International Symposium on Applied Sciences in Biomedical and Communication Technologies*, 2011.
29. Watts, C.M., Liu, X., Padilla, W.J., Metamaterial electromagnetic wave absorbers. *AM*, **24**, 23, OP98–OP120, 2012.
30. Zhu, W., *et al.*, Optical metamaterial absorber based on leaf-shaped cells. **102**, 147–151, 2011.
31. Gordon, O., *et al.*, Metamaterial absorbers realized in an X-band rectangular waveguide. **21**, 11, 117801, 2012.
32. Zhu, W., Rukhlenko, I.D., Premaratne, M., Graphene metamaterial for optical reflection modulation. *APL*, **102**, 24, 2013.
33. Ra'di, Y., Simovski, C.R., Tretyakov, S.A., Thin perfect absorbers for electromagnetic waves: theory, design, and realizations. *PRA*, **3**, 3, 037001, 2015.
34. Liu, X., *et al.*, Infrared spatial and frequency selective metamaterial with near-unity absorbance. **104**, 20, 207403, 2010.
35. Park, J.W., *et al.*, Multi-band metamaterial absorber based on the arrangement of donut-type resonators. **21**, 8, 9691–9702, 2013.
36. Zhou, W., *et al.*, Microwave metamaterial absorber based on multiple square ring structures. **5**, 11, 2015.
37. Gu, S., Su, B., Zhao, X., Planar isotropic broadband metamaterial absorber. *JAP*, **114**, 16, 2013.
38. Cui, Y., *et al.*, Ultrabroadband light absorption by a sawtooth anisotropic metamaterial slab. **12**, 3, 1443–1447, 2012.

39. Kim, Y.J., *et al.*, Dual broadband metamaterial absorber. **23**, 4, 3861–3868, 2015.
40. Shen, Y., *et al.*, Ultrabroadband terahertz absorption by uniaxial anisotropic nanowire metamaterials. **27**, 21, 2284–2287, 2015.
41. Chen, Q., *et al.*, Nanowire-based ultra-wideband absorber for visible and ultraviolet light. **105**, 102–105, 2018.
42. Chen, H., *et al.*, Equivalent circuit model for left-handed metamaterials. **100**, 2, 2006.
43. Yen, T.-J., *et al.*, Terahertz magnetic response from artificial materials. **303**, 5663, 1494–1496, 2004.
44. Baena, J.D., *et al.*, Artificial magnetic metamaterial design by using spiral resonators. **69**, 1, 014402, 2004.
45. Yang, J., *et al.*, Optical transparent infrared high absorption metamaterial absorbers. **8**, 01, 1850007, 2018.
46. La Spada, L. and Vegni, L., Metamaterial-based wideband electromagnetic wave absorber. *OE*, **24**, 6, 5763–5772, 2016.
47. Tyurnev, V., Direct derivation and refinement of generalized Cohn-Matthaei formulas for resonator coupling coefficients in a microwave filter. *JCTE*, **53**, 554–557, 2008.
48. Bahl, I.J., *Lumped elements for RF and microwave circuits*, Artech House, 2022.
49. Gilbert, E., Impedance matching with lossy components. *ITCS*, **22**, 2, 96–100, 1975.
50. Sharma, S., *et al.*, Impedance matching techniques for microstrip patch antenna. **10**, 28, 1–16, 2017.
51. Engheta, N., Thin absorbing screens using metamaterial surfaces, in: *IEEE Antennas and Propagation Society International Symposium*, (IEEE Cat. No. 02CH37313), IEEE, 2002.
52. Qin, G., *et al.*, Lowering plasma frequency by enhancing the effective mass of electrons: A route to deep sub-wavelength metamaterials. **22**, 8, 087302, 2013.
53. Hao, J., Zhou, L., Qiu, M., Nearly total absorption of light and heat generation by plasmonic metamaterials. *PRB*, **83**, 16, 165107, 2011.
54. Jain, P., *et al.*, Machine learning assisted hepta band THz metamaterial absorber for biomedical applications. **13**, 1, 1792, 2023.
55. Gu, L., *et al.*, Optimized Design of Plasma Metamaterial Absorber Based on Machine Learning. *Photonics*, 2023, MDPI.
56. Jain, P., *et al.*, Machine Learning Techniques for Predicting Metamaterial Microwave Absorption Performance: A Comparison. **11**, 128774–128783, 2023.
57. Jain, P., *et al.*, Multiband Metamaterial absorber with absorption prediction by assisted machine learning. **307**, 128180, 2023.
58. Al-badri, K.S.L., Multi band metamaterials absorber for stealth applications. *LSTR*, **11**, 1, 133–144, 2019.

59. Kim, J., Han, K., Hahn, J.W., Selective dual-band metamaterial perfect absorber for infrared stealth technology. *SR*, **7**, 1, 1–9, 2017.
60. Ozden, K., *et al.*, Metamaterial based broadband RF absorber at X-band. **70**, 8, 1062–1070, 2016.
61. Iwaszczuk, K., *et al.*, Flexible metamaterial absorbers for stealth applications at terahertz frequencies. **20**, 1, 635–643, 2012.
62. Dincer, F., *et al.*, Design and analysis of perfect metamaterial absorber in GHz and THz frequencies. **29**, 18, 2492–2500, 2015.
63. Quan, C., *et al.*, High-temperature resistant broadband infrared stealth metamaterial absorber. **156**, 108579, 2022.
64. Huang, Q., *et al.*, Metamaterial electromagnetic wave absorbers and devices: Design and 3D microarchitecture. **108**, 90–101, 2022.
65. Dincer, F., *et al.*, Polarization angle independent perfect metamaterial absorbers for solar cell applications in the microwave, infrared, and visible regime. **144**, 93–101, 2014.
66. Mulla, B. and Sabah, C., Perfect metamaterial absorber design for solar cell applications. *WRCM*, **25**, 3, 382–392, 2015.
67. Rufangura, P. and Sabah, C., Theoretical and thermal characterization of a wideband perfect absorber for application in solar cells. *APA*, **122**, 1–8, 2016.
68. Zhang, Y., *et al.*, Dual band visible metamaterial absorbers based on four identical ring patches. **127**, 114526, 2021.
69. Raza, H.M.T. and Rana, A.S., Metamaterial Absorber for Solar Thermophotovoltaic Systems, in: *2022 Third International Conference on Latest trends in Electrical Engineering and Computing Technologies (INTELLECT)*, IEEE, 2022.
70. Mohammed, A.S., *et al.*, Design and Development of Perfect Dual-band Metamaterial Absorber Array to Enhance the Efficiency of Solar Energy Harvesting in Infrared Radiation, in: *2022 39th National Radio Science Conference (NRSC)*, IEEE, 2022.
71. Kumar, R., *et al.*, Broadband metamaterial absorber in the visible region using a petal-shaped resonator for solar cell applications. **142**, 115327, 2022.
72. Narayan, S., *et al.*, Electromagnetic performance analysis of novel multiband metamaterial FSS for millimeter wave radome applications. **31**, 1, 1, 2012.
73. Narayan, S. and Jha, R., A novel metamaterial FSS-based structure for wideband radome applications. *CMC*, **37**, 2, 97–108, 2013.
74. Liu, L. and Cha, H., Analysis and design of the invisible radome by LLumar glass. *JPDAP*, **47**, 7, 075105, 2014.
75. Patel, S.K., *et al.*, Liquid metamaterial based radome design. **60**, 9, 2303–2309, 2018.
76. Narayan, S., *et al.*, Novel metamaterial-element-based FSS for airborne radome applications. **66**, 9, 4695–4707, 2018.

77. Han, Y., *et al.*, Multi-functional sandwich structure with metamaterial antenna lattice cores: protection, radiation and absorption. **14**, 7, 593–599, 2020.
78. Mirzapour, M.I., Ghorbani, A., Azadi Namin, F., Metasurface Radome to Achieve a Wideband High Gain, Low RCS, and Low SLL Antenna. *IJR*, 1–8, 2022.
79. Ha, T.D., *et al.*, Optically transparent metasurface radome for rcs reduction and gain enhancement of multifunctional antennas. **71**, 1, 67–77, 2022.
80. Chao, C.-P., *et al.*, A Method for Improving the Detection Range of the 60-GHz Radar with a Metamaterial Radome. **1**, 719–728, 2023.
81. Xing, Z., *et al.*, Low-RCS Ka-band receiving and transmitting satellite communication antennas co-designed with high-performance absorbent frequency-selective radomes. **37**, 2, 190–206, 2023.
82. Beeby, S.P., *et al.*, Energy harvesting vibration sources for microsystems applications. **17**, 12, R175, 2006.
83. Priya, S. and Inman, D.J., *Energy harvesting technologies*, vol. 21, Springer, 2009.
84. Karaaslan, M., *et al.*, Microwave energy harvesting based on metamaterial absorbers with multilayered square split rings for wireless communications. **392**, 31–38, 2017.
85. Fowler, C. and Zhou, J., A metamaterial-inspired approach to RF energy harvesting. *APA*, 2017.
86. Kaur, K.P., *et al.*, Ultrathin dual-layer triple-band flexible microwave metamaterial absorber for energy harvesting applications. **29**, 1, e21646, 2019.
87. Xiao, Z., *et al.*, A three-dimensional ultra-broadband and polarization insensitive metamaterial absorber and application for electromagnetic energy harvesting. **31**, 6, 2168–2176, 2021.
88. Shukoor, M.A., *et al.*, Compact polarisation insensitive wide angular stable triple band absorber for RF energy harvesting, RCS reduction, and sensor applications. **31**, 9, e22763, 2021.
89. Akarsu, G., *et al.*, A novel 5G wideband metamaterial based absorber for microwave energy harvesting applications, in: *2021 8th International Conference on Electrical and Electronics Engineering (ICEEE)*, IEEE, 2021.
90. Fowler, C., *et al.*, High efficiency ambient RF energy harvesting by a metamaterial perfect absorber. **12**, 3, 1242–1250, 2022.
91. Agrahari, R., *et al.*, Triple-band metasurface absorber for RF energy harvesting applications. **65**, 8, 2252–2261, 2023.
92. Tak, J. and Choi, J., A wearable metamaterial microwave absorber. *IAWPL*, **16**, 784–787, 2016.
93. Yang, Y., *et al.*, Electromagnetic shielding using flexible embroidery metamaterial absorbers: Design, analysis and experiments. **222**, 111079, 2022.
94. Yang, Y., *et al.*, Design, characterization and fabrication of a flexible broadband metamaterial absorber based on textile. **69**, 103537, 2023.

95. Zuo, W., *et al.*, A miniaturized metamaterial absorber for ultrahigh-frequency RFID system. **16**, 329–332, 2016.
96. Venneri, F., *et al.*, Fractal-shaped metamaterial absorbers for multireflections mitigation in the UHF band. **17**, 2, 255–258, 2017.
97. Ryu, Y.-H. and Kim, S.-S., Design and Fabrication of Metamaterial Absorbers Used for RF-ID. *Korean J. Met. Mater.*, **58**, 2, 131–136, 2020.
98. Koohestani, M. and Ghaneizadeh, A., An ultra-thin double-functional metasurface patch antenna for UHF RFID applications. *SR*, **11**, 1, 857, 2021.
99. Vaz, L., *et al.*, Chipless RFID tag based on metamaterial absorbers, 2022.
100. Wei, C.-Y., *et al.*, Improving RFID performance through enhanced electromagnetic wave absorption with Fe2O3 and polytetrafluoroethylene-based bilayer polydimethylsiloxane composites. 108157, 2024.
101. Moniruzzaman, M., *et al.*, Tuning metallic stub loaded symmetrical resonator based dual band metamaterial absorber for wave shielding from Wi-Fi frequencies. **63**, 399–414, 2023.
102. Niesler, F.B., *et al.*, Metamaterial metal-based bolometers. **100**, 20, 2012.
103. Grant, J., *et al.*, A monolithic resonant terahertz sensor element comprising a metamaterial absorber and micro-bolometer. **7**, 6, 1043–1048, 2013.
104. Du, K., *et al.*, Wavelength and thermal distribution selectable microbolometers based on metamaterial absorbers. **7**, 3, 1–8, 2015.
105. Ma, W., *et al.*, Diode-based microbolometer with performance enhanced by broadband metamaterial absorber. **41**, 13, 2974–2977, 2016.
106. Kim, Y., *et al.*, Single-layer metamaterial bolometer for sensitive detection of low-power terahertz waves at room temperature. **28**, 12, 17143–17152, 2020.
107. Jiang, S., *et al.*, Metamaterial microbolometers for multi-spectral infrared polarization imaging. **30**, 6, 9065–9087, 2022.
108. Raad, S.H., Analysis and design of absorbers for electromagnetic compatibility applications, in: *RTEC*, p. 123, 2022.
109. Wang, L.B., *et al.*, Ultrathin and flexible screen-printed metasurfaces for EMI shielding applications. **53**, 3, 700–705, 2011.
110. Sivasamy, R., *et al.*, A wideband frequency tunable FSS for electromagnetic shielding applications. **60**, 1, 280–283, 2017.
111. Khoshniat, A. and Abhari, R., Design and evaluation of radiated emission metamaterial absorbers. *ITEC*, **61**, 4, 1314–1321, 2019.
112. Khoshniat, A. and Abhari, R., Metamaterial absorbers for lining system shield box and packaging: Cavity analysis and equivalent material design. *ITEC*, **63**, 4, 1007–1014, 2020.
113. Chen, H., *et al.*, Metamaterial-inspired radiofrequency (RF) shield with reduced specific absorption rate (SAR) and improved transmit efficiency for UHF MRI. **68**, 4, 1178–1189, 2020.
114. Shukoor, M.A. and Dey, S., Novel dual-mode polarization insensitive wide angular stable circular ring based deca-band absorber for RCS and EMI shielding applications. *ITEC*, **64**, 5, 1337–1345, 2022.

115. Hossain, M.B., Faruque, M.R.I., Islam, M.T., Double elliptical resonator based quadruple band metamaterial absorber for EMI shielding applications in microwave regime. *AEJ*, **69**, 193–206, 2023.
116. Hasan, M.M., *et al.*, Frequency and bandwidth modulation of a wide band-stop metamaterial for EMI shielding applications. **172**, 110515, 2024.
117. Vafapour, Z., Troy, W., Rashidi, A., Colon cancer detection by designing and analytical evaluation of a water-based THz metamaterial perfect absorber. *ISJ*, **21**, 17, 19307–19313, 2021.
118. Azab, M.Y., *et al.*, Highly sensitive metamaterial biosensor for cancer early detection. **21**, 6, 7748–7755, 2021.
119. Banerjee, S., *et al.*, A biomedical sensor for detection of cancer cells based on terahertz metamaterial absorber. **6**, 6, 1–4, 2022.
120. Seyyedmasoumian, S., *et al.*, Refractive index biosensor using metamaterial perfect absorber based on graphene in near-infrared for disease diagnosis. **22**, 15, 14870–14877, 2022.
121. Mukherjee, P., *et al.*, Refractive index sensor based on terahertz epsilon negative metamaterial absorber for cancerous cell detection. **25**, 3-4, 128–135, 2023.
122. Teber, A., A Dual-Band Terahertz Metamaterial Absorber Using an All-Metal Aluminum Hexagonal Metasurface Structure for Sensing of Cancerous Cells. *JEM*, 1–16, 2024.
123. Shen, Y., *et al.*, An extremely wideband and lightweight metamaterial absorber. **117**, 22, 2015.
124. Yang, Z., *et al.*, Design of a broadband electromagnetic absorbers based on TiO2/Al2O3 ceramic coatings with metamaterial surfaces. **687**, 384–388, 2016.
125. Rance, O., *et al.*, Oblique wide-angle multi-sector metamaterial absorber for space applications. **9**, 16, 3425, 2019.
126. Winson, D., *et al.*, Design and development of a hybrid broadband radar absorber using metamaterial and graphene. **67**, 8, 5446–5452, 2019.
127. Sadadiwala, V., Singh, V., Sharma, D., Ku band metamaterial absorber for stealth applications against Radar and Military Satcom. *PSE*, **1**, 3, 2834–2550, 2022.
128. Priyanka, *et al.*, Design and Manufacturing of a Hexapattern Frequency Selective Surface Absorber for Aerospace Stealth Application. **15**, 30, 37107–37115, 2023.
129. Kuznetsov, S.A., *et al.*, Matrix structure of metamaterial absorbers for multispectral terahertz imaging. **122**, 93–103, 2012.
130. Carranza, I.E., *et al.*, Terahertz metamaterial absorbers implemented in CMOS technology for imaging applications: scaling to large format focal plane arrays. **23**, 4, 1–8, 2016.
131. Grant, J., *et al.*, CMOS compatible metamaterial absorbers for hyperspectral medium wave infrared imaging and sensing applications. **26**, 8, 10408–10420, 2018.

132. Molaei, A., *et al.*, Digitized metamaterial absorber-based compressive reflector antenna for high sensing capacity imaging. 7, 1160–1173, 2018.
133. Jiang, S., *et al.*, Genetic optimization of plasmonic metamaterial absorber towards dual-band infrared imaging polarimetry. **28**, 15, 22617–22629, 2020.
134. Alkurt, F.Ö., *et al.*, Microwave power imaging detector based on metamaterial absorber. **59**, 8, 087104–087104, 2020.
135. Padilla, W.J. and Averitt, R.D., Imaging with metamaterials. *NRP*, **4**, 2, 85–100, 2022.
136. Alipour, Z., Mirzaei, S.I., Fardmanesh, M., Design, Fabrication and Characterization of a Wideband Metamaterial Absorber for THz Imaging. *EP*, **58**, 1, 92, 2023.
137. Rengasamy, S., Natarajan, R., Kuttathati Srinivasan, V., A Miniaturized penta-band metamaterial THz absorber for sensing and imaging applications. *P*, **18**, 5, 1933–1940, 2023.
138. Ramachandran, T., Faruque, M.R.I., Al-Mugren, K., Asymmetric metamaterial sandwich structure with NIM characteristics for THz imaging application. *SR*, **14**, 1, 6258, 2024.

8

RF-Based Wearable PPG Sensor for Real-Time Cardiovascular Health Monitoring

Mohammed Arshad Ali Khan and Geetha Chakaravarthi*

Department of Instrumentation and Control Engineering, National Institute of Technology, Tiruchirappalli, Tamil Nadu, India

Abstract

The incorporation of Radio Frequency Identification (RFID) technology with wireless power transfer has substantial potential for continuous cardiac monitoring in the healthcare field. By harvesting energy from radio frequency (RF) signals, this work overcomes the challenges posed by battery constraints. It facilitates continuous monitoring of vital signs, such as heart rate (HR) and blood oxygen saturation level (SpO_2), which are crucial for identifying various health issues. The design emphasizes a non-invasive monitoring technique that consistently detects photoplethysmography (PPG) signals through the finger. PPG incorporates red and infrared light-emitting diodes (LEDs) to monitor variations in pulse rate and arterial oxygen levels. The proposed wearable PPG sensor integrated with RFID technology features an energy harvesting module, an in-built low-cost PPG sensor, and a microcontroller unit for the evaluation of the PPG signal. The meandering patterned antenna wirelessly harvests RF signals and converts them into DC voltage to deliver power to the PPG sensor and microcontroller. The system is designed for easy placement on the fingertip without the requirement of adhesives and ensures continuous monitoring of health status. Therefore, the demand for continuous, non-intrusive monitoring of the cardiovascular system prompted the incorporation of RF energy harvesting. This study demonstrates a wearable sensor that improves the reliability and comfort of monitoring cardiac parameters, particularly HR and SpO_2.

***Keywords*:** Antenna design, healthcare, photoplethysmography, Radio Frequency Identification (RFID), RF energy harvesting

**Corresponding author*: geethac@nitt.edu

Dilip Kumar Choudhary, Indrasen Singh, Manoj Kumar Singh and Amit Kumar Jain (eds.) Compact and Flexible Microwave Devices, (197–222) © 2025 Scrivener Publishing LLC

8.1 Introduction

Cardiovascular diseases (CVDs) are the most prevalent causes of death worldwide. According to data from the World Health Organization (WHO), 17.9 million people died from CVDs, accounting for 32% of all deaths globally. The surprising quantity mostly consists of cardiac arrest and stroke, accounting for a significant 85% of deaths associated with CVD [1]. Moreover, CVDs put a significant burden on the economy and healthcare systems [2]. Effective measures for early detection, prevention, and management are essential to lessen the economic burden of CVDs while enhancing overall public health outcomes, provided their widespread prevalence and significant impact.

The increasing requirement for real-time monitoring technologies in the management of the cardiovascular system has become more apparent in modern healthcare services [3]. As cardiovascular diseases (CVDs) tend to be the most common cause of fatalities throughout the world, it is important to emphasize the requirements for early identification and preventive actions. The conventional method for detecting cardiovascular problems involves analyzing the electrocardiogram (ECG) signals, which provide information about the heart's rhythm [4]. However, traditional ECG-based detection methods are constrained due to accessibility, cost, and the requirement of clinical supervision. Therefore, it is expensive for monitoring heart rate for the purpose of identifying potential cardiac problems. An alternative to electrocardiograms is to utilize wearable devices with PPG sensors [5], which can be used to continuously monitor health without the need for medical professionals. Wearable sensors are gaining substantial attention from the end users and funding because of their ability to potentially transform the healthcare industry by allowing for continuous online consultation, and non-invasive assessment of vital signs [6]. PPG-based monitoring devices are proving to be highly valuable instruments for cardiovascular assessment [7]. However, the limited battery lifespan of these devices necessitates regular recharging or battery replacements, potentially leading to performance interruptions [8]. In addition, the increased size and weight of batteries may compromise user comfort. Hence, standard PPG sensors have proven successful for numerous applications in the healthcare industry, and incorporating them with wireless radio-frequency (RF) technology provides significant opportunities for continuous monitoring of the cardiovascular system [9]. Hence, RF-based wearable sensors can address previously defined problems and carry out continuous monitoring

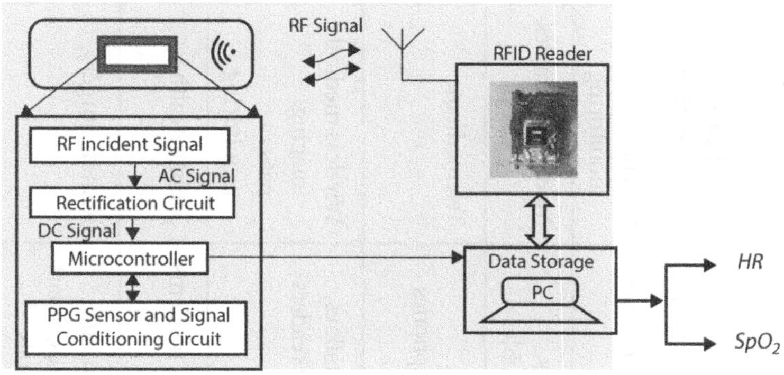

Figure 8.1 System architecture of RF-based wearable sensor for real-time monitoring of cardiac health.

of the cardiovascular system. Furthermore, it would be employed in the hospital environment to detect the abnormal heart rhythms.

The research investigates the development of a wearable sensor by integrating RF signals with a PPG sensor for continuous monitoring of vital signs, including HR and SpO_2. By comprehensively analysing current research, clinical studies, and market trends, a low-cost and battery-less wearable sensor is designed for indicating the health status of the cardiovascular system. Figure 8.1 shows the architecture of a complete RF-based wearable sensor.

This work contributes to the development of an RF-based wearable PPG sensor, enabling continuous and reliable cardiac monitoring for improved cardiovascular healthcare.

8.2 Motivation

The global burden of disease analysis revealed that 46.3 million people worldwide were affected by CVDs. Forecasts indicate that by 2050, the prevalence of these CVDs potentially grows approximately two-fold, with around 3 million strokes expected in Asia [10]. The purpose of the study is to design and develop an augmented RF-based wearable sensor system that employs RF technology for continuous monitoring of cardiovascular parameters, such as HR and SpO_2. Traditionally, HR is measured using electrocardiography (ECG) [11]. However, wearable devices are embedded with the PPG sensor for continuous and non-invasively monitoring of

Table 8.1 Comparison of distinct wireless technologies.

Technology	Frequency range	Data rate	Range	Power consumption	Typical devices	Healthcare applications
Zigbee [20]	2.4 GHz	Up to 250 kbps	100 ft (typical)	Low	Industrial sensors	Patient monitoring
Bluetooth [21]	2.4 GHz	Up to 3 Mbps	30 ft (typical)	Low	Headsets, Wearables	Medical wearables
Wi-Fi (802.11) [22]	2.4 GHz, 5 GHz	Up to several Gbps	100 ft (indoors)	Moderate to High	Laptops, smartphones	Telemedicine
UHF [23]	300 MHz - 3 GHz	Varies	Varies	Varies	Walkie-talkies, RFID readers	Wireless medical imaging, patient monitoring
4G LTE [24]	Multiple bands	Up to 1 Gbps (LTE-A)	Several miles	Moderate to High	Routers, modems	Mobile health
5G [25]	Multiple bands	Up to 10 Gbps (Theoretical)	Several miles	Moderate to High	Autonomous vehicles, Smart hospitals	Remote surgery

cardiovascular health [12–14]. The sensor developed effectively addresses issues like limited battery life frequently encountered in traditional wearable devices by capturing energy from interrogating RF sources [15–19]. Additionally, it offers a cost-effective, self-sustaining approach for ongoing real-time cardiovascular monitoring, enhancing patient comfort and expanding the possibilities of non-invasive healthcare.

8.3 The Fundamental of Photoplethysmography

Photoplethysmography (PPG) is a non-invasive optical technique used to measure blood volume fluctuation in the arteries or microvascular tissues. The word comes from the Greek terms "plethysmos" (becoming increasing) and "graphy" (to write). The popularity of PPG can be attributed to the realization that it has important implications for various healthcare applications, particularly in vital sign monitoring, blood oxygen detection, and cardiovascular health monitoring [26]. With the advancement in electronic circuits and miniature sensors over time, PPG transformed into a useful and adaptable technology. It has been employed in different areas, ranging from hospital environments to the fitness sector, where it is used

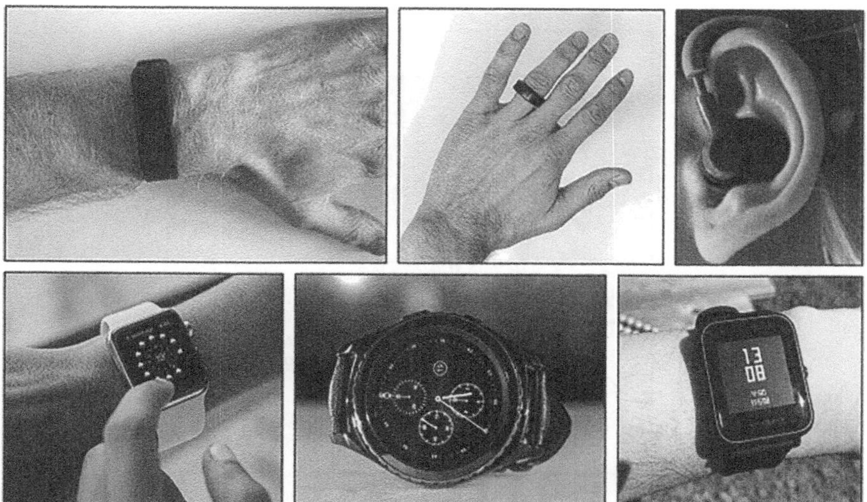

Figure 8.2 PPG-based wearable sensor: Examples of wrist-finger-ear worn devices that detect the PPG signal. (clockwise from top left), the Max-Health-Band, Oura Ring, Amazfit Bip, Samsung Gear Galaxy S2, and Apple Watch [26].

to continuously monitor distinct physiological parameters [27]. Figure 8.2 shows the distinct wearable devices for continuous healthcare monitoring.

8.3.1 PPG Basic Working Principle

PPG is a non-invasive optical technique used to measure blood volume changes in the arteries. The variations in blood volume within the tissue caused by cardiac activity alter the intensity of the light, which is either transmitted or reflected, and this change is subsequently measured by a photodetector. The detected signal comprises both AC and DC components. The AC component denotes the periodic changes attributed to the cardiac cycle, whereas the DC component demonstrates the steady variations from bloodless tissues, as shown in Figure 8.3. Signal processing procedures are employed to distinguish these elements, thereby facilitating the extraction of physiological measurements such as HR and SpO_2. The non-invasive and user-friendly characteristics of PPG provide its application as a versatile tool for continuous monitoring for numerous applications, including medical diagnosis, health monitoring, and wearable technology.

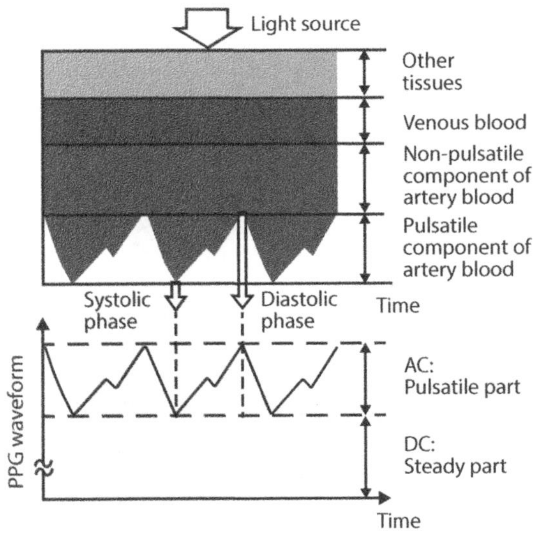

Figure 8.3 The representation of the PPG waveform generated by the absorption of light in tissue over time [3].

8.3.2 Relative Positioning of PPG Sensor

The relative position of the light-emitting diode (LED) and photodetector has significance in both transmittance and reflectance photoplethysmography (PPG) systems. In the transmittance photoplethysmography (PPG) process, an LED produces light on one side of the tissue, whereas a photodiode is installed on the opposite side to determine variations in the volume of blood. In contrast, reflectance photoplethysmography (PPG) is an approach where both the LED and photodetector are mounted on the same surface of the tissue at an optimized distance due to the maximum photons observed in the photodetector. The light travels through the tissues and is then reflected to the photodiode. Reflectance photoplethysmography (PPG) has proven particularly valuable in circumstances where it is challenging to approach the tissues from the opposite side [28]. It serves as an alternate perspective on the circulation of blood in the peripheral areas and facilitates understanding its characteristics. Reflectance photoplethysmography (PPG), because of its simple sensor integration and user-friendly form, has become prevalent in wearable devices, therefore serving as an indispensable tool for healthcare monitoring [29].

8.3.3 The Beer-Lambert Law in PPG

Beer-Lambert's law, particularly employed in photoplethysmography (PPG), demonstrates how the absorbed amount of light in biological tissue is correlated with the concentration of the component absorbing the radiation. Hemoglobin contributes a key part as a light absorber, and the concentration of hemoglobin in the bloodstream influences the extent to which light is transmitted or reflected. The correlation between blood concentration and fluctuations in light radiation can be comprehended by employing the Beer-Lambert law [30].

The Beer-Lambert equation is formulated as:

$$B = log_{10}\left(\frac{P_0}{P}\right) = k\varepsilon x \tag{12.1}$$

Where:
B denotes absorbance,
P_0 represent the intensity of incident light,
P stands for the intensity of transmitted or reflected light,

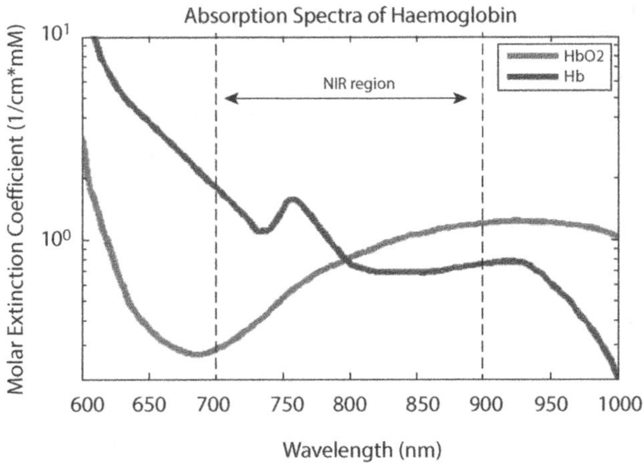

Figure 8.4 Oxy and Deoxy Hemoglobin Absorption for Red and IR Wavelength of Light [30].

ε signifies the molar absorptivity of the absorbing substance (hemoglobin),

k indicates the concentration of the absorbing substance, and

x refers to the path length of the light through the tissue.

In PPG, Beer-Lambert's law illustrates how changes in blood volume and hemoglobin concentration affect radiation absorption in tissue during the cardiac cycle. The PPG waveform reflects cardiovascular and blood flow characteristics. Hemoglobin, found in red blood cells, plays a pivotal role in oxygen transport and carbon dioxide removal. Pulse oximetry uses red (660 nm) and infrared (950 nm) light to measure oxygen saturation: Oxy-hemoglobin in the blood can absorb radiation with a wavelength of 660nm, while deoxy-hemoglobin absorbs radiation with a wavelength of 950nm (refer to Figure 8.4). The Beer-Lambert equation helps to understand these absorption variations to assess oxygenated and deoxygenated hemoglobin concentrations in tissues, which is crucial for healthcare monitoring.

8.3.4 Application of PPG

A. **Cardiovascular Assessment:** PPG assists in investigating the cardiovascular function by examining pulse wave structure and therefore provides for the recognition of irregularities and analysis of arterial stiffness.

B. **Health Monitoring:** Photoplethysmography (PPG) is often employed in wearable electronics for periodically examining physiological parameters like pulse rate and blood saturation levels.
C. **Blood Oxygen Detection:** Photoplethysmography (PPG) is implemented in pulse oximeters for non-invasively detecting bloodstream oxygenation saturation levels, which is significant for determining pulmonary and cardiovascular status.
D. **Fitness Tracking:** Wearable fitness devices incorporate photoplethysmography (PPG) to follow daily activity and assess caloric expenditure, as well as monitor exercise-induced physiological changes.
E. **Stress and Wellness Monitoring:** Sensors involving photoplethysmography regulate stress by monitoring heart rhythm fluctuations, offering information about the parasympathetic nervous system's function.
F. **Non-intrusive Blood Pressure Measurement:** Photoplethysmography (PPG) has been explored for its potential to assess blood pressure instead of the requirement for intrusive techniques, affording an alternative to traditional cuff-based assessments.
G. **Sleep Monitoring:** Photoplethysmography (PPG) is encompassed in sleep surveillance instruments to investigate sleep patterns by observing variations in pulse rhythm and oxygen saturation through distinct sleeping phases.
H. **Clinical Diagnostics:** PPG is used in clinical contexts for the diagnosis of cardiac issues and evaluating peripherals blood circulation, along with tracking patients through procedures.

8.4 RF-Based Wearable Sensors and Applications in Healthcare Monitoring

Table 8.2 explores the incorporation of RF technology into wearable sensors for providing continuous healthcare monitoring. These sensors leverage RF energy harvesting technique to produce power for healthcare monitoring systems, enabling non-invasive and convenient techniques for recording vital signs such as heart rate and blood oxygen saturation.

Table 8.2 RF-based wearable sensor in healthcare monitoring.

Application	Wearable sensor	Functionality
Heart Rhythm Monitoring [31]	Optical Heart Rate Sensor	Continuous cardiac monitoring provides insights into cardiovascular well-being and the amount of physical activity.
Activity Monitoring [32]	Accelerometer	Tracking physical activity, calculating steps, and forecasting consumption of energy helps foster an active and healthy lifestyle life.
Sleep Tracking [33]	Gyroscope, Accelerometer	Monitoring sleep patterns, encompassing the amount of time, quality, and characterization of various sleep stages for a comprehensive evaluation of holistic sleeping health.
Temperature Measurement [34]	Thermometer	Continuous monitoring of the temperature of the body proves helpful for identifying illness or variations that may indicate forthcoming medical issues.
Blood Oxygen Saturation Measurement [35]	Photoplethysmography (PPG)	Non-invasive monitoring of blood hemoglobin levels serves as vital for assessing cardiopulmonary and cardiovascular well-being.
Fall Detection [36]	Accelerometer, Gyroscope	Leveraging the detection of rapid shifts in acceleration or position to recognise events of collapsing in older or vulnerable groups, and consequently triggering alarms for intervention.

(*Continued*)

Table 8.2 RF-based wearable sensor in healthcare monitoring. (*Continued*)

Application	Wearable sensor	Functionality
Stress Level Evaluation [37]	Electrodermal Activity (EDA)	Integrating skin conductivity and sweat concentrations to gauge the amount of stress, fostering stress management regulations.
Remote Monitoring of Patient [38]	RFID-based temperature sensor integrated with a passive metal-free aortic valve prosthesis	Remote monitoring of various vital signs, which includes heart rhythm and temperature, permits healthcare professionals to keep track of patients with medical conditions.
Posture Detection [39]	Posture Sensors	Identifying healthy posture as well as providing users suggestions for maintaining it, consequently lessening the likelihood of muscular disorders.
Systolic and Diastolic Pressure Measurement [40]	Photoplethysmography (PPG)	PPG is being considered to provide a non-intrusive arterial pressure assessment technique that can replace cuff-based monitoring.
Gait Analysis [41]	Accelerometer, Gyroscope	Evaluating moving activities and noticing inconsistencies in gait could point to underlying psychological or muscular-skeletal disorders.

8.4.1 Requirement of Energy Harvesting Module

The incorporation of the significance of energy harvesting modules expands across several fields and applications. Considering the growing requirement for EH techniques, it is imperative to identify energy sources that can be sustained independently [42]. Energy harvesters represent an optimistic approach by acquiring the energy from the surrounding environment, for example, solar radiation, vibration, heat gradients, and kinetic motion, RF energy, and transforming it into suitable power for appliances. This inherent autonomy facilitates electronic devices to run without the requirement of regular replacements for batteries or another source of electrical power. Furthermore, energy-harvesting devices have played a vital part in promoting sustainability by minimizing reliance on conventional forms of energy and suppressing environmental impacts [43]. Because of their versatility and reliability, they are appropriately suited for multiple purposes such as wearable technology, wireless sensor networks, Internet of Things (IoT) products, and systems for remote monitoring. Energy harvesters harness ambient power sources to accomplish various advantages, notably enhanced system life expectancy, improved reliability, and lower operational expenses. It consequently promotes technological advancement and effectiveness in different domains [44].

8.4.2 Different Energy Harvesting Sources

The article presents a comprehensive overview of different energy harvesting sources and their applications across various domains, as depicted in Figure 8.5. These energy sources include piezoelectric crystals, solar power, thermal energy, and RF waves, which are harnessed to generate usable DC voltage. This voltage is then utilized to power sensors for real-time

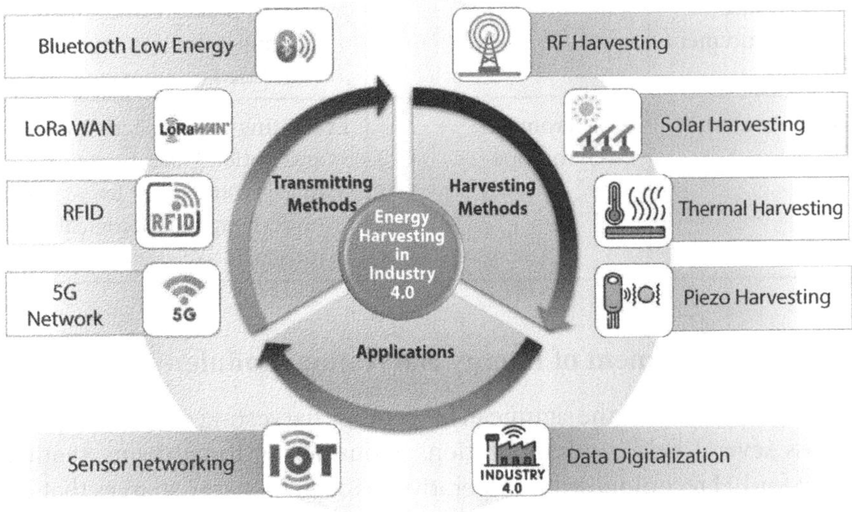

Figure 8.5 Overview of energy harvesting sources and their applications [46].

monitoring, facilitated through connectivity options such as Bluetooth, LoRa WAN (Long Range Wide Area Network), 5G, or RFID. Among these options, RFID technology emerges as the most suitable choice due to its reliable power and data transmission, along with consistent energy availability [45, 46].

Overall, the content offers insights into different RF sources and their applications, highlighting the transformative potential of these technologies in driving innovation, sustainability, and connectivity across various sectors.

8.5 Methodology

8.5.1 Development of Energy Harvesting Rectification Module

In Ultra-High-Frequency Radio-Frequency Identification (UHF-RFID) systems, the energy harvesting technique utilizes electromagnetic waves from the RFID reader to power low-power devices, eliminating the need for a battery source. This method improves the long-term reliability and sustainability of wireless sensor networks, providing them compatible with continuous health monitoring, asset tracking, and IoT applications. The semi-passive RFID uses both active and passive components to energise, while active RFID tags have the power source. Among them, the inherent qualities of passive RFID tags, such as being battery-free, affordable, low-weight, and long-duration. The integrated system consists of an antenna, impedance matching network, rectifier circuit, and PPG sensor, as depicted in Figure 8.6.

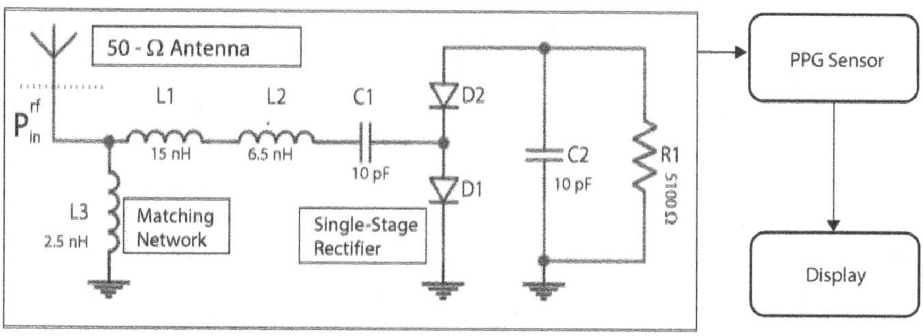

Figure 8.6 Block diagram of a complete passive sensing system.

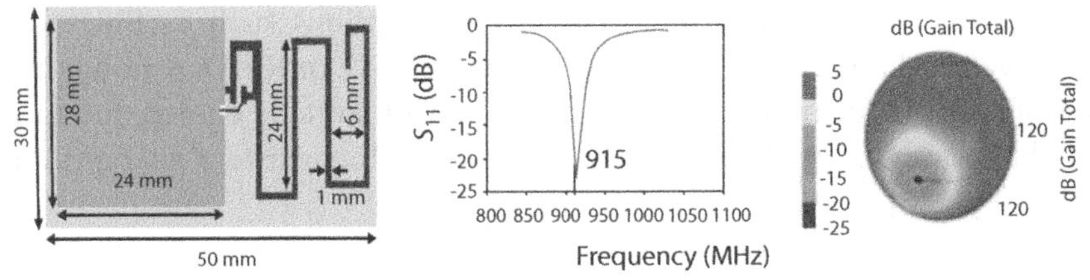

(**a**) Geometry of Antenna Design (**b**) Reflection Co-efficient (**c**) Gain

Figure 8.7 Antenna design and performance analysis. (a) Geometry of antenna design. (b) Reflection co-efficient. (c) Gain.

8.5.1.1 Design of Antenna

The antenna design is optimised at 915 MHz using ANSYS HFSS software on an FR4 substrate with a dielectric constant of 4.4, a substrate thickness of 1.6 mm, and a copper thickness of 35 um, ensuring reliable conductivity and less resistive loss. Figure 8.7(a) shows the geometry of a compact meandered antenna of 30 * 50 mm^2. Figure 8.7(b) depicts the simulated reflection coefficient (S11) is -23 dB at 915 MHz, which indicates the effective impedance matching and minimal signal loss. In addition, an antenna gain is 1.21 dBi, which shows the antenna's effectiveness for directing the RF signals, as shown in Figure 8.7(c).

8.5.1.2 Comprehensive Analysis of RF Circuit Characteristics Using Keysight ADS

Figure 8.8 shows the performance analysis of the RF circuit, such as reflection coefficient, output power, input power, output voltage, and efficiency in Keysight ADS software. The simulation results show the effective correlation between these parameters and efficiency of the circuit. Figure 8.8 (a) shows the reflection coefficient of -12 dB at the resonant frequency of 915 MHz. Further analysis emphasizes the direct correlation between input power (20 dBm) and output power (2.5 mW), as shown in Figure 8.8(b), as well as the influence of input power of 30 dBm on an output voltage of around 3.5 volts. Figure 8.8(c). The circuit's efficiency is determined to be approximately 44% at a certain 0 dBm of input power level (refer to Figure 8.8(d), which is quite less but sufficient to supply enough power to the PPG sensor).

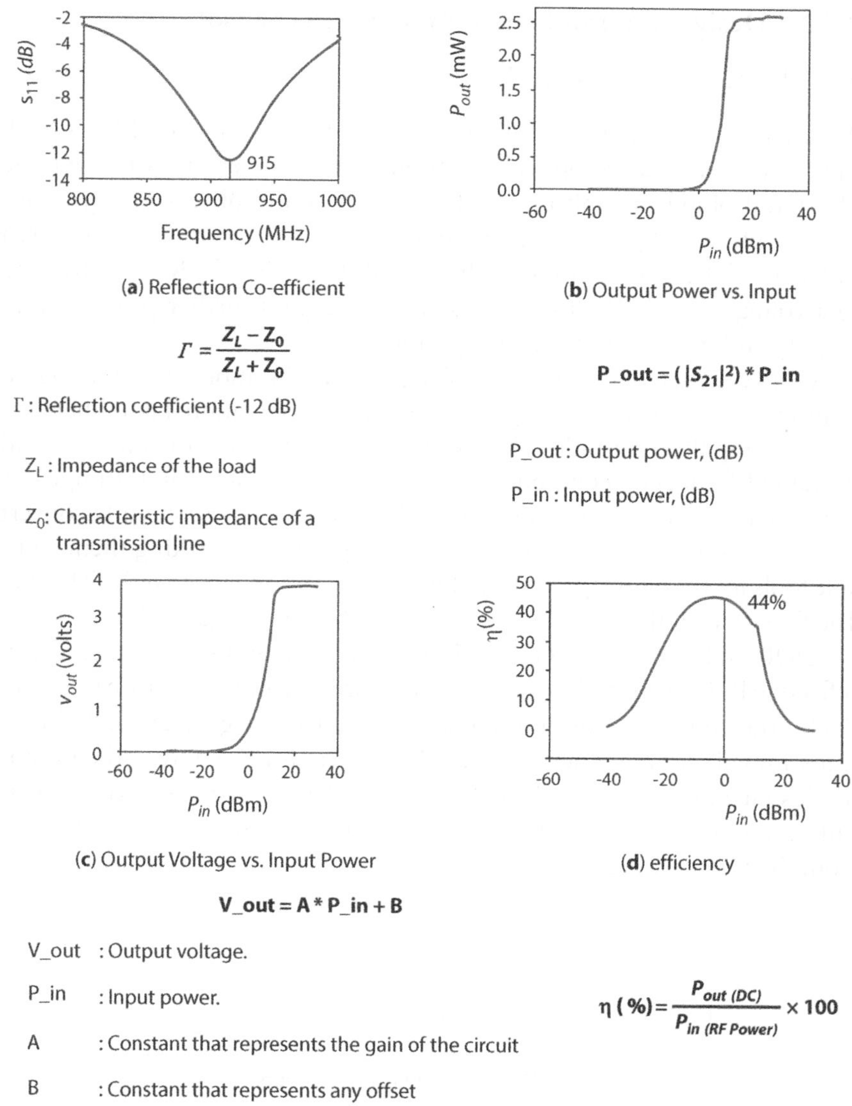

Figure 8.8 RF circuit performance analysis. (a) Reflection co-efficient. (b) Output power vs. input. (c) Output voltage vs. input power. (d) efficiency.

8.5.2 Design and Implementation of PPG Sensor

8.5.2.1 Signal Processing Circuit

A signal processing circuit (SPC) is designed to acquire the PPG signal. PPG is a non-invasive optical technique, which determines the volume of arterial blood by emitting light on the skin and observing variations in absorption of light induced by blood flow. The variation is measured in terms of the current signal, which, with the help of SPC, is converted to a voltage signal. The raw PPG signal undergoes further processing to amplify and filter it for detailed experimentation.

A PPG signal often consists of signal amplification and filtering to improve signal quality. Analog elements such as operational amplifiers are used for amplification and analog filters are employed for reducing noise and unwanted frequency components. The signal processing circuit improves the signal-to-noise ratio (SNR) for further analysis. These circuits convert the optical signals into meaningful physiological data, making them valuable tools for monitoring heart rhythm, SpO_2, and analyzing overall health. The flowchart of the PPG sensing system is shown in Figure 8.9.

A 940nm LED and a 640nm LED are employed in the experiment, with reflective PPG measured as depicted in Figures 8.10(a) and 8.10(b), respectively. The conversion of photodiode current to voltage is facilitated by a trans-impedance amplifier, illustrated in Figure 8.10(c). Given the photodiode's current range of 0.5 to 90 μA, a feedback resistor of 51k ohms is utilized, along with capacitors to mitigate thermal high-frequency noise from the photodiode.

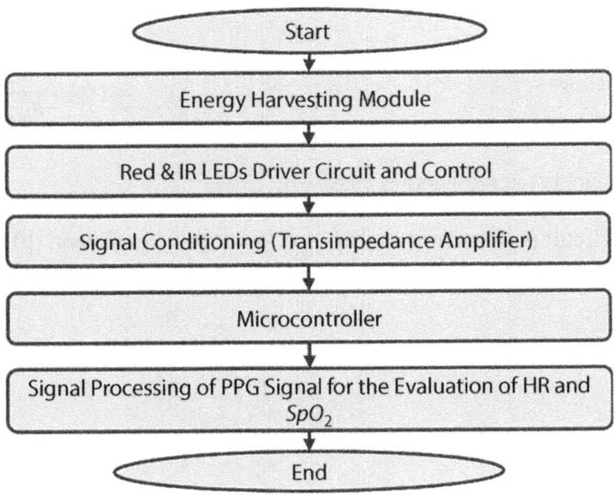

Figure 8.9 Flowchart of energy harvesting module integrated with PPG sensor.

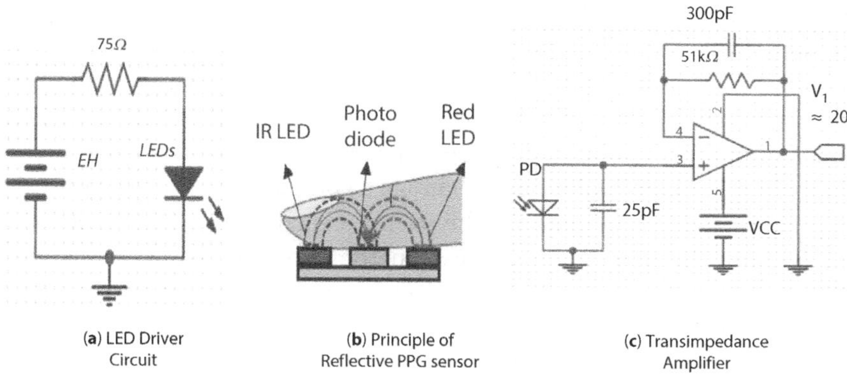

Figure 8.10 PPG sensor and signal conditioning circuits. (a) LED Driver Circuit (b) Principle of reflective PPG sensor. (c) Transimpedance Amplifier.

$$V_1 = I_{PD} * R_f \tag{12.2}$$

8.6 Experimental Setup of EH Module Integrated with PPG Sensor

Figure 8.11 shows the prototype of an integrated energy harvesting module with an in-house low-cost PPG sensor. The system leverages the standard RFID Gen2 ThingMagic M6e reader for wireless power harvesting. The antenna and rectification circuit are fabricated to transmit power to

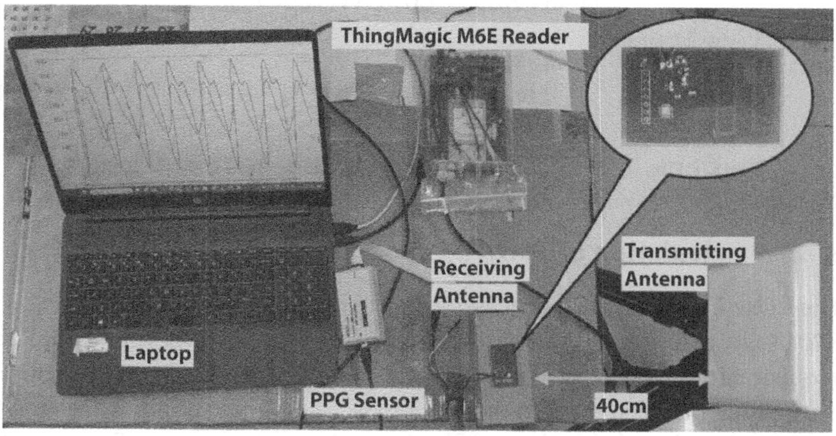

Figure 8.11 Measurement of real-time PPG signal using the proposed RF-based PPG sensor.

the PPG sensor. The Thingmagic M6e reader generates an interrogating RF signal through the transmitting antenna, allowing the EH circuit to acquire power using an RF-DC rectifier. The harvested energy is sufficient to supply the PPG sensor, MSP430FR2433 microcontroller, and the signal is acquired through the analog-to-digital converter (ADC) of the microcontroller. The designed module exhibits a compact design, which is suitable for wearable applications. The overall expenditure of the prototype, considering the fabrication process on the substrate, components, and PPG sensor, is low. The voltage requirement of the PPG sensor, voltage is between 1.95 and 2.5 volts, whereas the fabricated energy harvesting module gives a voltage of around 3.3 volts and current is 0.77mA for 30 dBm of power at a distance of 40cm.

8.7 Data Analysis

8.7.1 Calculation of Heart Rate

The estimation of heart rate from PPG signals is highly significant in cardiovascular monitoring and investigations. This procedure emphasizes recognizing the highest points in the PPG waveform, which represent individual heartbeats, and calculating the time intervals between them to assess the current heart rate. By leveraging signal processing techniques, such as peak identification algorithms, accurate heart rate data are extracted from the wearable PPG sensors. The equation 12.3 is mentioned below [47].

The formula for estimating heart rate is:

$$\text{Heart Rate} = 60 / (\text{Average } t_p) \tag{12.3}$$

$$\text{Heart Rate} = 75 \text{ BPM} \tag{12.4}$$

t_p : Peak time interval among the consecutive heart rhythms.

8.7.2 Calculation of SpO_2

The Pulse Oximetry data processing has been done offline using MATLAB R2013b, a proprietary software built by The MathWorks Inc. The data-acquiring framework had a sampling frequency of 25 Hz. Data is measured by toggling between the two pairs of LEDs. The signal at both wavelengths was processed with band-pass filtering using a 10th-order Butterworth

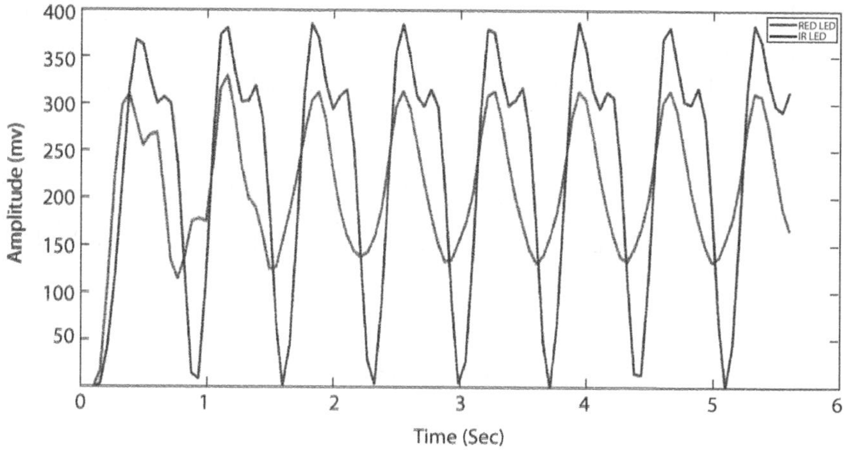

Figure 8.12 PPG signals obtained from the developed sensor.

digital filter with a bandwidth of 0.5-3 Hz. This filtering process extracted the pulsating portion of the signal (AC(t)). Following this, a low-pass filtering approach was performed using the 10th-order Butterworth digital filter with a cut-off frequency of 0.2 Hz. This filtering operation recovered the slow signal components that were not associated with pulsation (DC(t)). The corresponding pulsatile strength of the signal, represented as S(t) is determined by dividing the signals from both infrared and red wavelengths, relative waveforms are shown in Figure 8.12. The corresponding equations 12.5, 12.6 and 12.7 are used for calculating SpO_2 [48].

The formula for S(t) is

$$S(t) = \frac{\frac{PPG_{AC_R}}{PPG_{DC_R}}}{\frac{PPG_{AC_R}}{PPG_{DC_{IR}}}} \tag{12.5}$$

The ratio R(t) of the infrared and red pulsatile components was computed using an integration time window of 5 seconds, and at one-second intervals.

$$R(t) = \frac{\ln\left(rms\left(S(T)_R + 1\right)\right.}{\ln\left(rms\left(S(T)_{IR} + 1\right)\right.} \tag{12.6}$$

When red and infrared wavelengths are utilised, the equation 12.7 empirical calibration curves, which derived from healthy individuals, shows the strong correlation between R and arterial oxygen saturation SpO_2.

$$SpO_2(t) = \frac{\varepsilon_{Hb}(\lambda_R)DPF_{R-IR-\varepsilon_{Hb}}(\lambda_{IR})R(t)}{\left[\varepsilon_{Hb}(\lambda_R) - \varepsilon_{HbO_2}(\lambda_R)\right]DPF_{R-IR} + \left[\varepsilon_{HbO_2}(\lambda_{IR}) - \varepsilon_{Hb}(\lambda_{IR})\right]R(t)} \tag{12.7}$$

$$SpO_2 = 98\%$$

Where $\varepsilon_{Hb}(\lambda_R)$ and $\varepsilon_{HbO_2}(\lambda_R)$ are the extinction co-efficient of deoxyhaemoglobin and oxyhaemoglobin corresponding to red radiation (640 nm) and $\varepsilon_{Hb}(\lambda_{IR})$ *and* $\varepsilon_{HbO_2}(\lambda_{IR})$ are the extinction co-efficient of deoxyhaemoglobin and oxyhaemoglobin corresponding to Infrared radiation (950 nm). The extinction co-efficient for both types of haemoglobin is obtained from ref. [49] ($\varepsilon_{Hb}(\lambda_R) = 0.106\,mm^{-1}$, $\varepsilon_{HbO_2}(\lambda_R) = 0.011\,mm^{-1}$, $\varepsilon_{Hb}(\lambda_{IR}) = 0.018\,mm^{-1}$, and $\varepsilon_{HbO_2}(\lambda_{IR}) = 0.028\,mm^{-1}$). DPL_{R-IR} analyses the affect of distinct optical path lengths across two wavelengths. It is derived as the proportion of their corresponding differential path length factors (DPLs). The colour responsiveness of the optical path length is reliant on the biological tissue's scattering characteristics and varies with the wavelength of light. When DPL_{R-IR} is approximately 1, equation (12.7) illustrates the expression for measuring the SpO_2.

8.8 Impact of Wearable Sensors in the Market

Wearable sensors have substantially altered various sectors, such as healthcare, physical fitness, and safety at work. These devices offer up-to-the-minute information about users' health, enabling well-informed choices and enhanced health outcomes. In healthcare, continuous monitoring and prompt intervention facilitate patient care improvement. Similarly, wearable sensors in the realm of sports analytics assist in monitoring performance indicators, thus mitigating the risk of injuries and improving athlete performance. Further, they have an essential role in maintaining workplace safety through surveillance of environmental conditions and notifying staff of potential hazards. The market for wearable sensors is steadily growing due to technological advancements and increased consumer interest. The wearable sensors significantly influence industries and consumer behaviors as they are gradually integrated into everyday life.

A. **Health monitoring:** The incorporation of wearable technology within healthcare applications has resulted in a new phase of continuous health monitoring. These small devices can monitor a range of health characteristics, notably heart rate (HR), blood oxygen saturation level (SpO_2), glucose levels, and cardiovascular disease, and offer significant data for both individuals and healthcare professionals. By integrating attributes like health monitoring, virtual and augmented reality, and additional information, the sensors that are included in such devices enrich the user experience. The merging of technological advances and trends has offered possibilities regarding a broadening of sectors for both attractive and efficient devices that are worn.
B. **Sports and Performance Analytics:** Wearable sensors have become crucial in sports and athletic training as they offer athletes sophisticated equipment for tracking their performance parameters to prevent accidents. This equipment assesses movements and monitors health metrics, while offering useful information for athletes and coaches aspiring to outstanding performance. The incorporation of sensors into clothing has been demonstrated to be a transformative factor in the analysis of sports.
C. **Ensuring Safety in the Workplace:** Monitoring devices play an essential part for enhancing safety on the job in manufacturing environments. Smart helmets and coats, which are equipped with ambient detectors, have the ability to continuously track the circumstances to recognise potential threats. Workers have been provided with prompt updates, therefore decreasing the possibility of accidents and strengthening the level of security. Wearable sensors revolutionised industrial precautions in several industries.
D. **Augmented Reality (AR) and Virtual Reality (VR):** Virtual reality (VR) and augmented reality (AR) applications depend upon wearable technologies to improve the immersive experiences they are offering. AR glasses incorporate sensors that enable the detection of gestures, eye tracking, and awareness of location. This incorporation improves user participation

and involvement in virtual environments, demonstrating the revolutionary capability of wearable sensor technologies.

8.9 Conclusion and Future Scope

The integration of Radio Frequency Identification (RFID) technology and wireless power transmission exhibits outstanding prospects for continuous cardiac monitoring in healthcare, successfully addressing restrictions triggered by the limitation of batteries. This technique employs power derived from radio wave transmissions to serve as a sustainable power source to monitor important health indicators such as heart rate (HR) and blood oxygen saturation level SpO_2, which are imperative for diagnosing different health issues. The proposed sensor-augmented RFID system, comprising an energy harvesting module, low-power PPG sensor, and microcontroller unit, represents a non-intrusive monitoring strategy. The energy harvesting module provides a stable power supply and facilitates convenient attachment to the body without the requirement of adhesives. Consequently, the reliability of continuous cardiac parameter monitoring significantly improved. Future work comprises improving the system's efficiency and flexibility, collaborating with healthcare professionals for clinical trials, and evaluating its efficacy in continuous cardiac monitoring.

References

1. WHO, Getting your workplace ready for COVID-19. *World Heal. Organ.*, March, 1–8, 2020, [Online]. Available: https://www.who.int/docs/default-source/coronaviruse/getting-workplace-ready-for-covid-19.pdf.
2. Freedman, B., *et al.*, World Heart Federation roadmap on atrial fibrillation – A 2020 update. *Glob. Heart*, 16, 1, 1–36, 2021, doi: 10.5334/GH.1023.
3. Tamura, T., Maeda, Y., Sekine, M., Yoshida, M., Wearable photoplethysmographic sensors—past and present. *Electron.*, 3, 2, 282–302, 2014, doi: 10.3390/electronics3020282.
4. Vest, A.N., *et al.*, An open source benchmarked toolbox for cardiovascular waveform and interval analysis. *Physiol. Meas.*, 39, 10, aae021, 2018, doi: 10.1088/1361-6579/aae021.
5. Roy, Wearable Photoplethysmography for Cardiovascular Monitoring. *Proc. IEEE*, 110, 3, 355–381, 2022, doi: 10.1109/JPROC.2022.3149785.
6. Charlton, P.H., Kyriacou, P.A., Mant, J., Marozas, V., Chowienczyk, P., Alastruey, J., Wearable Photoplethysmography for Cardiovascular Monitoring. *Proc. IEEE*, 110, 3, 355–381, 2022, doi: 10.1109/JPROC.2022.3149785.

7. Jorge, J., *et al.*, Non-contact physiological monitoring of post-operative patients in the intensive care unit. *npj Digit. Med.*, 5, 1, 1–11, 2022, doi: 10.1038/s41746-021-00543-z.
8. Shuvo, M.M.H., Titirsha, T., Amin, N., Islam, S.K., Energy Harvesting in Implantable and Wearable Medical Devices for Enduring Precision Healthcare. *Energies*, 15, 20, 2022, doi: 10.3390/en15207495.
9. Hudak, N.S. and Amatucci, G.G., Small-scale energy harvesting through thermoelectric, vibration, and radiofrequency power conversion. *J. Appl. Phys.*, 103, 10, 2008, doi: 10.1063/1.2918987.
10. Kornej, J., Börschel, C.S., Benjamin, E.J., Schnabel, R.B., Epidemiology of Atrial Fibrillation in the 21st Century: Novel Methods and New Insights. *Circ. Res.*, 127, 1, 4–20, 2020, doi: 10.1161/CIRCRESAHA.120.316340.
11. Rachim, V.P. and Chung, W.Y., Wearable Noncontact Armband for Mobile ECG Monitoring System. *IEEE Trans. Biomed. Circuits Syst.*, 10, 6, 1112–1118, 2016, doi: 10.1109/TBCAS.2016.2519523.
12. Yang, C. and Rodr, J.J., Using PPG Signals and Wearable Devices for Atrial Fibrillation Screening, vol. 66, pp. 8832–8842, 2019.
13. Singh, W., Deb, S., Bahubalindruni, P., Low-Noise Energy Efficient Readout Front-End for Wearable Continuous Blood Pressure Monitoring Systems. *IEEE Trans. Consum. Electron.*, 66, 4, 318–326, 2020, doi: 10.1109/TCE.2020.3017282.
14. Kaisti, M., *et al.*, Clinical assessment of a non-invasive wearable MEMS pressure sensor array for monitoring of arterial pulse waveform, heart rate and detection of atrial fibrillation. *npj Digit. Med.*, 2, 1, 1–10, 2019, doi: 10.1038/s41746-019-0117-x.
15. Boukhayma, A., Barison, A., Haddad, S., Caizzone, A., Earbud-Embedded Micro-Power mm-Sized Optical Sensor for Accurate Heart Beat Monitoring. *IEEE Sens. J.*, 21, 18, 19967–19977, 2021, doi: 10.1109/JSEN.2021.3098861.
16. Cui, L., Zhang, Z., Gao, N., Meng, Z., Li, Z., Radio frequency identification and sensing techniques and their applications—A review of the state-of-the-art. *Sens. (Switzerland)*, 19, 18, 2019, doi: 10.3390/s19184012.
17. Escobedo, P., Bhattacharjee, M., Nikbakhtnasrabadi, F., Dahiya, R., Flexible Strain and Temperature Sensing NFC Tag for Smart Food Packaging Applications. *IEEE Sens. J.*, 21, 23, 26406–26414, 2021, doi: 10.1109/JSEN.2021.3100876.
18. Kang, M.H., Lee, G.J., Yun, J.H., Song, Y.M., Nfc-based wearable optoelectronics working with smartphone application for untact healthcare. *Sens. (Switzerland)*, 21, 3, 1–13, 2021, doi: 10.3390/s21030878.
19. Kim, J., *et al.*, Miniaturized Battery-Free Wireless Systems for Wearable Pulse Oximetry. *Adv. Funct. Mater.*, 27, 1, 1–8, 2017, doi: 10.1002/adfm.201604373.
20. Gil, J., *et al.*, A fully-integrated low-power high-coexistence 2.4-GHz ZigBee transceiver for biomedical applications. *2013 IEEE MTT-S Int. Microw. Work. Ser. RF Wirel. Technol. Biomed. Healthc. Appl. IMWS-BIO 2013 - Proc*, pp. 1–3, 2013, doi: 10.1109/IMWS-BIO.2013.6756235.

21. Thelen, S., Czaplik, M., Meisen, P., Schilberg, D., Jeschke, S., Using off-the-shelf medical devices for biomedical signal monitoring in a telemedicine system for emergency medical services. *IEEE J. Biomed. Heal. Inf.*, 19, 1, 117–123, 2015, doi: 10.1109/JBHI.2014.2361775.
22. Muaaz, M., Chelli, A., Abdelgawwad, A.A., Mallofré, A.C., Pätzold, M., WiWeHAR: Multimodal human activity recognition using Wi-Fi and wearable sensing modalities. *IEEE Access*, 8, 164453–164470, 2020, doi: 10.1109/ACCESS.2020.3022287.
23. Ramos, V., *et al.*, Electromagnetic Characterization of UHF-RFID Fixed Reader in Healthcare Centers Related to the Personal and Labor Health. *IEEE Access*, 10, 28614–28630, 2022, doi: 10.1109/ACCESS.2022.3156477.
24. Huang, C.C. and Lin, W.C., A radio transceiver architecture for coexistence of 4G-LTE and 5G systems used in mobile devices. *IEEE MTT-S Int. Microw. Symp. Dig.*, 2056–2058, 2017, doi: 10.1109/MWSYM.2017.8059075.
25. Yu, B.Y., *et al.*, Flexible and Wearable Hybrid RF and Solar Energy Harvesting System. *IEEE Trans. Antennas Propag.*, 70, 3, 2223–2233, 2022, doi: 10.1109/TAP.2021.3118814.
26. Nwibor, C., *et al.*, Remote Health Monitoring System for the Estimation of Blood Pressure, Heart Rate, and Blood Oxygen Saturation Level. *IEEE Sens. J.*, 23, 5, 5401–5411, 2023, doi: 10.1109/JSEN.2023.3235977.
27. Harju, J., Tarniceriu, A., Parak, J., Vehkaoja, A., Yli-Hankala, A., Korhonen, I., Monitoring of heart rate and inter-beat intervals with wrist plethysmography in patients with atrial fibrillation. *Physiol. Meas.*, 39, 6, 2018, doi: 10.1088/1361-6579/aac9a9.
28. Sidorov, I.S., Romashko, R.V., Koval, V.T., Giniatullin, R., Kamshilin, A.A., Origin of infrared light modulation in reflectance-mode photoplethysmography. *PLoS One*, 11, 10, 1–11, 2016, doi: 10.1371/journal.pone.0165413.
29. Krizea, M., Gialelis, J., Protopsaltis, G., Mountzouris, C., Theodorou, G., Empowering People with a User-Friendly Wearable Platform for Unobtrusive Monitoring of Vital Physiological Parameters. *Sensors*, 22, 14, 2022, doi: 10.3390/s22145226.
30. Nitzan, M., Nitzan, I., Arieli, Y., The various oximetric techniques used for the evaluation of blood oxygenation. *Sens. (Switzerland)*, 20, 17, 1–28, 2020, doi: 10.3390/s20174844.
31. Yang, C., Veiga, C., Rodríguez-Andina, J.J., Fariña, J., Iñiguez, A., Yin, S., Using PPG Signals and Wearable Devices for Atrial Fibrillation Screening. *IEEE Trans. Ind. Electron.*, 66, 11, 8832–8842, 2019, doi: 10.1109/TIE.2018.2889614.
32. Naranjo-Hernández, D., Roa, L.M., Reina-Tosina, J., Estudillo-Valderrama, M.A., SoM: A smart sensor for human activity monitoring and assisted healthy ageing. *IEEE Trans. Biomed. Eng.*, 59, 12 PART2, 3177–3184, 2012, doi: 10.1109/TBME.2012.2206384.
33. Jaworski, D.J. and Park, E.J., Apple Watch Sleep and Physiological Tracking Compared to Clinically Validated Actigraphy, Ballistocardiography and

Polysomnography. *Proc. Annu. Int. Conf. IEEE Eng. Med. Biol. Soc. EMBS*, 1–4, 2023, doi: 10.1109/EMBC40787.2023.10340725.
34. Yu, M., Yu, G., Dai, B., Graphene fiber-based strain-insensitive wearable temperature sensor. *IEEE Sens. Lett.*, 4, 10, 30–33, 2020, doi: 10.1109/LSENS.2020.3026671.
35. Berwal, D., Kuruba, A., Shaikh, A.M., Udupa, A., Baghini, M.S., SpO2Measurement: Non-Idealities and Ways to Improve Estimation Accuracy in Wearable Pulse Oximeters. *IEEE Sens. J.*, 22, 12, 11653–11664, 2022, doi: 10.1109/JSEN.2022.3170069.
36. Wickramasinghe, A., Ranasinghe, D.C., Fumeaux, C., Hill, K.D., Visvanathan, R., Sequence Learning with Passive RFID Sensors for Real-Time Bed-Egress Recognition in Older People. *IEEE J. Biomed. Heal. Inf.*, 21, 4, 917–929, 2017, doi: 10.1109/JBHI.2016.2576285.
37. Wang, Y., Cao, J., Zheng, Y., Toward a Low-Cost Software-Defined UHF RFID System for Distributed Parallel Sensing. *IEEE Internet Things J.*, 8, 17, 13664–13676, 2021, doi: 10.1109/JIOT.2021.3067379.
38. Naccarata, F. and Marrocco, G., Integrated Wireless RFID Temperature Sensor for Biological Aortic Valve Prostheses. *IEEE J. Radio Freq. Identif.*, 7, 293–300, 2023, doi: 10.1109/JRFID.2023.3264557.
39. Feng, L., Li, Z., Liu, C., Chen, X., Yin, X., Fang, D., SitR: Sitting Posture Recognition Using RF Signals. *IEEE Internet Things J.*, 7, 12, 11492–11504, 2020, doi: 10.1109/JIOT.2020.3019280.
40. Gao, S., *et al.*, Different effects of intravenous and local anesthesia in patients undergoing ultrasound-guided radiofrequency ablation of thyroid nodules: a prospective cohort study. *Int. J. Hyperth.*, 39, 1, 1036–1043, 2022, doi: 10.1080/02656736.2022.2106384.
41. Yang, X., Liu, J., Chen, Y., Guo, X., Xie, Y., MU-ID: Multi-user Identification Through Gaits Using Millimeter Wave Radios. *Proc. - IEEE INFOCOM*, 2020, July, 2589–2598, 2020, doi: 10.1109/INFOCOM41043.2020.9155471.
42. Eid, A., *et al.*, Inkjet-/3D-/4D-Printed perpetual electronics and modules. *IEEE Microw. Mag.*, 21, 12, 87–103, 2020, doi: 10.1109/MMM.2020.3023310.
43. Matiko, J.W., Grabham, N.J., Beeby, S.P., Tudor, M.J., Review of the application of energy harvesting in buildings. *Meas. Sci. Technol.*, 25, 1, 2014, doi: 10.1088/0957-0233/25/1/012002.
44. Lazaro, A., Villarino, R., Girbau, D., A survey of NFC sensors based on energy harvesting for IoT applications. *Sens. (Switzerland)*, 18, 11, 2018, doi: 10.3390/s18113746.
45. Sidhu, R.K., Singh Ubhi, J., Aggarwal, A., A Survey Study of Different RF Energy Sources for RF Energy Harvesting. *2019 Int. Conf. Autom. Comput. Technol. Manag. ICACTM 2019*, pp. 530–533, 2019, doi: 10.1109/ICACTM.2019.8776726.
46. Moloudian, G., *et al.*, RF Energy Harvesting Techniques for Battery-Less Wireless Sensing, Industry 4.0, and Internet of Things: A Review. *IEEE Sens. J.*, 24, 5, 5732–5745, 2024, doi: 10.1109/JSEN.2024.3352402.

47. Boukhayma, A., Barison, A., Haddad, S., Caizzone, A., Ring-Embedded Micro-Power mm-Sized Optical Sensor for Accurate Heart Beat Monitoring. *IEEE Access*, 9, 127217–127225, 2021, doi: 10.1109/ACCESS.2021.3111956.
48. Haque, C.A., Hossain, S., Kwon, T.H., Kim, K.D., Comparison of Different Methods to Estimate Blood Oxygen Saturation using PPG. *Int. Conf. ICT Converg.*, 2021-Octob, 792–794, 2021, doi: 10.1109/ICTC52510.2021.9621142.
49. Zijlstra, W.G., Buursma, A., Meeuwsen-Van Der Roest, W.P., Absorption spectra of human fetal and adult oxyhemoglobin, de-oxyhemoglobin, carboxyhemoglobin, and methemoglobin. *Clin. Chem.*, 37, 9, 1633–1638, 1991, doi: 10.1093/clinchem/37.9.1633.

Index

Also of Interest

Check out these other related titles from Scrivener Publishing

Controller Design for Industrial Applications, Edited by Arindam Mondal & Souvik Ganguli, ISBN: 9781394287079. Controller Design for Industrial Applications is essential for anyone looking to master the advanced techniques of intelligent controller design, enabling you to effectively tackle the complexities of modern industrial processes and optimize performance in an ever-evolving landscape.

Special Electrical Machinery, Edited by Dr. Jigneshkumar P. Desai, ISBN: 9781394193912. This book is a comprehensive guide to specialized motors, covering everything from switched reluctance motors to axial flux ironless PM motors, giving in-depth information on their operating principles, applications, and controls.

DESIGN, MODELING AND RELIABILITY IN ROTATING MACHINERY, Edited by Robert X. Perez, ISBN: 9781119631682. This broad collection of current rotating machinery topics, written by industry experts, is a must-have for rotating equipment engineers, maintenance personnel, students, and anyone else wanting to stay abreast with current rotating machinery concepts and technology.

MAINTENANCE, RELIABILITY AND TROUBLESHOOTING IN ROTATING AND PROCESS MACHINERY, Edited by Robert X. Perez, ISBN: 9781119631644. For Rotating equipment professionals, maintenance personnel, project engineers, process engineers, mechanical engineering students, and anyone working around critical rotating equipment.

Troubleshooting Rotating Machinery: Including Centrifugal Pumps and Compressors, Reciprocating Pumps and Compressors, Fans, Steam Turbines, Electric Motors, and More, by Robert X. Perez and Andrew P. Conkey, ISBN: 9781119294139. A must-read for anyone whose job depends on operating or maintaining safe, reliable, and efficient machinery in a process facility, this volume shows the newcomer and veteran alike how you can start troubleshooting rotating equipment problems immediately by implementing this book's common-sense methodology. *NOW AVAILABLE!*

Operator's Guide to Process Compressors, by Robert X. Perez, ISBN: 9781119580614. The perfect primer for anyone responsible for operating or maintaining process gas compressors. *NOW AVAILABLE!*

Operator's Guide to General Purpose Steam Turbines: An Overview of Operating Principles, Construction, Best Practices, and Troubleshooting, by Robert X. Perez and David W. Lawhon, ISBN: 9781119294214. A must-read book for anyone operating or maintaining general purpose steam turbines in a process setting, this is a practical reference that includes a collection of field-tested procedures aimed at ensuring safe general purpose steam turbines start-ups, shutdowns, and over-speed tests. *NOW AVAILABLE!*

Dictionary of Industrial Terminology 2nd Edition, by Michael D. Holloway and Emma Holloway, ISBN: 9781119363446. Greatly expanded and revised, this second edition is the most comprehensive and in-depth dictionary of industrial terms available, a must-have for any engineer, scientist, technician, or operator working in industry. *NOW AVAILABLE!*

Basic Electrical and Instrumentation Engineering, by P. Sivaraman, C. Sharmeela, A. Thaiyal Nayagi, and R. Mahendran, ISBN: 9781119764465. Offering the most up-to-date coverage on the subject available, this new volume provides detailed concepts of AC circuits and power systems, transformers, DC machines, AC machines, measurement and instrumentation, and many other practical concepts for the engineer or engineering student. *NOW AVAILABLE!*

ELECTRIC VEHICLE DESIGN: Design, Simulation and Applications, Edited by Krishan Arora, Suman Lata Tripathi, and Himashu Sharma, ISBN: 9781394204373. This book will serve as a definitive guide to conceptual and practical knowledge about the design of hybrid electrical vehicles (HEV), battery electrical vehicles (BEV), fuel cell electrical vehicles (FCEV), plug-in hybrid electrical vehicles (PHEV), and efficient EV charging techniques with advanced tools and methodologies for students, engineers, and academics alike.

INDUSTRIAL CONTROL SYSTEMS, Edited by Vipin Chandra Pal, Suman Lata Tripathi, and Souvik Ganguli, ISBN: 9781119829256. This volume serves as a comprehensive guide in the journey of industrial control systems with a multidisciplinary approach to the key engineering problems in the 21st century.

MODERN AUTOMOTIVE ELECTRICAL SYSTEMS: Theory and Applications, Edited by Pedram Asef, Sanjeevikumar Padmanaban, and Andrew Lapthorn, ISBN: 1119801047. Presenting the concepts and advances of modern automotive electrical systems, this volume, written and edited by a global team of experts, also goes into the practical applications for the engineer, student, and other industry professionals.

NANODEVICES FOR INTEGRATED CIRCUIT DESIGN, Edited by Suman Lata Tripathi, Abhishek Kumar, K. Srinivasa Rao, and Prasantha R. Mudimela, ISBN: 9781394185788. Written and edited by a team of experts in the field, this important new volume broadly covers the design of nano-devices and their integrated applications in digital and analog integrated circuits (IC) design.

DESIGN AND DEVELOPMENT OF EFFICIENT ENERGY SYSTEMS, Edited by Suman Lata Tripathi, Dushyant Kumar Singh, Sanjeevikumar Padmanaban, and P. Raja, ISBN: 9781119761631. Covering the concepts and fundamentals of efficient energy systems, this volume, written and edited by a global team of experts, also goes into the practical applications that can be utilized across multiple industries, for both the engineer and the student.

Electrical and Electronic Devices, Circuits, and Materials: Technical Challenges and Solutions, Edited by Suman Lata Tripathi, Parvej Ahmad Alvi, and Umashankar Subramaniam, ISBN: 9781119750369. Covering every aspect of the design and improvement needed for solid-state electronic devices and circuit and their reliability issues, this new volume also includes overall system design for all kinds of analog and digital applications and developments in power systems.

Printed and bound by CPI Group (UK) Ltd, Croydon, CR0 4YY

17/09/2026

14964262-0001